Well-Being in Adolescent Girls

This book equips school psychologists and other mental health professionals with a comprehensive understanding of mental health and well-being in adolescent girls.

The text places adolescent girls in a developmental and social-cultural context and outlines factors that can shape girls' well-being including family, peers, and media. Chapters discuss trajectories that might result in mental distress and dysfunction in adolescent girls and identify pathways to their optimal development. Additionally, the book reviews the domains of well-being including physical health and habits, emotional well-being, healthy relationships, and identity and agency. Each chapter includes theory-informed and empirically supported interventions to help promote girls' positive physical and socio-emotional development and culminates in a list of further recommended resources for the reader.

Well-Being in Adolescent Girls is a valuable resource for school psychologists, counselors, and other mental health professionals working with adolescents along with those in graduate-level courses in school psychology and school counseling programs.

Elena Savina, **PhD**, is a professor at the Department of Graduate Psychology at James Madison University. She teaches courses and supervises clinical practica at the Combined-Integrated Doctoral Program in Clinical and School Psychology.

Jennifer M. Moran, **PsyD**, is a licensed clinical and school psychologist. She currently works as a psychologist at a children's hospital where she provides services to children and adolescents in both inpatient and outpatient settings.

Well-Being in Adolescent Girls

From Theory to Interventions

Elena Savina and Jennifer M. Moran

Routledge
Taylor & Francis Group

NEW YORK AND LONDON

First published 2022
by Routledge
605 Third Avenue, New York, NY 10158

and by Routledge
2 Park Square, Milton Park, Abingdon, Oxon, OX14 4RN

Routledge is an imprint of the Taylor & Francis Group, an informa business

Library of Congress Cataloging-in-Publication Data
Names: Savina, Elena A., author. | Moran, Jennifer M., author.
Title: Well-being in adolescent girls : from theory to
interventions / Elena Savina and Jennifer M. Moran.
Identifiers: LCCN 2021020368 (print) | LCCN 2021020369
(ebook) | ISBN 9780367615666 (hardback) |
ISBN 9780367615659 (paperback) | ISBN 9781003105534 (ebook)
Subjects: LCSH: Teenage girls—Psychology. | Well-being. |
Emotions in adolescence. | Positive psychology.
Classification: LCC HQ798.S258 2022 (print) |
LCC HQ798 (ebook) | DDC 155.5/33—dc23
LC record available at https://lccn.loc.gov/2021020368
LC ebook record available at https://lccn.loc.gov/2021020369

ISBN: 978-0-367-61566-6 (hbk)
ISBN: 978-0-367-61565-9 (pbk)
ISBN: 978-1-003-10553-4 (ebk)

DOI: 10.4324/9781003105534

Typeset in Times New Roman
by codeMantra

"An excellent resource for mental health practitioners and anyone else interested in understanding and enhancing adolescent girls' well-being. The balanced blend of contemporary research, theory, and practical interventions makes for a highly relevant book on a much-needed topic."

John J. Murphy, PhD, *author of* Solution-Focused Counseling in Schools, *professor of Psychology, University of Central Arkansas, AR*

"The authors take the fluid, overwhelming, and often confusing period of adolescence and break it down into easy-to-understand and applicable domains. Not only do they provide comprehensive overviews of the unique challenges and opportunities for girls in this phase of life, but they also provide real world and practical strategies for educators, therapists, and parents to apply to maximize well-being. I recommend this book for anyone who works with or spends time with adolescent girls."

Rachel G. Lilly, PhD, *psychologist, Geisinger Lewistown— Pediatric Psychology, Lewistown, PA*

"This book provides a refreshingly holistic approach to understanding health and wellness among adolescent girls in today's society. I especially appreciate the authors' careful consideration of the developmental and socio-cultural context in which girls are living in and how these factors impact well-being. The interventions outlined are thoughtful, evidence-based, and applicable across a wide range of educational and clinical settings. While adolescence can be a time of complex transitions and stress, I appreciate the authors outlining the inherent resilience in adolescent girls and focusing on promoting well-being from a preventative perspective as well as an intervention. This book is such a valuable resource in my clinical practice."

Toni P. Boos, PsyD, *associate director of Child Program- Compass Health Center, Northbrook, IL*

"*Well-Being in Adolescent Girls: From Theory to Interventions* provides not only theoretical frameworks and supporting research, but it also offers practical interventions to foster well-being in adolescent girls. This is the resource I was looking for and I recommend it for any mental health professional who is focusing on assisting our girls in finding their voice and cultivating their strengths."

Virginia Gallup Larsen, PsyD, *school psychologist, Loudoun County Public Schools, VA*

"Now more than ever, adolescent mental health is rising to the forefront of today's headlines. This book views adolescent girls' health and well-being through a biopsychosocial lens and equips professionals across disciplines with practical recommendations to best meet the needs of today's youth. The authors also adequately address the developmental complexities impacting adolescent girls and provide easy to understand theories to behaviors that equip readers with evidenced-based interventions that can be used across settings."

Kelsie-Marie Offenwanger, PsyD, *child and adolescent psychologist at Marshfield Clinic Health System, Marshfield, WI*

Contents

About the Authors   xi

1   Well-Being: Definitions and Frameworks   1
Hedonic Well-Being 2
Eudaimonic Well-Being 3
Integrative Models of Well-Being 6
Models of Well-Being in Adolescents 7
Well-Being Interventions 8
    Positive Education 10
Recommended Resources 11

2   Adolescence: Risks and Opportunities   15
Brain Development in Adolescence: A Window
   of Opportunity 16
Puberty in Adolescent Girls 18
Adolescents' Mental Health 20
    Barriers to Adolescents' Health and Well-Being 21
    Digital Media and Adolescents' Mental Health 23
Pathways to Optimal Adolescent Development 24
    Positive Youth Development 24
    Resilience as an Integral Part of Youth Optimal
       Development 26
    Activities that Foster Positive Youth Development 28
Recommended Resources 30

3   Sociocultural Construction of Girls and Girlhood   36
Gender Socialization 37
Sexualization and Body Image in Adolescent Girls 38
Appearance and the Ideal of Femininity 40
"Mean Girls" 41
Power and Agency in Adolescent Girls 42

Experiences of Ethnic and Racial Minority Girls 43
Identity in Adolescent Girls 45
Recommended Resources 46

4   Physical Health and Healthy Habits in Adolescent Girls   50
Physical Activity in Adolescent Girls 50
Eating Habits in Adolescent Girls 51
Body Image 52
   Factors Contributing to Body Dissatisfaction 53
Interventions to Support Physical Activity, Healthy Eating,
   and Body Image 54
      Strategies to Motivate Girls to Stay Physically Active 55
      Programs and Curricular to Support Healthy Habits 56
      Specific Body Image Interventions 57
Sleep Habits 59
      Factors Contributing to Inadequate Sleep in Adolescence 60
      Interventions to Support Sleep Hygiene 61
How to Make Healthy Habits Interventions Work 62
Recommended Resources 64

5   Emotional Well-Being   73
Emotion Regulation 74
      Emotion Regulation in Adolescents 76
Depression in Adolescent Girls 76
      Interventions to Reduce Depression 78
Stress and Anxiety 80
      Sources of Stress 81
      Test Anxiety 82
      Interventions to Reduce Stress and Anxiety 82
      Fostering Emotional Awareness and Acceptance 84
Positive Emotions and Well-Being 85
Recommended Resources 87

6   Interpersonal Relationships in Adolescent Girls as a
Pathway to Well-Being   98
Relationships with Parents 98
      Recommendations for Parents to Support Positive
         Parent-Adolescent Relationships 101
      Interventions to Support Positive Parent-Adolescent
         Relationships 103
Relationships with Peers 104
      Relational Aggression in Adolescent Girls 105

Romantic Relationships in Adolescent Girls 106
Social Media and Relationships with Peers 108
Recommendations to Support Girls' Healthy
    Relationships with Peers 110
Interventions to Support Girls' Healthy Relationships
    with Peers 111
Promoting Healthy Relationships through Mentoring 112
Creating Caring Communities to Promote Healthy Relationships 113
Recommended Resources 114

7   **Purpose, Agency, and Identity**   121
Purpose 121
    How to Foster Purpose in Adolescents 123
Character Strengths 124
    Strength Building Interventions 125
Goal Pursuit 125
    Developmental Goals 126
    Growth Mindset 128
    Hope and Goal Pursuit 128
Agency in Adolescence 129
Identity Development 130
    Possible Selves 131
    Social Identity 132
    Interventions to Support Identity Development in
        Girls of Color 134
Recommended Resources 135

Index   143

Authors

Elena Savina received a PhD in developmental and educational psychology from Moscow State Pedagogical University, Russia, and a PhD in school psychology from the University of Central Arkansas, USA. Presently, she is a professor at the Department of Graduate Psychology at James Madison University. She teaches courses in the Combined-Integrated Doctoral Program in Clinical and School Psychology. Throughout her career, Dr. Savina has provided mental health services to children and adolescents, parent education, and teacher training. She served as a psychologist at Children's Village-SOS (Lavrovo, Russia), the world's largest child charity dedicated to orphans and abandoned children. Dr. Savina is the author of books and articles on children's self-regulation and socio-emotional development and learning.

Jennifer M. Moran received a PsyD in clinical and school psychology from James Madison University, USA. Presently, she is a clinical psychologist at a children's hospital where she provides services to children and adolescents in inpatient and outpatient settings. Dr. Moran previously worked as a psychologist in public schools. Dr. Moran's research interests include developing interventions to promote mental health and well-being in children and adolescents and training community and school personnel to implement programs to enhance youth well-being.

1 Well-Being

Definitions and Frameworks

In 1948, the World Health Organization defined health as a "state of complete physical, mental and social well-being and not merely the absence of disease or infirmity" (WHO, 1948, p. 28). This definition provided a vision for the mental health field delineating positive aspects of human functioning. Nevertheless, for many years a medical model dominated the field. This model defined health as the absence of illness, rather than the presence of wellness. This medical model "narrows our focus on what is weak and defective about people to the exclusion of what is strong and healthy. It emphasizes abnormality over normality, poor adjustment over healthy adjustment and sickness over health" (Maddux, 2008, p. 56). Furthermore, the medical model places adjustment and maladjustment inside the person, but disregards complex person-environment interactions, social and cultural values, and the role of societal institutions in human functioning.

In the 1990s, the positive psychology movement shifted the focus away from pathology and toward human strength, resiliency, and positive functioning. One of the founders of positive psychology, Martin Seligman, argued that:

> psychology is not just the study of disease, weakness, and damage; it is also the study of strength and virtue. Treatment is not just fixing what is wrong; it is also building what is right. Psychology is not just about illness or health; it also is about work, education, insight, love, growth, and play.
>
> (Seligman, 2002, p. 4)

Positive psychology became the study of the strengths and virtues that allow both individuals and communities to thrive (Seligman & Csikszentmihalyi, 2000). Seligman (2002) further proposed a concept of positive mental health that delineated human flourishing and living a fulfilled life. This concept places human functioning on a continuum, with mental illness representing one end of the continuum and optimal psychological health the other. Human well-being became a central concept in positive psychology (Seligman, 2011).

DOI: 10.4324/9781003105534-1

The construct of well-being defies precise definition. Rather, it encompasses a broad range of characteristics and processes related to human optimal psychological functioning. Well-being is not synonymous with happiness, though the experience of happiness is important for well-being. It includes an individual's strengths and virtues, meaning, purpose, and life satisfaction. It is further concerned with identifying outcomes of well-being for overall human functioning and conditions that can promote or undermine well-being. The latter is especially important for designing well-being interventions.

The study of well-being in psychology stems from two philosophical traditions: one emphasizing the pursuit of pleasure and life satisfaction (hedonic well-being) and the other emphasizing the pursuit of a meaningful life and optimal functioning (eudaimonic well-being; Ryan & Deci, 2001). While hedonic and eudaimonic perspectives represent two distinct understandings of well-being, experiences of pleasure and living a meaningful life are related. Individuals experience positive emotions in response to meaningful achievements, and these positive experiences likely lead to the pursuit of meaningful and fulfilling opportunities in the future. Thus, the hedonic and eudaimonic perspectives are in many ways complementary. Both perspectives are briefly discussed below.

Hedonic Well-Being

The hedonic perspective on well-being focuses on subjective experiences associated with well-being:

> The centrality of hedonic well-being in everyday discourse, at least in Western society, is well illustrated by the omnipresent greeting, "How are you?" Although the answer to this question may draw upon either physical (e.g., "I'm just getting over the flu") or psychological experiences (e.g., "I am so relaxed from our vacation"), or may involve a pro forma reply ("Fine, thanks"), the frequency with which we ask one another this question reflects a common preoccupation with hedonic well-being.
>
> (Lent, 2004, p. 484)

Diener's (2009) theory of subjective well-being (SWB) is one example of the hedonic tradition. The term subjective means that well-being is based on the self-appraisal of an individual's life and emotional experiences. More specifically, well-being is determined by how people evaluate their current affect (positive vs. negative), their overall life satisfaction, and satisfaction in specific domains. Positive and negative affect reflect basic appraisals of ongoing events and life circumstances (Diener et al., 2003). Global estimates of life satisfaction are cognitive judgments about an individuals' life condition, weighing the importance of the conditions and evaluation of lives as satisfied or unsatisfied. In addition to global life satisfaction, it is important to consider an individual's satisfaction in all relevant domains. These may include work, relationships, or education. In sum, the SWB framework considers well-being as experiences of high levels of positive affect, low levels of negative affect, and high satisfaction, both in general and in specific life domains. In general, younger people experience more positive affect, but older people experience greater life satisfaction (Diener, 2009). Several variables contribute to SWB, such as level of income, employment, religion, and marriage/family status. Among personal variables affecting SWB are high self-esteem and an internal locus of control.

Eudaimonic Well-Being

The eudaimonic framework claims that well-being is much more than the subjective experience of happiness or life satisfaction. It is also about living a good and meaningful life (Ryff, 2014):

> The eudaimonic view may be seen as somewhat broader and more amorphous than the hedonic position in that it involves a diverse set of experiences and mechanisms (e.g., personal goals, values) through which people achieve psychological growth, make meaning, and seek purpose in their lives.
>
> (Lent, 2004, p. 484)

Within the eudaimonic tradition, there are three models of well-being. The first model is based on self-determination theory (Ryan et al., 2008). According to this theory, well-being results from satisfying basic psychological needs for competence, relatedness, and autonomy. The need for autonomy is related to choice and volition; relatedness reflects a need for close connection to and being cared for by others; and the need for competence is a sense of efficacy when managing internal and external environments (Ryan et al., 2008). Furthermore, well-being is associated with pursuing intrinsic (e.g., personal growth or relationships) rather than extrinsic goals and values (e.g., wealth or fame). Other important contributors to well-being are the ability to be autonomous and act on one's own volition and the ability to be mindful and self-aware.

A second model of well-being is the human flourishing framework proposed by Seligman (2011). Seligman identified the following elements associated with well-being, abbreviated as PERMA: Positive emotion, Engagement, Relationships, Meaning, and Accomplishment. Positive emotion is characterized by feeling good about present, past, and future, experiencing more positive affect and less negative affect, and having skills that amplify positive emotions and lessen negative emotions. Engagement reflects one's ability to be actively involved in and absorbed by an activity, while Positive Relationships reflect the benefits of having good relationships with others. Meaning, another important element of well-being, can be attained by serving something that is bigger than oneself. Finally, Accomplishment reflects success within a particular domain or activity and involves motivation for mastery and competence (Seligman, 2011). According to Seligman, flourishing can be achieved through increasing positive emotions, engaging with the world, and finding meaning and purpose in life. It also involves cultivating and applying strengths and talents to accomplish worthwhile tasks and connecting with others at a deeper level. These strivings constitute living the "good life" (Seligman, 2011).

The last eudaimonic model of well-being is represented by Ryff (1989; 2014), the psychological well-being (PWB) framework. She defined well-being and optimal mental health as resulting from the "processes of setting and pursuing goals, attempting to realize one's potential, experiencing deep connections to others, managing surrounding demands and opportunities, exercising self-direction, and possessing positive self-regard" (Ryff, 1989, p. 1072). She identified six major domains characterizing optimal mental health: (1) Self-acceptance; (2) Positive relations with others; (3) Autonomy; (4) Environmental mastery; (5) Purpose in life; and (6) Personal growth. Striving toward excellence in these areas is associated with well-being.

Ruini and Fava (2014) further developed well-being therapy (WBT) based on Ryff's conceptualization. WBT leads a client from an impaired level to an optimal level of functioning in the six dimensions of PWB. It emphasizes balanced functioning and the idea that the various dimensions of positive functioning can compensate for each other. It also takes a dialectical approach to the dimensions of well-being outlined by Ryff (2014), demonstrating that both low and very high levels of those dimensions can be problematic for one's well-being. Below are detailed descriptions of each domain based on Ryff's and Ruini and Fava's conceptualizations.

Self-acceptance refers to positive attitudes toward oneself (Ryff, 2014). On the one hand, individuals with high self-acceptance acknowledge and accept both positive and negative aspects of self and feel good about their past. On the other hand, inflated self-esteem might cause distress when reality does not support it (Ruini & Fava, 2014). Individuals with low self-acceptance feel dissatisfied with themselves and disappointed with the past; they wish to be different than who they are (Ryff, 2014). Furthermore, they may hold unrealistically high standards and expectations for their performance.

Positive relations with others reflect the importance of warm, trusting relationships with others (Ryff, 2014). Those who score high in this area have satisfying interpersonal relationships and are concerned about the welfare of others. They further have capacity for empathy, affection, and intimacy. On the other hand, over-involvement with others' well-being might result from low self-esteem and can be distressing (Ruini & Fava, 2014). Those who score low do not have close relationships with others and have difficulty being warm and empathetic with others (Ryff, 2014). They may feel isolated and are not willing to compromise for the sake of good interpersonal relationships. A lack of positive relationships with others is associated with low social integration and perceived support.

Autonomy reflects the degree of independence that individuals experience (Ryff, 2014). Individuals who score high are self-determining, can resist social pressures, and have a strong ability to self-regulate and evaluate themselves using personal standards. At the same time, having too much autonomy and self-reliance may prevent individuals from seeking support from others (Ruini & Fava, 2014). Individuals with low autonomy are concerned about the expectations and evaluations of others, often rely on others to make decisions, and have difficulty resisting social pressures to think and act in certain ways (Ryff, 2014). A lack of autonomy can compromise well-being through difficulty asserting oneself and having one's needs met.

Environmental mastery refers to the individual's ability to choose or create environments beneficial to their well-being (Ryff, 2014). Those who score high on this dimension feel competent in managing their environment, create a context to have their needs met, and use opportunities effectively. Very high levels of environmental mastery (e.g., being too engaged in work or other activities) might become a source of stress and allostatic load, leading to an inability to relax and enjoy daily life (Ruini & Fava, 2014). Those who score low have difficulty managing everyday life and feel ineffective in changing or improving their environment (Ryff, 2014). They may not see and/or use opportunities and are lacking a sense of control over their external world. Low levels of environmental mastery manifests as a lack of sense of control and might lead to missed opportunities.

Purpose in life is a sense of having direction in one's life (Ryff, 2014). Individuals who score high have clear purpose and direction in their life. On the other hand, those with a strong determination to realize their goals might become rigid and overcommit themselves in goals that are not achievable (Ruini & Fava, 2014). Individuals who score low on the purpose dimension are lacking direction and a sense of purpose. Those with impaired environmental mastery and sense of personal growth often lack a sense of purpose.

Finally, personal growth reflects the need to continue developing potential and to grow personally. Individuals who score high on this dimension are open to new experiences and are engaged in self-development and self-improvement. At the same time, those with dysfunctionally high levels of personal growth might be very future-oriented but underestimate the role of negative experiences and learning from those experiences

(Ruini & Fava, 2014). Individuals who score low on the personal growth dimension may experience a sense of personal stagnation and lack interest in expanding personal horizons (Ryff, 2014). They also tend to focus more on their distance from their goals rather than on the progress toward goals (Ruini & Fava, 2014).

Integrative Models of Well-Being

Several scholars have criticized the dichotomous, hedonic versus eudaimonic, approach to well-being. For example, Kashdan and colleagues (2008) argued that hedonic and eudaimonic well-being overlap conceptually and may represent psychological mechanisms that work in synergy. Several integrative well-being models have been proposed to bring together hedonic and eudaimonic traditions in well-being research. One model, proposed by Keyes (2007), considered mental health as flourishing. It comprises both hedonic and eudaimonic indices of functioning and delineates three dimensions, including emotional, psychological, and social well-being. Emotional well-being includes positive affect and satisfaction with one's own life, while PWB is characterized by positive psychological functioning in the domains outlined by Ryff (2014) (e.g., self-acceptance, personal growth, a sense of purpose, environmental mastery, autonomy, and positive relationships with others). Finally, the social well-being domain consists of positive engagement with the community and society at large and includes a sense of belonging and seeing one's actions as being valued by the community.

Another integrative well-being model, called the engine model, distinguishes between inputs, processes, and outcome variables (Jayawickreme et al., 2012). The input variables consist of exogenous and endogenous predictors of well-being. Exogenous predictors include income and level of education, as they give an opportunity for people to engage in valuable activities and healthy lifestyles. The endogenous predictors include personality variables such as optimism, curiosity, strengths, and talents. The process variables comprise internal states that influence people's choices and behavior. These may include emotional states, motivation, and explanations people make about their choices. Finally, the outcome variables include behaviors resulting from well-being, for example, accomplishment, positive relationships with others, and engagement in meaningful activity.

The last integrative model discussed here is the Nested Model of Well-Being (Henriques et al., 2014). This model is based on Bronfenbrenner's socio-ecological systems framework that places an individual's functioning within a broader context of nested systems (Bronfenbrenner, 1979). The Nested Model conceptualizes well-being across four domains: Subjective, Health and Functioning, Environmental, and Values and Ideology. The *Subjective Domain* is concerned with the frequency, intensity, and duration of an individual's positive and negative emotional states and a sense of satisfaction with his/her life. This SWB can be assessed by both affective indices (e.g., positive vs. negative affect) and cognitive appraisals (e.g., level of self-reflective satisfaction). The *Health and Functioning* domain acknowledges health as the essential element of overall well-being and distinguishes two components: biological and psychological. The biological component includes habits and lifestyle (e.g., eating habits, sleeping, etc.), while the psychological component comprises emotional and relational functioning, coping and defenses, identity, self-esteem, and worldview. The *Environmental* domain points at the centrality of the relationship between person and environment for an individual's adaptive functioning and well-being. This includes the material environment with presence or absence of resources (e.g., financial or technological) and stressors (e.g., pollutants or crowding) and the social environment defined by social networks and interpersonal relationships. The final domain, *Values and Ideology*, highlights a broader context that shape one's appraisals of well-being. It acknowledges that well-being is an inherently evaluative concept that is linked to underlying societal values and ideologies (Henriques et al., 2014).

Models of Well-Being in Adolescents

In 2015, the UN recognized the unique need to support the health and well-being of adolescents in its 2030 Agenda for Sustainable Development (Ross et al., 2020). This led experts from around the world to examine and address the health and well-being needs of adolescents:

> Adolescent well-being is a personal and societal good in its own right, and at the same time, adolescence is a critical period of the life course when many of the factors that contribute to lifelong well-being are, or are not, acquired or solidified.
>
> (Ross et al., 2020, p. 472)

Ross and colleagues (2020) proposed a comprehensive framework for adolescents' well-being consisting of five interconnected domains. The first domain, *Good health and optimum nutrition*, includes access to valid and relevant health information, affordable health services, a healthy physical environment, opportunity for adequate physical exercise, and access to a healthy diet. The second domain, *Connectedness, positive values, and contribution to society*, emphasizes the importance for adolescents to have access to positive social and cultural networks, develop meaningful relationships with others; and be valued and respected by others. It also emphasizes respect for others, good interpersonal skills, and engagement in socially valuable activities through which youth can contribute to the common good. The third domain, *Safety and a supportive environment*, includes emotional and physical safety, adequate material conditions in the physical environment, equity, equality, nondiscrimination, and respect for privacy. The fourth domain, *Learning, competence, education, skills, and employability*, reflects motivation and support for education, access to resources and opportunities to learn life skills, employability, and also an adolescent's self-confidence to be successful. The final domain, *Agency and resilience*, encompasses self-esteem, a sense of agency, identity, purpose, and resilience.

Mastorci, Bastiani, Trivellini and colleagues (2020) argued that various components of health and well-being have synergistic effects on each other. For example, they found that adolescents' health is affected by lifestyle habits, social context, emotional status, and cognitive abilities. Lifestyle habits and social relationships have the strongest bidirectional association with adolescents' health and well-being (Mastorci, Bastiani, Trivellini et al., 2020). The social relationships factor was also strongly associated with emotional health, which in turn was bidirectionally associated with lifestyle habits. Another research study found that the social component was the most important indicator of perceived well-being in adolescents, followed by autonomy, lifestyle, and emotional health (Mastorci, Bastiani, Doveri et al., 2020). For the lifestyle component, leisure time had greater weight in comparison to diet and physical activity.

In a similar vein, Renshaw and colleagues (2014) proposed a concept of covitality, which reflects the synergistic effect of multiple positive psychological indicators on positive mental health. The authors argued that a combination of strengths and positive traits is stronger than individual components. In a sense, covitality is similar to the concept of comorbidity, but with a focus on the co-occurrence of positive traits contributing to well-being. The model identified 12 psychological building blocks of covitality making up four positive mental health domains (Renshaw et al., 2014). The first domain, *Belief-in-self*, is made up of self-efficacy, self-awareness, and persistence, while the second domain, *Belief-in-others*, comprises school, peer, and family support. The third domain, *Emotional competence*, includes the ability of youth to regulate their emotions and behaviors, as well as their capacity for empathy. The final domain, *Engaged living*, comprises gratitude, zest, and optimism. The covitality model was used to develop the Social Emotional Health Survey (SEHS), a strengths-based assessment that examines multiple areas of positive functioning that contribute to overall youth mental health (Furlong, You et al., 2014). The authors suggest that since a combination of strengths and positive traits is most influential in well-being, interventions should target them in tandem rather separately (Furlong, Dowdy et al., 2014).

Well-Being Interventions

Family, school, and community are essential for promoting adolescents' well-being. Among variables contributing to well-being are connection to family and school, experiencing caring relationships, safety, prosocial norms, high expectations, structure and guidance, and opportunities to contribute to communities (Gillham et al., 2013). Even though prevention programs often target high-risk youth, well-being interventions should reach all youth as many young people, regardless of their background and demographics, experience stressors at some point in their life. Furthermore, these interventions should target a broad range of potential challenges including academic difficulties, life transition, and conflicts with peers. They should further focus on teaching adolescents important life skills, cultivating strengths, and promoting a nurturing school climate (Gillham et al., 2013).

Positive psychology interventions (PPIs) are one avenue to increase well-being in youth. These interventions are easily implemented activities aimed at increasing positive emotions (Lyubomirsky & Layous, 2013). PPIs that target gratitude, hope, and character strengths were found to be effective in increasing SWB (Marques et al., 2011; Seligman et al., 2009). For example, Suldo and colleagues (2014) implemented a school-based program that combined several PPIs, including gratitude, simple acts of kindness, character strengths, optimistic thinking, and focusing on positive emotions. The program outcome study found that adolescents who participated in the intervention reported increased life satisfaction. There is additional evidence that these PPIs can be implemented with both adolescents and their parents. In one multi-target intervention, adolescents demonstrated significant gains in life satisfaction and positive affect and decrease in negative affect (Roth et al., 2017).

Social-Emotional Learning (SEL) is another avenue to promote well-being in youth. The Collaborative for Academic, Social, and Emotional Learning (CASEL, 2003) identified five interrelated sets of competencies essential for youth's positive functioning, including self-awareness, self-management, social awareness, relationship skills, and responsible decision-making. A meta-analytic study of universal school-based SEL initiatives evidenced their effectiveness in improving youths' socioemotional skills, reducing behavioral problems, and promoting academic learning (Durlak et al., 2011).

The Penn Resiliency Program (PRP) is an evidence-based program that supports well-being (Gillham et al., 2013). The PRP is a school-based, small group intervention delivered by teachers and counselors. Initially developed as a depression prevention program, the PRP expanded to incorporate a broader set of skills essential for well-being. More specifically, the program focused on building relational skills, character strengths, and positive thinking. It trains youth to identify and use their personal strengths and develop social-emotional and self-regulation skills. It further targets problem-solving and decision-making skills, social awareness, self-efficacy, and realistic optimism. Program evaluation studies evidence an increase in positive thinking and decrease in depressive symptoms among youth who participated in the program (Gillham et al., 2013).

There is evidence that WBT implemented in the school setting can also be effective in increasing personal growth and decreasing negative emotions in young people (Ruini et al., 2009). The school WBT protocol consists of six two-hour sessions, held once a week. Sessions focus on training emotional skills, cognitive restructuring and positive thinking, healthy relationships, autonomy, purpose, and happiness (Visani et al., 2014).

Positive Education

Positive education is aimed at the integration of well-being initiatives into academic curriculum (Noble & McGrath, 2014). Initiatives posit that fostering young people's well-being along with academic skills should become a new philosophy of education (Seligman et al., 2009). Positive education strives to:

> develop resilient and effective learners as well as productive, caring, achieving, healthy and responsible adults with sound levels of well-being. An investment in positive education at the school, system and national level, and in educational policies and practices for student well-being produce long-term benefits for individual students, for school communities and for the whole of society.
>
> (Noble & McGrath, 2014, p. 149)

Noble and McGrath (2014) identified several directions for school-based positive education, including teaching youth social-emotional competencies and resiliency skills; skills for self-management and self-discipline; the ability to amplify positive emotions; interpersonal skills; character strengths; fostering a sense of meaning and purpose; and creating an optimal learning environment. Positive education can include topics about nutrition and its connection to mood and learning, the role of sleep in well-being, and the role of the brain in learning, executive functioning and delayed gratification, and stress reduction strategies (Morris, 2013). Promoting well-being education and teaching positive dispositions may require a significant reform of the curriculum currently in place.

One unique initiative in positive education is the *Geelong Grammar School Project*. The Geelong Grammar School in Australia incorporates positive education in all courses and school practices (Norrish, 2015). The aim of the program is to promote resilience, strengths, gratitude, and positive relationships. Teachers receive a comprehensive training in positive psychology and create their own ways to incorporate positive psychology principles and methods into their teaching. Several frameworks were used to guide this positive education program including PERMA (Seligman, 2011), the Values in Action framework of strengths (Peterson & Seligman, 2004), and the broaden-and-build theory of positive emotions (Fredrickson, 2013). Both students and educational staff are trained to understand their own character strengths and to identify strengths in others. The Geelong Grammar School Project recognizes the fundamental importance of interpersonal connection and belonging for youth well-being (Norrish, 2015). It focuses on cultivating positive relationships and building a strong school community. The project further promotes emotional well-being through teaching youth to accept their emotions and increase positive emotions including love, joy, contentment, gratitude, and hope. Both staff and students are educated about the intrinsic link between physical and psychological health and are committed to developing and maintaining healthy habits. Students and staff also strive to have meaning in their lives and pursue goals that are personally rewarding and valuable for the community.

Another example of positive education is a high school curriculum based on Seligman's (2011) pathways to happiness, including life of pleasure, life of engagement, and life of meaning (Gillham et al., 2013). Accordingly, the program includes three units: The Pleasant Life focusing on positive emotions, The Engaged Life promoting strengths, and The Meaningful Life during which students reflect on purpose and meaning. This program yielded promising results in increasing youth's social skills and their school engagement.

Recently, positive education has gained international recognition and development. One initiative is the International Positive Education Network (IPEN, 2020) which aims to unite students, teachers, parents, schools, private companies, and governments to promote positive education. IPEN (2020) suggests a two-prong approach to education where academic learning and well-being education go hand-in-hand.

Recommended Resources

Positive Psychology Center at the University of Pennsylvania – https://ppc.sas.upenn.edu/services/penn-resilience-training

The Penn Positive Psychology Center provides evidence-based resilience and positive psychology programs. These programs equip individuals with a set of practical skills that can be applied in everyday life to navigate adversity and thrive in challenging environments. The programs have been found to build resilience, well-being, and optimism. They can be offered to individuals, teams, and leadership from a variety of sectors, including healthcare, education, and the military.

References

Bronfenbrenner, U. (1979). *The ecology of human development: Experiments by nature and design*. Cambridge, MA: Harvard University Press.

Collaborative for Academic, Social, and Emotional Learning. (2003). Safe and sound: An educational leader's guide to evidence-based social and emotional learning (SEL) programs. Collaborative for Academic, Social, and Emotional Learning. https://casel.org/wp-content/uploads/2016/06/safe-and-sound.pdf

Diener, E. (2009). Subjective well-being. In E. Diener (Ed.), *The science of well-being: The collected works of Ed Diener. Social indicators research series: Vol. 37* (pp. 11–58). Springer Science + Business Media. https://doi.org/10.1007/978-90-481-2350-6_2

Diener, E., Scollon, C. N., & Lucas, R. E. (2003). The evolving concept of subjective well-being: The multifaceted nature of happiness. *Advances in Cell Aging and Gerontology, 15*, 187–219. https://doi.org/10.1016/S1566-3124(03)15007-9

Durlak, J. A., Weissberg, R. P., Dymnicki, A. B., Taylor, R. D., & Schellinger, K. B. (2011). The impact of enhancing students' social and emotional learning: A meta-analysis of school-based universal interventions. *Child Development, 82*, 405–432. https://doi.org/10.1111/j.1467-8624.2010.01564.x

Fredrickson, B. L. (2013). Positive emotions broaden and build. *Advances in Experimental Social Psychology, 47*, 1–53. https://doi.org/10.1016/B978-0-12-407236-7.00001-2

Furlong, M., Dowdy, E., Carnazzo, K., Bovery, B. L., & Kim, E. (2014). Covitality: Fostering the building blocks of complete mental health. *Communique, 42*(8), 28–29.

Furlong, M. J., You, S., Renshaw, T. L., Smith, D. C., & O'Malley, M. D. (2014). Preliminary development and validation of the Social and Emotional Health Survey for secondary school students. *Social Indicators Research, 117*(3), 1011–1032. https://doi.org/10.1007/s11205-013-0373-0

Gillham, J., Abenavoli, R. M., Brunwasser, S. M., Linkins, M., Reivich, K. J., & Seligman, M. E. P. (2013). Resilience education. In I. Boniwell, S. A. David, & A. C. Ayers (Eds.), *Oxford handbook of happiness (pp. 609–630)*. Oxford University Press. https://doi.org/10.1093/oxfordhb/9780199557257.013.0046

Henriques, G., Klineman, K., & Asselin, C. (2014). The nested model of well-being: A unified approach. *Review of General Psychology, 18*(1), 7–18. https://doi.org/10.1037/a0036288

International Positive Education Network (2020). *About us.* https://www.ipen-network.com/about-us

Jayawickreme, E., Forgeard, M. J. C., & Seligman, M. E. P. (2012). The engine of well-being. *Review of General Psychology, 16*(4), 327–342. https://doi.org/10.1037/a0027990

Kashdan, T. B., Biswas-Diener, R., & King, L. A. (2008). Reconsidering happiness: The costs of distinguishing between hedonics and eudaimonia. *The Journal of Positive Psychology, 3*(4), 219–233. https://doi.org/10.1080/17439760802303044

Keyes, C. L. M. (2007). Promoting and protecting mental health as flourishing: A complementary strategy for improving national mental health. *American Psychologist, 62*(2), 95–108. https://doi.org/10.1037/0003-066X.62.2.95

Lent, R. W. (2004). Toward a unifying theoretical and practical perspective on well-being and psychosocial adjustment. *Journal of Counseling Psychology, 51*(4), 482–509. https://doi.org/10.1037/0022-0167.51.4.482

Lyubomirsky, S., & Layous, K. (2013). How do simple positive activities increase well-being? *Current Directions in Psychological Science, 22*(1), 57–62. https://doi.org/10.1177/0963721412469809

Maddux, J. E. (2008). Positive psychology and the illness ideology: Toward a positive clinical psychology. *Applied Psychology: An International Review, 57*, 54–70. https://doi.org/10.1111/j.1464-0597.2008.00354.x

Marques, S. C., Lopez, S. J., & Pais-Ribero, J. L. (2011). "Building Hope for the Future": A program to foster strengths in middle-school students. *Journal of Happiness Studies, 12*, 139–152. https://doi.org/10.1007/s10902-009-9180-3

Mastorci, F., Bastiani, L., Doveri, C., Trivellini, G., Casu, A., Vassalle, C., & Pingitore, A. (2020). Adolescent health: A framework for developing an innovative personalized well-being index. *Frontiers in Pediatrics, 8*, Article 18. https://doi.org/10.3389/fped.2020.00181

Mastorci, F., Bastiani, L., Trivellini, G., Doveri, C., Vassalle, C., & Pingitore, A. (2020). A new integrated approach for adolescent health and well-being: The AVATAR project. *Health and Quality of Life Outcomes, 18*(77). https://doi.org/10.1186/s12955-020-01291-6

Morris, I. (2013). A place for well-being in the classroom? In C. Proctor & P. A. Linley (Eds.), *Research, applications, and interventions for children and adolescents: A positive psychology perspective* (pp. 185–198). Springer Science + Business Media. https://doi.org/10.1007/978-94-007-6398-2_11

Noble, T., & McGrath, H. (2014). Well-being and resilience in school settings. In G. Fava & C. Ruini (Eds.), *Increasing psychological well-being in clinical and educational settings* (pp. 135–152). Dordrecht: Springer. https://doi.org/10.1007/978-94-017-8669-0_9

Norrish, J. (2015). *Positive education: The Geelong Grammar School journey.* Oxford University Press. https://doi.org/10.1093/acprof:oso/9780198702580.001.0001

Peterson, C., & Seligman, M. E. P. (2004). *Character strengths and virtues: A handbook and classification.* Oxford University Press and American Psychological Association.

Renshaw, T. L., Furlong, M. J., Dowdy, E., Rebelez, J., Smith, D. C., O'Malley, M. D., Lee, S.-Y., & Strøm, I. F. (2014). Covitality: A synergistic conception of adolescents' mental health. In M. J. Furlong, R. Gilman, & E. S. Huebner (Eds.), *Educational psychology handbook series. Handbook of positive psychology in schools* (pp. 12–32). New York: Routledge/Taylor & Francis Group.

Ross, D. A., Hinton, R., Melles-Brewer, M., Engel, D., Zeck, W., Fagan, L., Herat, J., Phaladi, G., Imbago-Jácome, D., Anyona, P., Sanchez, A., Damji, N., Terki, F., Baltag, V., Patton, G., Silverman, A., Fogstad, H., Banerjee, A., & Mohan, A. (2020). Adolescent well-being: A definition and conceptual framework. *Journal of Adolescent Health, 67*(4), 472–476. https://doi.org/10.1016/j.jadohealth.2020.06.042

Roth, R. A., Suldo, S. M., & Ferron, J. M. (2017). Improving middle school students' subjective well-being: Efficacy of a multicomponent positive psychology intervention targeting small groups of youth. *School Psychology Review, 46*(1), 21–41. https://doi.org/10.17105/10.17105/SPR46-1.21-41

Ruini, C., & Fava, G. A. (2014). *The individualized and cross-cultural roots of well-being therapy.* In G. A. Fava & C. Ruini (Eds.), *Cross-cultural advancements in positive psychology: Vol. 8. Increasing psychological well-being in clinical and educational settings: Interventions and cultural contexts* (pp. 21–39). Springer Science + Business Media. https://doi.org/10.1007/978-94-017-8669-0_2

Ruini, C., Ottolini, F., Tomba, E., Belaise, C., Albieri, E., Visani, D., Offidani, E., Caffo, E., & Fava, G. A. (2009). School intervention for promoting psychological well-being in adolescence. *Journal of Behavior Therapy and Experimental Psychiatry, 40*(4), 522–532. https://doi.org/10.1016/j.jbtep.2009.07.002

Ryan, R. M., & Deci, E. L. (2001). On happiness and human potentials: A review of research on hedonic and eudaimonic well-being. *Annual Review of Psychology, 52*(1), 141–166. https://doi.org/10.1146/annurev.psych.52.1.141

Ryan, R. M., Huta, V., & Deci, E. L. (2008). Living well: A self-determination theory perspective on eudaimonia. *Journal of Happiness Studies: An Interdisciplinary Forum on Subjective Well-being, 9*(1), 139–170. https://doi.org/10.1007/s10902-006-9023-4

Ryff, C. D. (1989). Happiness is everything, or is it? Explorations on the meaning of psychological well-being. *Journal of Personality and Social Psychology, 57*(6), 1069–1081. https://doi.org/10.1037/0022-3514.57.6.1069

Ryff, C. D. (2014). Psychological well-being revisited: Advances in the science and practice of eudaimonia. *Psychotherapy and Psychosomatics, 83*, 10–28. https://doi.org/10.1159/000353263

Seligman, M. E. P. (2002). Positive psychology, positive prevention, and positive therapy. In C. R. Snyder & S. J. Lopez (Eds.), *Handbook of Positive Psychology* (pp. 3–9). Oxford: Oxford University Press.

Seligman, M. E. P. (2011). *Flourish: A visionary new understanding of happiness and well-being.* Free Press.

Seligman, M. E. P., & Csikszentmihalyi, M. (2000). Positive psychology: An introduction. *American Psychologist, 55*(1), 5–14. https://doi.org/10.1037/0003-066X.55.1.5

Seligman, M. P., Ernst, R. M., Gillham, J., Reivich, K., & Linkins, M. (2009). Positive education: Positive psychology and classroom interventions. *Oxford Review of Education, 35*(3), 293–311. https://doi.org/10.1080/03054980902934563

Suldo, S. M., Savage, J. A., & Mercer, S. H. (2014). Increasing middle school students' life satisfaction: Efficacy of a positive psychology group intervention. *Journal of Happiness Studies, 15*(1), 19–42. https://doi.org/10.1007/s10902-013-9414-2

Visani, D., Albieri, E., & Ruini, C. (2014). *School programs for the prevention of mental health problems and the promotion of psychological well-being in children.* In G. A. Fava & C. Ruini (Eds.), *Cross-cultural advancements in positive psychology: Vol. 8. Increasing psychological well-being in clinical and educational settings: Interventions and cultural contexts* (pp. 177–185). Springer Science + Business Media. https://doi.org/10.1007/978-94-017-8669-0_11

World Health Organization. (1948). *World Health Organization constitution.* World Health Organization.

2 Adolescence

Risks and Opportunities

Adolescence is the developmental period characterized by the transition from childhood to adulthood. It begins around the onset of puberty and ends when young people become relatively independent from their parents (Casey, 2015). In adolescence, biological, cognitive, psychological, and social functions are changing in an interrelated manner. Youth have to master many developmental tasks, including identity formation, intentional self-regulation, attaining autonomy-with-connection with family, and preparation for the adult world (Crocetti, 2017; Ferrer-Wreder & Kroger, 2020; Larson & Tran, 2014). Developmental tasks are often not well specified, which adds more complexity in mastering them (Larson & Tran, 2014). Moreover, young people often have to define these tasks, which they need to do or learn in order to be effective in their developmental trajectory. They also must navigate challenges associated with growing up in a rapidly changing world and increasingly fluid and heterogeneous societies.

Adolescence is a period of significant reorganization of biological, psychological, and social functioning that poses challenges for young people to adapt to new cultural expectations and demands (Susman & Rogol, 2004). At the same time, this reorganization leads to changes in the social environment that adolescents seek or create for themselves. While adolescence is marked by significant biological changes, these changes are not the primary factors responsible for psychological or social development. Adolescents' developmental trajectories result from complex interactions among biological changes, cultural expectations, and immediate social contexts (Lerner et al., 2013). There are individual differences in how youths navigate this developmental period, stemming from differences in the timing of changes in biological, psychological, and societal systems. Different configurations of person-context relationships in adolescence (i.e., relationships with family, community, or peers) lead to multiple pathways that young people take during this developmental stage (Lerner et al., 2013).

Adolescents actively participate in multiple ecologies (e.g., family, school, peer group, community) where each might have a different set of values and expectations (Larson, 2011). Therefore, they need strategic

DOI: 10.4324/9781003105534-2

thinking skills in order to capture the dynamic elements of these systems and to function well in those systems. This might be especially important for youths of color or living in poverty. Advances in cognitive abilities provide a basis for identity development and exploration of goals, values, and beliefs (Crocetti, 2017; Ferrer-Wreder & Kroger, 2020; Harter, 2012). Adolescents begin to ponder about social justice, agency, and their own role in society (Larson, 2011). They are becoming increasingly capable of engaging in reflection and taking critical perspectives on complex matters about the world, people, and themselves. Furthermore, they begin to reflect on the kind of people they want to become, their roles, and their place in society. During adolescence, youths begin to integrate their earlier disjointed ideas of themselves into a more coherent identity and sense of self (Ferrer-Wreder & Kroger, 2020; Harter, 2012).

Brain Development in Adolescence: A Window of Opportunity

The public often views adolescence as a time of vulnerability and risk. For example, the title of a popular book *The Teenage Brain: A Neuroscientist's Survival Guide to Raising Adolescents and Young Adult*s by Frances Jensen speaks for itself – adolescence is presented as a time parents have to survive given the "underdeveloped" nature of the adolescent brain (Choudhury & Ferranti, 2018). Furthermore, the author suggests that parents should become the adolescents' frontal lobes. This idea of adolescence as a troubled time is further propagated by media. One example is the article "The Terrible Teens" (2015) published by *The New Yorker* (Choudhury & Ferranti, 2018). The concept of adolescence in popular culture draws on simplified interpretations of research on adolescent brain development, specifically the popular science idea about a "mismatch" between adolescents' desire for autonomy and intensified emotional reactivity on the one hand and slower developing capacity for self-regulation on the other. Such rhetoric leads to stigmatizing adolescents as immature and troubled and maintains long-standing societal stereotypes about them (National Academies of Sciences, Engineering, and Medicine, 2019). Furthermore, it informs practices and policies geared toward protecting adolescents from potential harm, but inadvertently limits their opportunity to learn from experience.

Recent advances in developmental neuroscience evidenced that the adolescent brain is characterized by malleability and plasticity that primes it for learning and experiences (Fuhrmann et al., 2015). Neural plasticity is a "window of opportunity for specialized learning – a maturational interval when patterns of experience are shaping patterns of neural connections in the developing brain" (Dahl & Suleiman, 2017, p. 23). While this can set the stage for negative outcomes, it can also create many opportunities for learning, exploration, and growth. Heightened neuroplasticity in adolescence represents a second window of opportunity in brain development and therefore for environmental interventions (Fuhrmann et al., 2015). The adolescent brain is especially sensitive to experiential input affecting self-regulation and socio-emotional functioning (Choudhury, 2017). Therefore, policies and practices regarding adolescents should "better leverage these developmental opportunities to harness the promise of adolescence – rather than focusing myopically on containing its risks" (National Academies of Sciences, Engineering, and Medicine, 2019, p. 1).

Social context plays a central role in understanding adolescents' behavior. Not only the mind, but the human brain is also situated in a sociocultural context (Choudhury, 2017). "Sociocultural and biological forces are inextricably entwined and mutually shape brain development and activity" (Choudhury & Ferranti, 2018, p. 41). Biological changes only create particular behavioral tendencies, whereas actual behavior is determined by the complex interaction of social, emotional, psychological, behavioral, and neurodevelopmental processes in a particular sociocultural context (Dahl & Suleiman, 2017). For example, pubertal changes in sleep/wake regulation might lead to preferences to stay up later and sleep in later. However, habits associated with digital media use at bedtime might amplify those biological tendencies and lead to problematic behaviors.

Hormonal changes associated with puberty stimulate many changes in the brain by reorganizing neural circuitry, especially those involved in processing rewards, emotions, and social relationships (Dahl & Suleiman, 2017). These neural changes propel adolescents' motivation to explore their boundaries and engage in novel experiences. During adolescence the dopaminergic system that mediates orientation toward rewards undergoes significant changes, including the projection of dopaminergic neurons to various subcortical and cortical brain regions (Telzer, 2016). The adolescent brain is especially wired for social and emotional learning (Casey, 2015; Dahl & Suleiman, 2017). Heightened dopaminergic activity is associated with motivation for exploration, novelty, and risk-taking and increased sensitivity to social evaluation and rejection (Telzer, 2016). This might result in poor well-being or serve as an adaptive function, steering adolescents toward positive behaviors. Adolescents are highly motivated to engage in interpersonal relationships with peers and romantic partners and to learn about the social world and their place in it (Dahl & Suleiman, 2017). They have a strong motivation to be accepted, belong, and feel respected; but may also experience anxiety associated with potential rejection and humiliation. From an evolutionary perspective, such an amplified interest in social interactions coincides with sexual maturity and prepares adolescents to find a mate and raise children. However, in modern society, these biological changes typically do not come to completion. Instead, they are open opportunities for exploration and experimentation (Dahl & Suleiman, 2017).

Adolescents may have difficulty controlling impulses and demonstrate an intensified limbic response to threats (Casey, 2015). These characteristics can be attributed to the asynchronous development of the subcortical region of the brain, which is involved in emotions and motivation, and the cortical region responsible for cognitive control. The asynchrony between bottom-up limbic and top-down prefrontal control regions explains adolescents' bias toward socio-emotional and reward-based information. Nevertheless, it does not necessarily imply negative outcomes associated with difficulty regulating one's emotions and drives (Casey, 2015). Instead, a decreased fear of novelty can propel exploratory behavior and learning. However, the kind of exploratory behavior adolescents will be involved in depends on their socialization. Socialization practices in family and school should take advantage of adolescents' readiness to learn and steer them toward positive trajectories. However, when not being monitored, adolescents' propensity toward emotional and motivational sensitivity can lead to substance abuse, risky sexual behavior, and mental health problems (Casey, 2015). For example, the heightened response in the dopamine-rich region of the ventral striatum might lead adolescents to experiment with illicit drugs that can cause addiction (Casey, 2015). However, one study showed that the activation in the ventral striatum was higher in the presence of peers but lower in the presence of one's mother (Telzer, 2016). Therefore, parental supervision can be an important protective factor against risk-taking behavior.

With the maturation of the cortical region and increased synchronization of brain regions, adolescents gain a better ability to self-regulate and make decisions that consider future outcomes (Casey, 2015). For example, a longitudinal study demonstrated that fun-seeking can predict both prosocial and rebellious behaviors while a faster maturing prefrontal cortex leads to less rebellious behavior (Blankenstein et al., 2020). The popular perception that adolescents lack self-regulation due to an immature brain is not accurate (Casey, 2015). Indeed, adolescents are able to demonstrate adequate self-regulation unless strong environmental cues are present. When these cues are present (regardless of their valence), adolescents might show heightened reactivity which may contribute to difficulty in suppressing inappropriate emotions, desires, and an inability to engage in appropriate actions (Casey, 2015).

Puberty in Adolescent Girls

Puberty is defined as the period of biopsychosocial transition from childhood to adulthood initiated by significant neuroendocrine changes (Susman & Dorn, 2013). In girls, physical changes associated with puberty (i.e., increase in breast tissue) appear earlier than in boys. Puberty is both a biological and sociocultural construct. While biological and physical changes are universal, the meaning of puberty and its associated behavioral expectations are different across cultures and time. Puberty brings about changes in how adolescents view themselves, their bodies, and their relationships with others. The earlier view of adolescence (stemming from work of Freud and Hall) considered puberty as the beginning of a turbulent and stressful developmental period (Susman & Dorn, 2013). However, research indicates that the majority of adolescents do not experience "storminess" and "turbulence," but adjust rather well to the changes associated with this developmental period.

Today, girls enter puberty earlier compared to their peers from previous generations (Susman & Dorn, 2013). Obesity might be one initiator of earlier puberty. Another proposed mechanism is endocrine disruption, an alteration of endocrine function by estrogen contained in household cleaning products, cosmetics, or food. The presence of family stressors is also associated with earlier puberty. When a father is absent and male-female relationships in the family are conflictual, girls might perceive relationships with a male as unstable and unreliable. As a result, they may start puberty earlier and engage in early sexual activity to maximize their reproductive capability (Susman & Dorn, 2013). However, high parental investment in child rearing, warmth, and father involvement creates a different social context for girls, leading them to believe in their worth and competitiveness. Girls from such families have the opportunity for a longer childhood.

In girls, earlier onset of puberty is associated with negative outcomes, including an increased risk for depression, negative emotions, problematic alcohol use, and behavioral problems (Susman & Dorn, 2013). However, such risks are present for girls who had behavioral problems before puberty. Increases of the hormone estradiol may heighten girls' sensitivity to emotionally upsetting events. Girls may feel isolated when around other girls who mature at a more typical pace. Unfortunately, having earlier puberty is often associated with earlier pregnancy, low-paying jobs, and consequently increased life stressors (Mendle et al., 2007). It is also associated with a higher risk of bulimia. Early maturation coupled with feminine gender role identity and a stressful environment increase the likelihood of internalizing symptoms (Natsuaki et al., 2015).

One reason why early maturation might negatively impact girls' well-being is that these girls transition to the next developmental period too quickly, without being fully prepared. With changes in physical appearance, girls must navigate new social norms and expectations placed on them by their parents and other adults which leads to changes in their self-perception and identity (Mendle et al., 2007). Girls with a more mature physical appearance might lead adults to place greater expectations and pressure on them; however, these girls may not have the cognitive and emotional resources yet to meet those expectations (Susman & Dorn, 2013). Social context plays an important role in how girls navigate the challenges associated with early puberty, leading to either resilience or vulnerability (Mendle et al., 2007). Given these findings, girls with earlier puberty may benefit from working with a mental health professional to reduce the risk of significant emotional and behavioral problems.

Adolescents' Mental Health

Adolescence is a time of increased susceptibility to psychopathology (Powers & Casey, 2015). Early adolescence is associated with an onset of mental disorders, substance use, suicides, eating disorders, sexually transmitted infections, and unwanted pregnancy (Dahl & Suleiman, 2017). Adolescents' low fear extinction, or difficulty regulating fear when a threat is no longer present, puts them at greater risk for anxiety and stress-related disorders (Powers & Casey, 2015). Difficulty regulating fear expression is associated with immature fronto-amygdala neurocircuitry. Fear extinction is also important to recover from stress; therefore, adolescents might not recover quickly from stressful events. Given that, exposure-based treatment of anxiety may not be effective for the adolescent population (Powers & Casey, 2015).

In adolescence, depression is often precipitated by social rejection or a loss of status in social relationships (Davey et al., 2008). During this age, reward is often associated with positive social relationships, including love, feelings of belonging, and acceptance. However, such rewards may not be immediately available. Given the still maturing prefrontal cortex, adolescents may have difficulty pursuing distal rewards. If the reward system has been suppressed for a long time, it might lead to depression (Davey et al., 2008).

Stress exposure also makes adolescents susceptible to depression (Andersen & Teicher, 2008). Exposure to a stressful event during adolescence likely results in alterations in prefrontal development which weakens the capacity of the prefrontal cortex to regulate the overactivated amygdala. An overactivated amygdala is responsible for social anxiety that often precedes depression in adolescence (Andersen & Teicher, 2008). Furthermore, early exposure to stress alters hippocampal development, which leads to failing to accurately evaluate contexts when emotionally laden stimuli are present (Andersen & Teicher, 2008).

Rapee and colleagues (2019) explained how the interaction of developmental processes in adolescence and risk factors existing prior to the onset of adolescence could trigger socio-emotional disorders. Hormonal changes coupled with morphological changes represent one risk pathway. Hormonal changes are linked to emotional reactivity and sensitivity to social rewards. These changes are also associated with diminished sleep quality and heightened emotionality. Sleep deficit is one factor that makes adolescents vulnerable to emotional disorders. These factors, coupled with preexisting risks and a diminished emotion regulation capacity, might trigger emotional disorders. The morphological changes during puberty (e.g., changes in physical appearance) often lead to changes in self-perception and social interactions. If observable physical changes are not desirable (e.g., gained weight), then they present a risk for emotional problems, especially when coupled with heightened self-consciousness (Rapee et al., 2019).

Adolescents with temperamentally based heightened emotionality are less successful in social interactions and more likely to be rejected by peers, which increases the risk for depression (Rapee et al., 2019). Emotional difficulties negatively impact relationships and school performance which, in turn, further lead to negative emotions. A lack of support from peers, peer rejection, and social comparison are among the social risk factors for emotional problems, especially in adolescents with preexisting vulnerabilities (e.g., lack of social competence or low self-esteem and popularity). These social risk factors are more salient for girls than for boys (Rapee et al., 2019).

There are significant gender differences in adolescent psychopathology. While early onset disorders (e.g., conduct disorder, autism, developmental language disorders, ADHD) are more common in males, adolescent-onset emotional disorders (e.g., mood disorders, anxiety disorders, and eating disorders) are more common in females (Zahn-Waxler et al., 2008). Sex differences in behavioral and emotional problems and disorders can be attributed to different environmental risk factors, biological processes, and their combination. Certain brain structures, including the frontal cortex, caudate, and temporal lobes, develop much faster in girls than in boys, which leads to better decision-making, judgment, and inhibitory control. These developments decrease the risk for externalizing problems in girls. At the same time, rapid physical maturation and the tendency to overprocess emotional cues might increase the risk for internalizing problems. Additionally, earlier onset of puberty increases the risk to develop depressive symptoms (Zahn-Waxler et al., 2008). Girls are more invested and at the same time more sensitive to interpersonal relationships, which is why disruption in relationships is more stressful for girls than for boys. Additionally, they may over-rely on others, which can decrease their agency and ability to cope effectively, thus contributing to feeling depressed. Heightened vulnerability to interpersonal stressors might also create anxiety associated with potential rejection and not being liked by others. Additionally, girls tend to ruminate more than boys and are more sensitive to reactions of others such as approval/disapproval and acceptance/rejection. Unfortunately, the internalizing nature of girls' problems make them less "visible" as having difficulty; as a result, they may not receive necessary help from mental health professionals (Zahn-Waxler et al., 2008).

Barriers to Adolescents' Health and Well-Being

The health of adolescents…is integrally shaped by the daily contexts in which they grow and develop. Transformations in world economics, government, families, and technology, among other things, are altering societies around the world, and, in turn, reshaping the contexts of adolescents' lives.

(Call et al., 2002, p. 77)

Economic, social, and structural barriers can significantly compromise adolescents' healthy development by reducing access to the opportunities and services and exposing youth to risks and stresses. Adolescents are characterized by heightened sensitivity to environmental influences; therefore, their development can be compromised by adversities such as resource deprivation, unhealthy relationships, and exposure to drugs or violence (National Academies of Sciences, Engineering, and Medicine, 2019). Environmental pressures can "get under the skin" and negatively affect adolescents' brain development leading to a wide range of problems. Disparities based on socioeconomic status, race, and ethnicity exist in adolescents' health, mental health, and educational outcomes. A meta-analytic study by Benner and colleagues (2018) showed that greater perceptions of racial/ethnic discrimination were linked to greater psychological distress, more depressive and other internalizing symptoms, poor self-esteem, lower academic achievement and engagement, and greater engagement in risky sexual behaviors, externalizing behaviors, and substance use. Identity coherence is especially important at the time of cultural transition. White and high-SES status youth not only have better outcomes, but also have better access to opportunities to achieve those outcomes. At the same time, social connectedness is an important factor for psychosocial well-being in adolescents of color. A large-scale study ($N = 1170$) with African American and Caribbean Black adolescents found that those well connected to their family, peer, school, religion, and neighborhood had higher life satisfaction, self-esteem, mastery, and coping, and lower depression and perceived stress compared to not well connected youth (Rose et al., 2019). Therefore, promoting connectedness is a promising intervention avenue.

In the US, more than nine million children and youth live in households with incomes below the poverty level, with the rates higher for racial and ethnic minority youth (National Academies of Sciences, Engineering, and Medicine, 2019). Growing up in poverty is associated with increased stress levels, risky behaviors including delinquency, and worse physical and mental health. As a result of residential segregation in the US, adolescents from poor or minority families often live in poor and segregated neighborhoods with a lack of access to educational and social resources necessary for healthy development (National Academies of Sciences, Engineering, and Medicine, 2019). Living in poverty is associated with high-risk behaviors, including substance abuse, delinquency, early pregnancy, poor nutrition, school failure, and a pessimistic outlook (Call et al., 2002). Low-income urban youth of color often experience elevated levels of stress associated with poverty, exposure to drugs, violence, unwanted pregnancies, and sexual harassment (Berg et al., 2009). Youth from immigrant families experience additional stress from acculturation and breaking ties with their home culture (Call et al., 2002). LGBTQ youth are also at higher risk of mental health problems than their heterosexual peers (National Academies of Sciences, Engineering, and Medicine, 2019).

Digital Media and Adolescents' Mental Health

The growing proliferation of digital media has brought both promise and risks to youth's development. Digital media is a ubiquitous part of youth's lives: About 97% of adolescents use a social media platform such as YouTube, Instagram, Snapchat, or Facebook (Anderson & Jiang, 2018). Approximately 45% of teens report being "almost constantly" online, with girls being more likely than boys (50% vs. 39%) to report being "almost constantly" online (Anderson & Jiang, 2018). Over 95% of teens have access to smartphones (Anderson & Jiang, 2018) and over half of US children own their own smartphones by age 11 (Rideout & Robb, 2019).

Digital media allow youth access to a vast amount of information, create opportunities for learning, and expand social interaction. Adolescents consider the Internet as a private space for practicing autonomy, identity exploration, developing interests, and connecting with peers (Borca et al., 2015). Moreover, it can be a safe place for interactions for youth with social anxiety and underdeveloped socio-emotional skills (Pierce, 2009; Ziv & Kiasi, 2016).

At the same time, the excessive use of digital media is associated with many risks for adolescents' well-being. A large-scale study in the UK ($N = 9,859$) found that adolescent girls used social media more than boys (Booker et al., 2018). In girls, spending a lot of time on social media in early adolescence was associated with diminished well-being later on. Throughout adolescence, well-being declines in both boys and girls (Booker et al., 2018). A national survey in the US found that youth with lower life satisfaction tend to be the heaviest media users (Roberts & Foehr, 2008). Adolescents using social media for more than two hours a day reported more significant mental health problems, including psychological distress and suicidal ideation (Sampasa-Kanyinga & Lewis, 2015). The association between social media usage and symptoms of depression is stronger for girls compared to boys (Kelly et al., 2018). A longitudinal study with adolescents found that compulsive Internet use predicted mental health problems, especially in adolescent girls (Ciarrochi et al., 2016). Problematic smartphone use is associated with poorer mental health and well-being, including higher symptoms of anxiety (Sohn et al., 2019). Low academic performance and poor relationships with parents were both predictive of greater levels of smartphone overuse (Lee & Lee, 2017).

Rosen and colleagues (2013) argue that screen technology created so-called "iDisorders." The authors found that youth with a greater number of Facebook friends and higher rates of Facebook use also have more significant mental health problems. Adolescents with higher levels of daily stress often use Facebook for social support. Although the perceived support is associated with less depression, seeking but not receiving support can exacerbate depressive symptoms (Frison & Eggermont, 2015). Adolescents with stronger needs for belonging and popularity also use Facebook more often (Beyens et al., 2016). A Fear of Missing Out (FoMO) can also contribute to social media overuse. FoMO is a pervasive apprehension that others may have enjoyable experiences from which one is absent. It leads to the desire to stay continuously connected with others in order to avoid missing potentially positive experiences (Przybylski et al., 2013). Those with stronger FoMO use Facebook more frequently and experience greater stress related to Facebook use. Females are especially susceptible to FoMO and problematic Instagram use (Balta et al., 2020).

The overuse of screen media may reduce the quality of adolescents' relationships with their families and peers (Morimoto & Friedland, 2011; Steiner-Adair & Barker, 2013; Subrahmanyam & Greenfield, 2008). Furthermore, anonymity in online social networking can disinhibit racist behavior, sexual harassment and solicitation, and cyberbullying (Subrahmanyam & Greenfield, 2008). Multitasking, prompted by digital media, can overtax mental resources and compromise executive functioning (Baumgartner et al., 2014; Courage et al., 2015). Excessive use of screen media also reduces quality of sleep, which has a downward spiral effect on academic performance and emotional health (Hysing et al., 2016; Zaccaro et al., 2019). Elevated exposure on social media is a risk factor for negative body image and eating disorders (McLean et al., 2015; Mingoia et al., 2017).

Social media may encourage ego enhancement and unrealistic self-evaluation through participation in behaviors that yield approval, adoration, and compliments (e.g., posting selfies, updating status, and counting "likes"; Adreassen et al., 2017; Lee & Sung, 2016). These behaviors provide adolescents with transient confirmation of their value and worth and maintain an elevated sense of self through the nearly instantaneous feedback from large user communities.

Unfortunately, many adolescents are unaware of the potential negative effects of screen media on their well-being: Forty-five percent believe that social media use has neither a positive nor a negative effect; 31% reported mostly positive effects; and only 24% reported mostly negative effects (Anderson & Jiang, 2018).

Pathways to Optimal Adolescent Development

Positive Youth Development

Adolescence is a developmental period that opens windows of opportunity for positive development:

A close understanding of these windows of opportunity, and how they are shaped by the environment and by experience, can have enormous implications for the ways in which we–in research, policy, advocacy, education, families, mental health and medicine–can provide protective, nurturing and empowering environments for adolescents.

(Choudhury, 2017, p. 40)

Adolescents are very responsive to psychosocial interventions aimed at mastering adaptive skills and preventing emotional and behavioral risks. Therefore, more attention should be given to developing policies and interventions aimed at creating opportunities for exploration, discovery, and innovation.

Positive Youth Development (PYD) is an evidence-based framework that delineates optimal development for adolescents (Lerner et al., 2013). PYD conceptualizes positive adolescent development with the "Five Cs": Competence, confidence, connection, character, and caring. These characteristics add to the definition of a "thriving youth" (Lerner et al., 2013). The presence of the "Five Cs" allows youth to be active agents in their own development and contribute to family, community, and society. Contribution to community is a key indicator of youth positive development (Lerner et al., 2013). The PYD framework considers young people to be producers of their own development, meaning that they are conscious agents in developing their knowledge, skills, and attitudes that help them navigate a complex world. The PYD framework approaches youth from a strengths perspective and seeks to identify mediators or environmental factors that result in positive developmental outcomes (Larson & Tran, 2014).

Adolescent development involves mutually influential relationships between a developing person and his or her context (Lerner et al., 2013). A person-and-context relationship regulates the directions and outcomes of the developmental course. The complexity and diversity of the developmental system creates many opportunities for change by finding the best alignment between a person's characteristics and contextual resources. The PYD framework states that thriving is possible for all adolescents by aligning their strengths with resources present in their social and physical environment. The plasticity of the adolescent brain opens many opportunities for positive development. However, the realization of these opportunities depends on how the environment meets adolescents' needs and capitalizes on their strengths. Therefore, it is important to align the resources for healthy growth present in the home, school, and community with the strengths of the youth (Lerner et al., 2013).

Positive development in adolescence depends on the presence, quality, and accessibility of ecological resources. Theokas and Lerner (2006) identified several ecological resources that can promote positive change, including human and physical/institutional resources, collective activity, and accessibility of resources. Human resources comprise strengths, talents, and abilities of people with whom adolescents interact. Examples include people (e.g., mentors in community-based or after-school programs) who can model positive behavior and reflect on youth's maladaptive behaviors. Physical/institutional resources include opportunities for learning, recreation, and engagement present in the community. The proximity of such resources increases the likelihood of youth's involvement. The collective activity resource includes the combined efforts of all parties involved in youth development, for example, the engagement between community members, parents, youth, schools, and youth organizations (Theokas & Lerner, 2006). Finally, resources must be accessible to youth, including transportation, hours of operation of youth-serving programs, infrastructure, ratio of adults to children in a neighborhood, and safety of the physical environment.

Benson and colleagues (2011) named the social and ecological resources that promote youths' physical and mental growth as "developmental assets." These assets can be external and internal. External assets include supportive relationships with familiar and non-familiar adults, caring schools and neighborhoods, and parental involvement in schooling. They also include empowerment by a community that is safe and values youth and their contribution. The presence of boundaries in family, community, and school, characterized by appropriate supervision, clear rules, and consequences for breaking those rules are among other external assets. Additional external assets include spending at least three hours a week in meaningful and creative activities and having high expectations and encouragement to do well from adults. Internal assets comprise commitment to learning, positive values, social competence, and positive identity, including a sense of purpose, a positive view of the future, and agency.

In one study, developmental assets were positively linked to life satisfaction, with self-esteem being the largest contributor (Soares et al., 2019). Among the assets contributing to life satisfaction were family support, planning and decision-making, a sense of purpose, positive family communication, caring, and school engagement. Nationally recognized, community-based organizations (e.g., Boys and Girls Clubs, Scouting, Big Brothers/Big Sisters, YMCA, or Girls, Inc.) and programs offered by local after-school programs are vital sources of developmental assets (Lerner et al., 2013). Programs that draw on the PYD framework are the most successful in yielding positive outcomes.

Resilience as an Integral Part of Youth Optimal Development

Resilience is defined as "patterns of positive adaptation in the context of risk or adversity" (Masten & Tellegen, 2012, p. 347). It is "an achievement-oriented sense of self attained by the individual to overcome obstacles (risks) by drawing on available resources (protective factors)" (Spencer et al., 2006, p. 635). Resilience is not a static phenomenon but develops and changes over time (Masten & Tellegen, 2012). Resilient youth who had adverse experiences have similar positive cognitive and socio-emotional outcomes as youth who did not experience much adversity. At the same time, youth who lack adaptive capacity experience significant stress when facing adversity.

Youth's adaptation is intrinsically connected with the achievement of developmental tasks. These tasks are culturally constructed and represent societal expectations about one's performance and behaviors (Masten & Tellegen, 2012). Healthy development depends on how effectively youth can meet the demands of developmental tasks at different stages of development. Furthermore, it "involves *negotiating some level of stage-specific threat* (i.e., given available and honed competencies of salience to the risks confronted) and *demonstrating a degree of resilience* (i.e., successful outcomes) in the face of challenge" (Spencer et al., 2006, p. 628). Adolescents' capacity for adaptive behavior is an important competence closely related to mastering developmental tasks (Masten & Tellegen, 2012). Being competent in mastering developmental tasks makes youth more resistant to stress.

Spencer and colleagues (2006) assert that in order to understand youth's adaptive development, we need to understand how adolescents perceive and construct their own worlds. Overlooking this aspect of adolescent lives may result in misunderstanding of adolescents' experiences. Accurate understanding of adolescents' lives, especially those of minority groups, requires attention to cultural values intrinsically embedded in adolescents' experiences. Youth of color frequently live in high-risk environments and experience systemic and structural barriers to individual success. Unfortunately, resilience in vulnerable youth often goes unrecognized. Ignoring resilience stemming from aversive life conditions linked to race and ethnicity leads to misinterpretation of youth coping efforts (Spencer et al., 2006). Limiting the protective function of recognized resiliency can further weaken a sense of agency and success. Deficit perspectives on minority youth originate from comparing them to the dominant culture and fail to recognize intragroup diversity and cultural strengths (Berg et al., 2009).

Spencer and colleagues (2006) emphasized the importance of understanding the interplay between contextual factors, their perceptions and appraisals, and emerging identity in adolescence. More specifically, attention should be paid to the risk and protective factors present at a particular developmental stage and to how youth perceive and experience challenging situations and available resources. Perception and appraisal of risks and available resources become an integral part of emerging identity in adolescents. Additionally, adolescents' responses to stressors, whether in adaptive or maladaptive ways, become stable over time and form part of one's emerging identity.

Activities that Foster Positive Youth Development

The "potential for change represents a fundamental strength of human development" (Lerner et al., 2013, p. 366). Adolescents' desire to take risks, the importance of social relationships and status, and heightened sensitivity to reward make them open to learning new experiences (National Academies of Sciences, Engineering, and Medicine, 2019). Furthermore, they are equipped intellectually to navigate complex human and societal issues (Larson, 2011). They can reflect on their experiences, have more advanced inductive and deductive reasoning skills, and more mature executive functions. All these cognitive advances allow youth to generate goals, exercise agency, and deal with various emotional and motivational challenges. Participation in positive activities represents a natural lab to foster the aforementioned skills (Larson, 2011).

Youth programs are an important avenue to promote positive development and well-being in adolescents. These include extracurricular activities, volunteering, youth activism programs, and youth participatory action research. Providing youth with a wide range of activities is an important developmental asset associated with positive development (Lerner et al., 2013). Experiencing a capacity to bring social change, contributing to others' well-being, and making a difference in society contributes to adolescents' empowerment. Lerner and colleagues (2013) identified the key features of effective youth programs, including positive and sustained relationships between youth and adults; promotion of important life skills; and creating opportunities to use these skills in valued community activities. Youth's psychological engagement in these activities (e.g., enjoyment) rather than simple physical presence is essential for positive developmental outcomes (Ramey et al., 2019). Program leaders are very important for engaging adolescents in positive activities. They can support youth's experience of ownership and agency while providing scaffolded guidance (Larson, 2011).

A large-scale longitudinal study, the 4-H Study of Positive Youth Development, demonstrated that extracurricular activities that capitalize on developmental assets and youth strengths promote positive development (Lerner et al., 2013). Participation in organized activities also helps reduce relational aggression through the joint effect of competence, peer connection, and contribution (Eisman et al., 2018). However, reducing the range of out-of-school activities is likely associated with increased depressive symptoms and risk-taking behaviors, including substance use (Agans et al., 2014).

Larson (2000, 2006) argued that participation in positive activities requires and simultaneously fosters the motivational and cognitive skills necessary for successful development. Engagement in positive activities calls for initiative, that is, internal motivation to pursue a challenging goal. In order to develop initiative, adolescents need not only opportunities for extracurricular voluntary activities, but supportive mentoring from adults as well. Youth's motivation to participate in positive activities can be weakened by various barriers, including boredom (Larson, 2000). Boredom arises when young people are not challenged enough. For that reason, matching the level of skills with the level of challenge is important. Furthermore, motivation is a dynamic process: It can be low at the beginning of a project but can pick up as the project unfolds. That is why it is important to make activities personally meaningful for adolescents and foster their sense of ownership in order for motivation to emerge.

During adolescence, young people become increasingly capable of prospective cognition. This means that they can reason about the future, anticipate events, and formulate flexible plans (Larson et al., 2014). Adolescents need strategic thinking in order to exercise agency within multiple social systems in which they are embedded (Larson & Hansen, 2005). Youth activism programs are a promising context to foster strategic thinking. In one program, Hispanic and African American youth worked together to bring positive social change in their school (Larson & Hansen, 2005). Participation in that program allowed youth to develop strategic thinking skills and transfer those skills from the context of the program to schoolwork and planning for their future.

Another project, a theater program, can provide youth with real-life contexts to learn emotional skills. Larson and Brown (2007) studied the effectiveness of high school theater programs on socio-emotional learning. Youths who participated in the program reflected that they learned about emotional elicitors and how to manage their emotions effectively. They became aware of the causes of emotions, learned how emotions unfold (e.g., through contagion), and how emotions influence one's behavior (e.g., positive emotions can help to combat anxiety and fear).

Adolescents' positive development can also be promoted through Youth Participatory Action Research (Youth-PAR). Youth-PAR is an advocacy-based approach to working with young people that integrates PYD, experiential education, prevention, and service-learning frameworks (Schensul et al., 2004). In Youth-PAR, adolescents act as advocates for social change. This is especially beneficial for marginalized youth as it helps them gain a sense of agency in shaping their own and their communities' future. Core elements of Youth-PAR include identity formation and building culture-specific socio-emotional and cognitive competencies. It further focuses on the development of a strong sense of group identity, promotes the understanding and value of diverse perspectives, and bridges cultural differences.

The Youth-PAR teaches young people skills to identify risks and protective factors, conduct community-based research, and generate a grounded theory of change (Schensul et al., 2004). In Youth-PAR, adolescents explore policies, laws, and cultural practices that affect their lives and take actions to improve life quality and opportunities (Berg et al., 2009). They build positive youth community as they learn to negotiate with each other and capitalize on their individual and collective efficacy. In one Youth-PAR project that lasted three years, low-income African Caribbean and Latino high school youth researched their needs and the needs of their communities as well as barriers to a successful life (Berg et al., 2009). Youths were engaged in social actions aimed at changing policies toward better serving young people at their schools and communities. This project helped participants explore their identities and opportunities and had a positive effect on youth's attitudes and behaviors.

Recommended Resources

Search Institute – https://www.search-institute.org/

Search Institute is a nonprofit organization that focuses on promoting PYD, especially in marginalized communities. It designs and delivers workshops, surveys, programs, and other practical resources to help improve the relationships between adults and youth in various settings.

Act for Youth – http://actforyouth.net/youth_development/professionals/manual.cfm

The Assets Coming Together for Youth Center for Community Action is an organization that connects research to practice for PYD and mental health. It provides resources, training, evaluative services, and consultations. This organization offers the PYD 101 curriculum, which provides an orientation for professionals on the youth development approach. The curriculum is structured in five sections focused on PYD, positive youth outcomes, youth voice and engagement, youth development programming, and youth worker competencies.

4-H Positive Youth Development – https://4-h.org/

This organization strives to provide youth with community, mentors, and learning opportunities to develop the skills they need to create positive change in their lives and communities. In 4-H programs, children and adolescents complete hands-on projects in areas such as health, science, agriculture, and civic engagement in a positive and supportive atmosphere where they receive guidance from adult mentors and are encouraged to explore interests, learn new skills, and take on leadership roles.

References

Adreassen, C. S., Pallesen, S., & Griffiths, M. D. (2017). The relationship between addictive use of social media, narcissism, and self-esteem: Findings from a large national survey. *Addictive Behaviors, 64*, 287–293. https://doi.org/10.1016/j.addbeh.2016.03.006

Agans, J. P., Champine, R. B., DeSouza, L. M., Mueller, M. K., Johnson, S. K., & Lerner, R. M. (2014). Activity involvement as an ecological asset: Profiles of participation and youth outcomes. *Journal of Youth and Adolescence, 43,* 919–932. https://doi.org/10.1007/s10964-014-0091-1

Anderson, M., & Jiang, J. (2018). Teens, social media and technology overview 2018. *Pew Internet & American Life Project.* https://www.pewresearch.org/internet/2018/05/31/teens-social-media-technology-2018/

Andersen, S. L., & Teicher, M. H. (2008). Stress, sensitive periods and maturational events in adolescent depression. *Trends in Neurosciences, 31*(4), 183–191. https://doi.org/10.1016/j.tins.2008.01.004

Balta, S., Emirtekin, E., Kircaburun, K., & Griffiths, M. D. (2020). Neuroticism, trait fear of missing out, and phubbing: The mediating role of state fear of missing out and problematic Instagram use. *International Journal of Mental Health and Addiction, 18,* 628–639. https://doi.org/10.1007/s11469-018-9959-8

Baumgartner, S. E., Weeda, W. D., van der Heijden, L. L., & Huizinga, M. (2014). The relationship between media multitasking and executive function in early adolescents. *The Journal of Early Adolescence, 34*(8), 1120–1144. https://doi.org/10.1177/0272431614523133

Benner, A. D., Wang, Y., Shen, Y., Boyle, A. E., Polk, R., & Cheng, Y. P. (2018). Racial/ethnic discrimination and well-being during adolescence: A meta-analytic review. *The American Psychologist, 73*(7), 855–883. doi:10.1037/amp0000204

Benson, P. L., Scales, P. C., & Syvertsen, A. K. (2011). The contribution of the developmental assets framework to positive youth development theory and practice. *Advances in child development and behavior, 41,* 197–230. Academic Press. https://doi.org/10.1016/b978-0-12-386492-5.00008-7

Berg, M., Coman, E., & Schensul, J. J. (2009). Youth action research for prevention: A multi-level intervention designed to increase efficacy and empowerment among urban youth. *American Journal of Community Psychology, 43*(3–4), 345–359. https://doi.org/10.1007/s10464-009-9231-2

Beyens, I., Frison, E., & Eggermont, S. (2016). "I don't want to miss a thing": Adolescents' fear of missing out and its relationship to adolescents' social needs, Facebook use, and Facebook related stress. *Computers in Human Behavior, 64,* 1–8. https://doi.org/10.1016/j.chb.2016.05.083

Blankenstein, N. E., Telzer, E. H., Do, K. T., van Duijvenvoorde, A. C. K., & Crone, E. A. (2020). Behavioral and neural pathways supporting the development of prosocial and risk-taking behavior across adolescence. *Child Development, 91*(3), e665–e681. https://doi.org/10.1111/cdev.13292

Booker, C. L., Kelly, Y. J., Sacker, A. (2018). Gender differences in the associations between age trends of social media interaction and well-being among 10–15 year olds in the UK. *BMC Public Health, 18*(321). https://doi.org/10.1186/s12889-018-5220-4

Borca, G., Bina, M., Keller, P. S., Gilbert, L. R., & Begotti, T. (2015). Internet use and developmental tasks: Adolescents' point of view. *Computers in Human Behavior, 52,* 49–58. https://doi.org/10.1016/j.chb.2015.05.029

Call, K. T., Riedel, A. A., Hein, K., McLoyd, V., Petersen, A., & Kipke, M. (2002). Adolescent health and well-being in the twenty-first century: A global perspective. *Journal of Research on Adolescence, 12*(1), 69–98. https://doi.org/10.1111/1532-7795.00025

Casey, B. J. (2015). Beyond simple models of self-control to circuit-based accounts of adolescent behavior. *Annual Review of Psychology, 66*(1), 295–319. https://doi.org/10.1146/annurev-psych-010814-015156

Choudhury, S. (2017). Situating the adolescent brain: The developing brain in its cultural contexts. In N. Balvin & P. Banati (Eds.), *The adolescent brain: A second window of opportunity* (pp. 39–45). UNICEF Office of Research.

Choudhury S., & Ferranti, N. (2018). The science of the adolescent brain and its cultural implications. In G. Anca, C. Gideon, & De W. Jurgen (Eds.), *The Routledge handbook of the philosophy of childhood and children* (pp. 33–44). Routledge Publisher. https://doi.org/10.4324/9781351055987-4

Ciarrochi, J., Parker, P., Sahdra, B., Marshall, S., Jackson, C., Gloster, A. T., & Heaven, P. (2016). The development of compulsive internet use and mental health: A four-year study of adolescence. *Developmental Psychology, 52*(2), 272–283. https://doi.org/10.1037/dev0000070

Courage, M. L., Bakhtiar, A., Fitzpatrick, C., Kenny, S., & Brandeau, K. (2015). Growing up multitasking: The costs and benefits for cognitive development. *Developmental Review, 35*, 5–41. https://doi.org/10.1016/j.dr.2014.12.002

Crocetti, E. (2017). Identity formation in adolescence: The dynamic of forming and consolidating identity commitments. *Child Development Perspectives, 11*(2), 145–150. https://doi.org/10.1111/cdep.12226

Dahl, R., & Suleiman, A. (2017). Adolescent brain development: Window for opportunity. In N. Balvin & P. Banati (Eds.), *The adolescent brain: A second window of opportunity* (pp. 21–25). UNICEF Office of Research.

Davey, C. G., Yücel, M., & Allen, N. B. (2008). The emergence of depression in adolescence: Development of the prefrontal cortex and the representation of reward. *Neuroscience and Biobehavioral Reviews, 32*(1), 1–19. https://doi.org/10.1016/j.neubiorev.2007.04.016

Eisman, A. B., Stoddard, S. A., Bauermeister, J. A., Caldwell, C. H., & Zimmerman, M. A. (2018). Organized activity participation and relational aggression: The role of positive youth development. *Violence and Victims, 33*(1), 91–108. https://doi.org/10.1891/0886-6708.VV-D-16-00208

Ferrer-Wreder, L., & Kroger, J. (2020). *Identity in adolescence: The balance between self and other* (4th ed.). Routledge.

Frison, E., & Eggermont, S. (2015). The impact of daily stress on adolescents' depressed mood: The role of social support seeking through Facebook. *Computers in Human Behavior, 44*, 315–325. https://doi.org/10.1016/j.chb.2014.11.070

Fuhrmann, D., Knoll, L. J., & Blakemore, S. J. (2015). Adolescence as a sensitive period of brain development. *Trends in Cognitive Sciences, 19*(10), 558–566. https://doi.org/10.1016/j.tics.2015.07.008

Harter, S. (2012). *The construction of the self: Developmental and sociocultural foundations* (2nd ed.). New York & London: The Guilford Press.

Hysing, M., Harvey, A. G., Linton, S. J., Askeland, K. G., & Sivertsen, B. (2016). Sleep and academic performance in later adolescence: results from a large population-based study. *Journal of Sleep Research, 25*(3), 318–324. https://doi.org/10.1111/jsr.12373

Kelly, Y., Zilanawala, A., Booker, C., & Sacker, A. (2018). Social media use and adolescent mental health: Findings from the UK Millennium Cohort Study. *EClinicalMedicine, 6*, 59–68. https://doi.org/10.1016/j.eclinm.2018.12.005

Larson, R. W. (2000). Toward a psychology of positive youth development. *American Psychologist, 55*(1), 170–183. https://doi.org/10.1037/0003-066X.55.1.170

Larson, R. (2006). Positive youth development, willful adolescents, and mentoring. *Journal of Community Psychology, 34*(6), 677–689. https://doi.org/10.1002/jcop.20123

Larson, R. W. (2011). Positive development in a disorderly world: SRA presidential address. *Journal of Research on Adolescence, 21*(2), 317–334. https://doi.org/10.1111/j.1532-7795.2010.00707.x

Larson, R. W., & Brown, J. R. (2007). Emotional development in adolescence: What can be learned from a high school theater program. *Child Development, 78*(4), 1083–1099. https://doi.org/10.1111/j.1467-8624.2007.01054.x

Larson, R., & Hansen, D. M. (2005). The development of strategic thinking: Learning to impact human systems in a youth activism program. *Human Development, 48*(6), 327–349. https://doi.org/10.1159/000088251

Larson, R. W., Lampkins-Uthando, S., & Armstrong, J. (2014). Adolescents' development of new skills for prospective cognition: Learning to anticipate, plan, and think strategically. *Journal of Cognitive Education and Psychology, 13*(2), 232–244. https://doi.org/10.1891/1945-8959.13.2.232

Larson, R. W., & Tran, S. P. (2014). Invited commentary: Positive youth development and human complexity. *Journal of Youth and Adolescence, 43*, 1012–1017. https://doi.org/10.1007/s10964-014-0124-9

Lee, C., & Lee, S.-J. (2017). Prevalence and predictors of smartphone addiction proneness among Korean adolescents. *Children and Youth Services Review, 77*, 10–17. https://doi.org/10.1016/j.childyouth.2017.04.002

Lee, J-A., & Sung, Y. (2016). Hide-and-Seek: Narcissism and 'selfie'-related behavior. *Cyberpsychology, Behavior & Social Networking, 19*(5), 347–351. https://doi.org/10.1089/cyber.2015.0486

Lerner, J. V., Bowers, E. P., Minor, K., Boyd, M. J., Mueller, M. K., Schmid, K. L., Napolitano, C. M., Lewin-Bizan, S., & Lerner, R. M. (2013). Positive youth development: Processes, philosophies, and programs. In R. M. Lerner, M. A., Easterbrooks, J. Mistry, & I. B. Weiner (Eds.), *Handbook of psychology, Vol. 6: Developmental psychology* (pp. 365–392). John Wiley & Sons, Inc.

McLean, S. A., Paxton, S. J., Wertheim, E. H., & Masters, J. (2015). Photoshopping the selfie: Selfphoto editing and photo investment are associated with body dissatisfaction in adolescent girls. *The International Journal of Eating Disorders, 48*(8), 1132–1140. https://doi.org/10.1002/eat.22449

Masten, A. S., & Tellegen, A. (2012). Resilience in developmental psychopathology: Contributions of the project competence longitudinal study. *Development and Psychopathology, 24*(2), 345–361. https://doi.org/10.1017/S095457941200003X

Mendle, J., Turkheimer, E., & Emery, R. E. (2007). Detrimental psychological outcomes associated with early pubertal timing in adolescent girls. *Developmental Review, 27*(2), 151–171. https://doi.org/10.1016/j.dr.2006.11.001

Mingoia, J., Hutchinson, A. D., Wilson, C., & Gleaves, D. H. (2017). The relationship between social networking site use and the internalization of a thin ideal in females: A meta-analytic review. *Frontiers in Psychology, 8,* 1351. https://doi.org/10.3389/fpsyg.2017.01351

Morimoto, S. A., & Friedland, L. A. (2011). The lifeworld of youth in the information society. *Youth & Society, 43*(2), 549–567. https://doi.org/10.1177/0044118X10383655

National Academies of Sciences, Engineering, and Medicine (2019). *The promise of adolescence: Realizing opportunity for all youth.* The National Academies Press. https://doi.org/10.17226/25388

Natsuaki, M. N., Samuels, D., & Leve, L. D. (2015). Puberty, identity, and context: A biopsychosocial perspective on internalizing psychopathology in early adolescent girls. In K. C. McLean & M. Syed (Eds.), *Oxford library of psychology. The Oxford handbook of identity development* (pp. 389–405). Oxford University Press.

Pierce, T. (2009). Social anxiety and technology: Face-to-face communication versus technological communication among teens. *Computers in Human Behavior, 25*(6), 1367–1372. https://doi.org/10.1016/j.chb.2009.06.003

Powers, A., & Casey, B. J. (2015). The adolescent brain and the emergence and peak of psychopathology. *Journal of Infant, Child, and Adolescent Psychotherapy, 14*(1), 3–15. https://doi.org/10.1080/15289168.2015.1004889

Przybylski, A. K., Murayama, K., DeHaan, C. R., & Gladwell, V. (2013). Motivational, emotional, and behavioral correlates of fear of missing out. *Computers in Human Behavior, 29*(4), 1841–1848. doi:10.1016/j.chb.2013.02.014

Ramey, H. L., Lawford, H. L., & Rose-Krasnor, L. (2019). Psychological engagement and behavioral activity participation as predictors of positive youth development. *Journal of Youth Development, 14*(3), 88–109. https://doi.org/10.5195/jyd.2019.769

Rapee, R. M., Oar, E. L., Johnco, C. J., Forbes, M. K., Fardouly, J., Magson, N. R., & Richardson, C. E. (2019). Adolescent development and risk for the onset of social-emotional disorders: A review and conceptual model. *Behaviour Research and Therapy, 123*, 103501. https://doi.org/10.1016/j.brat.2019.103501

Rideout, V., & Robb, M. B. (2019). *The common sense census: Media use by tweens and teens, 2019.* Common Sense Media.

Roberts, D. F., & Foehr, U. G. (2008). Trends in media use. *The Future of Children, 18*(1), 11–37. https://doi.org/10.1353/foc.0.0000

Rose, T., McDonald, A., Von Mach, T., Witherspoon, D. P., & Lambert, S. (2019). Patterns of social connectedness and psychosocial wellbeing among African American and Caribbean Black adolescents. *Journal of Youth and Adolescence, 48*(11), 2271–2291. https://doi.org/10.1007/s10964-019-01135-7

Rosen, L. D., Whaling, K., Rab, S., Carrier, L. M., & Cheever, N. A. (2013). Is Facebook creating "iDisorders"? The link between clinical symptoms of psychiatric disorders and technology use, attitudes and anxiety. *Computers in Human Behavior, 29*(3), 1243–1254. https://doi.org/10.1016/j.chb.2012.11.012

Sampasa-Kanyinga, H., & Lewis, R. F. (2015). Frequent use of social networking sites is associated with poor psychological functioning among children and adolescents. *Cyberpsychology, Behavior, and Social Networking, 18*(7), 380–385. https://doi.org/10.1089/ cyber .2015.0055

Schensul, J., Berg, M. J., Schensul, D., & Sydlo, S. (2004). Core elements of participatory action research for educational empowerment and risk prevention with urban youth. *Practicing Anthropology, 26*(2), 5–9. https://doi.org/10.17730/praa.26.2.k287g8jh47855437

Soares, A. S., Pais-Ribeiro, J. L., & Silva, I. (2019). Developmental assets predictors of life satisfaction in adolescents. *Frontiers in Psychology, 10*, 236. https://doi.org/10.3389/fpsyg.2019.00236

Sohn, S. Y., Rees, P., Wildridge, B., Kalk, N. J., & Carter, B. (2019). Prevalence of problematic smartphone usage and associated mental health outcomes amongst children and young people: A systematic review, meta-analysis and GRADE of the evidence. *BMC Psychiatry, 19*, 356. https://doi.org/10.1186/s12888-019-2350-x

Spencer, M. B., Harpalani, V., Cassidy, E., Jacobs, C., Donde, S., Goss, T. N., et al. (2006). Understanding vulnerability and resilience from a normative development perspective: Implications for racially and ethnically diverse youth. In D. Cicchetti, & D. Cohen. (Eds.), *Handbook of Developmental Psychopathology: Vol. 1. Theory and Method* (2nd ed., pp. 627–672). Wiley.

Steiner-Adair, C., & Barker, T. (2013). *The big disconnect: Protecting childhood and family relationships in the digital age.* HarperCollins Publishers.

Subrahmanyam, K., & Greenfield, P. (2008). Online communication and adolescent relationships. *The Future of Children, 18*(1), 119–146. https://doi.org/10.1353/foc.0.0006

Susman, E. J., & Dorn, L. D. (2013). Puberty: Its role in development. In R. M. Lerner, M. A. Easterbrooks, J. Mistry, & I. B. Weiner (Eds.), *Handbook of psychology: Developmental psychology* (pp. 289–320). John Wiley & Sons, Inc.

Susman, E. J., & Rogol, A. (2004). Puberty and psychological development. In R. M. Lerner & L. Steinberg (Eds.), *Handbook of adolescent psychology* (pp. 15–44). John Wiley & Sons Inc.

Telzer, E. H. (2016). Dopaminergic reward sensitivity can promote adolescent health: A new perspective on the mechanism of ventral striatum activation. *Developmental Cognitive Neuroscience, 17*, 57–67. https://doi.org/10.1016/j.dcn.2015.10.010

Theokas, C., & Lerner, R. M. (2006). Observed ecological assets in families, schools, and neighborhoods: Conceptualization, measurement, and relations with positive and negative developmental outcomes. *Applied Developmental Science, 10*(2), 61–74. https://doi.org/10.1207/s1532480xads1002_2

Zaccaro, A., Conversano, C., Lai, E., & Gemignani, A. (2019). Relationship between emotions, sleep and well-being. In A. Pingitore, F. Mastorci & C. Vassalle (Eds.), *Adolescent health and well-being* (pp. 153–166). Springer.

Zahn-Waxler, C., Shirtcliff, E. A., & Marceau, K. (2008). Disorders of childhood and adolescence: Gender and psychopathology. *Annual Review of Clinical Psychology, 4*, 275–303. https://doi.org/10.1146/annurev.clinpsy.3.022806.091358

Ziv, I., & Kiasi, M. (2016). Facebook's contribution to well-being among adolescent and young adults as a function of mental resilience. *The Journal of Psychology, 150*(4), 527–541. https://doi.org/10.1080/00223980.2015.1110556

3 Sociocultural Construction of Girls and Girlhood

Girls exist within several cultural ideologies such as family, school, or religion which shape their beliefs and identities (Stern, 2007). Ignoring the role of those ideologies in girls' socialization results in an incomplete and simplified picture of girlhood. Furthermore, interventions aimed at promoting well-being in adolescent girls may be less effective if they are not grounded in the sociocultural context of contemporary girls. That is why it is important for mental health professionals to understand socializing forces in adolescent girls' lives and the messages girls receive from media and adults.

For many years, girls were not visible in social research. Starting in the 1980s, scholars began to realize the distinctiveness of girls' lives and tried to understand the lives of girls located in particular political and historical contexts (Griffin, 2004). In 1982, a groundbreaking work by Carol Gilligan *In a Different Voice: Psychological Theory and Women's Development* started a new era in studying girls and women. Gilligan demonstrated the unique life experiences of girls and their quest to have a voice in a male-dominated society. She and her colleagues further explored in-depth the relational world of adolescent girls (Gilligan et al., 1990, 1991). Gilligan argued that adolescence is a critical time for girls' development. This is when they can lose their voices and connection with others when they are unseen and unheard. They face a difficult dilemma of staying connected with others and being themselves (Gilligan et al., 1991). Adolescent girls begin to experience a disparity between their own views and the views of others around them. They have to decide what they can say and what they cannot, and have to hold themselves in trying to be "good girls." Girls' resistance to the idea of being a "good girl" at the cost of losing their voice can take the form of standing up for their ideas and opinions. It can also take the form of devaluing themselves, ultimately leading to maladaptive behaviors (Gilligan et al., 1991).

Mary Pipher in her influential book *Reviving Ophelia: Saving the Selves of Adolescent Girls* made the observation that "something dramatic happens to girls in early adolescence…They lose their resilience and optimism and become less curious and inclined to take risks" (Pipher, 1994, p. 19).

DOI: 10.4324/9781003105534-3

They also become less assertive and more depressed. Girls are often aware of these changes, as one girl lamented, "Everything good in me died in junior high" (p. 20). Another scholar in girls' research, Lyn Brown (2003), interviewed over 400 girls of diverse backgrounds. She documented how young girls who trust and act friendly toward other girls transform into distrusting and competitive young women.

Several factors can make girls vulnerable (Pipher, 1994). First, girls undergo significant physical and physiological changes associated with puberty which leads to changes in girls' self-perception and relationships with others. Second, they are moving to a broader culture where girls are often evaluated on the basis of their appearance. Finally, girls may lose parental support when they most need it due to the cultural expectations that adolescence is a time when children begin to distance themselves from their parents. While individuation from parents is a normal developmental task, girls still need to be connected to and supported by their parents.

Gender Socialization

Socialization practices directed toward girls and boys reflect cultural beliefs about male and female roles, responsibilities, and behaviors as well as the division of labor in society (Leaper, 2002). Since women are typically expected to be primary caregivers, girls are socialized to be nurturing and caring, while boys are socialized to be more independent and risk-taking. Agency in men manifests as assertiveness and performance, while in women greater communality manifests as warmth and care for others (Ellemers, 2018). Starting in early childhood, parents tend to talk more to their daughters than to sons. Gender differences are observed regarding how emotions are discussed in families. Parents discuss emotions more often with girls than with boys; they also tend to discourage anger in daughters but not in sons (Miller-Slough & Dunsmore, 2016). However, boys receive fewer directives than girls which might positively contribute to their cognitive development, especially problem-solving skills. Gender stereotyping is evident in assigning chores with girls, in general, having more chores than boys (Leaper, 2002). Furthermore, parents make more frequent comments about girls' physical appearance than about boys' appearance.

Gender stereotypes transcend into beliefs about academic performance. In general, parents expect sons to do better in math and science compared to daughters, consequently influencing children's confidence (or lack thereof) and later career choice (Leaper, 2002). Furthermore, considering task performance is important when judging men, whereas social relationships are considered when judging women (Ellemers, 2018). Additionally, women are less likely than men to be promoted and elected to prestigious positions (Ellemers, 2018). Gender stereotypes can be harmful when they are used to estimate females' performance potential. They also may justify social inequality associated with gender.

Female students are often seen as less talented, especially in the areas of math and science. Girls who experience academic sexism perceive themselves as less competent in those areas (Brown & Leaper, 2010). Popular media may play a role in the construction and transmission of stereotypes regarding gender in the fields of science, technology, engineering, and mathematics (STEM):

> Images of STEM professionals in popular media have for many years both created and perpetuated a cultural stereotype that depicts women as less likely than men to be present in STEM fields as well as less likely to be talented, successful, and valued in STEM fields.
>
> (Steinke, 2017, p. 2)

Stereotype threat, when an individual becomes concerned about or at risk of conforming to stereotypes about their social group, might negatively influence adolescent girls' math achievement, reduce their desire to enroll in STEM courses, and eventually limit their career choices. Fortunately, these stereotypes are responsive to intervention. In one study, girls participated in a program aimed at encouraging their self-affirmation, changing the implicit attitude about girls not being good at math, and fostering an intellectual growth mindset (Zhao et al., 2018). Girls further discussed the injustices associated with gender stereotypes regarding math performance and identified female scientists who could be selected as their role models. This intervention resulted in a reduction of math-gender stereotypes and improvement in girls' math scores.

Sexualization and Body Image in Adolescent Girls

Girls have to navigate the contradictory and often impossible ideals of "sexy femininity" (Ringrose et al., 2018). "The societal encouragement of sexualization practices for young girls might lead them to accept a sexualized role as both normative and ideal without realizing that there might be negative consequences associated with a sexualized appearance" (Graff et al., 2013, p. 572). Several risk factors can be contributed to self-objectification in adolescent girls, including the Internet and social media, girls and women's magazines, conversations about appearance with peers, and watching TV programs with sexualized content.

Lamb and Koven (2019), in their comprehensive analysis of studies related to the sexualization of girls in media and pop culture, found that media products have a high level of sexual content and frequently depict women as sexual objects. Media often include body exposure and proliferate an unrealistically thin body ideal. Through interaction with media, adolescent girls internalize cultural messages about sex, gender, and relationships. Another cultural channel through which girls receive messages about gender and sex is popular music. Many contemporary pop music lyrics allude to sexual intercourse. In addition, music videos often objectify and degrade women and show them revealing themselves (Lamb & Koven, 2019). Features revealing girls' bodies are even present in Halloween costumes. Furthermore, adult video games stereotype female characters as attractive, sexy, and helpless, while male characters as muscular and powerful. Sexualized female images can be found in sports marketing and advertising as well, which portray women wearing sexualized uniforms and in sexualized poses (Lamb & Koven, 2019). Graff and colleagues (2013), in their analysis of the magazines *Seventeen* and *Girls' Life*, found a significant number of sexualizing characteristics of girls. These characteristics included low-cut and tight clothing associated with exposing the body and emphasizing breasts. These images supply girls with sexualizing cues and encourage sexual objectification.

Powerful, violent, and hypersexualized female character typology is becoming more frequent in action movies (Heldman et al., 2016). However, it is debatable whether such images can be empowering for women. While women are portrayed as agentic, their agentivity is closely tied to their hypersexuality. Exposure to powerful and hypersexualized female characters causes "girls and women to internalize the heterosexual male gaze," that is, to self-objectify themselves (Heldman et al., 2016, p. 10). A good example is the movie *Catwoman*, in which a female character undergoes a significant transformation. A shy, meek, and soft-spoken young woman gets involved in a troubling affair and eventually is killed by a group of criminals. She is then reborn as "Catwoman," who is powerful, sexual, and seductive. Eventually, she kills the men who "killed" her when she was a human. Those who watched this movie remember her tight black leather outfit revealing her body and her hip swinging walk – all pointing to body objectification. Although the female character enjoys her agency and power, those qualities are achieved through her hypersexualization (Heldman et al., 2016):

> This demonstrates that, no matter how powerful a woman becomes in traditionally masculine domains (action films) and on men's terms (e.g., using violence), she will remain in an inferior position within the confines of acceptable femininity. She will continue to serve as an object, rather than a subject.
>
> (Heldman et al., 2016, p. 11)

According to objectification theory, girls internalize cultural standards about their physical appearance and worth and overemphasize their sexualized outlook (Fredrickson & Roberts, 1997). When living in a culture that sexually objectifies women and girls, they eventually adopt an observer's perspective of their physical appearance. Girls became more concerned about how they look to others, particularly males, rather than focusing on their own feelings and experiences. They begin to self-objectify *themselves*, that is, view themselves as primarily an object to be looked at and evaluated based solely on appearance. McKinley and Hyde (1996) identified three aspects of self-objectification, including body surveillance, body shame, and control beliefs. Body surveillance refers to a tendency to engage in frequent self-monitoring of one's appearance and a fear of negative evaluation of one's appearance by others. Body surveillance is associated with body shame, when girls perceive themselves as not meeting idealized cultural and media beauty standards. Control beliefs, the last aspect of self-objectification, refers to the idea that reaching a beauty ideal is possible if an individual works hard perfecting their appearance.

Girls with higher levels of internalized self-sexualization wear more sexualized clothing, demonstrate more body surveillance, body shame, and appearance anxiety (Lamb & Koven, 2019). Self-objectification is also associated with habitual and constant monitoring of one's physical appearance, increased shame, and appearance anxiety. It further increases the risk for eating disorders, depression, and sexual problems (Fredrickson & Roberts, 1997). Self-objectification is positively associated with body shame, which in turn predicts restricted eating and depressive symptoms (Tiggemann & Slater, 2015). Self-objectification may also have a negative impact on girls' academic performance and career goals. Preoccupation with appearance may limit mental resources needed for academic tasks. Additionally, girls with stronger self-objectification tendencies are more vulnerable in terms of sexual harassment and victimization (Choate & Curry, 2009).

Appearance and the Ideal of Femininity

Girls learn very early that attractiveness is important for success (Pipher, 1994). Teen magazines and advertisements perpetuate their desire for attractiveness. In post-feminist media, the female body is considered empowering and gives agency, but it is also an object of self-surveillance and scrutinizing (Jackson & Vares, 2015). Agency can be partially achieved through "body work" aimed at beautification, taking care of oneself, and self-indulgence. These self-improvement practices are propelled by consumerism. There has been a significant shift to offering beauty products not only to adult women, but to young girls as well. In television makeover shows, beauty experts subject the female body to intense scrutiny. They further identify appearance flaws and offer advice on how to achieve beauty ideals (Jackson & Vares, 2015). Evans and Riley (as cited in Jackson & Vares, 2015) called this consumer-oriented construct of femininity a "technology of sexiness." A study with preteen girls found that girls are pressed to conform to these beauty practices (Jackson & Vares, 2015). They are engaged in relentlessly perfecting themselves by using creams and scrubs to achieve "flawless" skin. Girls often used the word "perfect" when talking about their skin. Furthermore, they considered achieving "pretty" and "skinny" body ideals as a personal accomplishment and marker of success. Girls reported feeling sad when they could not achieve a desired ideal. At the same time, they recognized that the beautiful skin of females portrayed in advertising and media can be a result of photoshopping, surgical procedures, and/or make-up (Jackson & Vares, 2015). Additionally, girls resisted such pressures and critiqued unrealistic beauty ideals.

White and Black girls may have different ways to navigate their femininity and construct body image. In one study, White girls reported that sexy femininity brings them confidence and they try to achieve their appearance ideals through the use of beauty products (Ringrose et al., 2018). Black girls, on the other hand, demonstrated a heightened awareness of how their bodies are viewed by others and oscillated between feeling not sexy enough and being hypersexualized. They were also concerned about negative messages they receive from others in school and other public spaces regarding their bodies (Ringrose et al., 2018). Another study revealed that African American adolescent girls associated the idea of a beautiful body with its large size (Lamb & Plocha, 2015). Furthermore, they reported having a big body as a source of pride. At the same time, girls expressed concern that their "sexy" outlook often evokes negative comments from peers and even potential for assaults. The girls also believed that for White girls, being sexy does not bring negative consequences.

"Mean Girls"

Brown (2003) argued that pop culture greatly affects how girls view themselves and construct their identity. It is not uncommon for some reality TV, talk shows, and soap operas to proliferate images of competitive and mean women and girls. She further claimed that being gossipy, competitive, cliquish, and backstabbing is not part of the normal development of girls. In many modern societies, girls experience significant pressure to be popular and fulfill unrealistic expectations, often perpetuated by media. At the same time, girls are discouraged from expressing strong feelings, especially anger. It is possible that for girls, it is safer to express their negative feelings toward other girls instead of challenging boys:

> While peers can be satisfying and growth-producing, they can also be growth-destroying...Many girls can describe a universal American phenomenon—the scapegoating of girls by one another. Many girls become good haters of those who do not conform sufficiently to our culture's ideas about femininity.
>
> (Pipher, 1994, p. 68)

Ringrose (2006), in her extensive review, illustrated how popular culture shifted from the notion of girls as vulnerable to girls as mean. "The indirectly aggressive girl is now operating as a normal template of girlhood restaging an age-old metaphor of femininity as repression by moving from the pole of nice to that of mean" (p. 419). Some romance-based reality TV shows construct and reinforce stereotypes about women's interpersonal relationships with men and other women. More specifically, they normalize aggression and reframe the image of a "mean girl" from being negative to empowering for adult women, especially in relationships with male partners (Downing, 2018). One example is the young adult series *Pretty Little Liars*, where adolescent females are presented as "mean girls" (Whitney, 2017). Furthermore, the series presents adolescent girls in a condescending manner, as mentally unhealthy. For example, female characters exemplify stereotypical ideas about women, including having an eating disorder, suppressed sexuality, disrupted family relationships, and early sexualization.

Another media example is the Hollywood blockbuster movie *Mean Girls* (Ringrose, 2006). This movie portrays middle-class girls as superficial, cruel, and manipulative. The storyline focuses on a group of schoolgirls involved in spreading nasty rumors about other girls in the school, which eventually leads to vicious girl fighting. The girls then confess, apologize, and rebuild trust with each other. Ringrose argues that such a portrayal pathologizes girls.

Power and Agency in Adolescent Girls

In Western societies, beginning around the 1990s, a new discourse about girls has emerged called Girl Power (Griffin, 2004). The origin of this discourse can be traced to the British pop group the Spice Girls. Girl Power centered on elevating and pleasing oneself through fun, sassiness, and dressing up. It further underscored girls' friendship, even above relationships with boyfriends. Additionally, Girl Power promoted a particular style that involved heavy makeup, glitter, and tight clothes (Griffin, 2004). Such an image of teenage girls constructs the power of the girl as a consumer who can "get what she wants." For example:

> one of the Spice Girls' early hits, which is frequently cited as a key text of Girl Power, is immortalized in the words of their song 'Wannabe,' with the refs in, 'Tell me what you want, what you really, really want'
>
> (Griffin, 2004, p. 35)

The discourse of Girl Power is based on the self-evident assumption that girls and women are already "equal" to boys and men (Griffin, 2004). Therefore, they do not need to challenge the existing power hierarchy system existing in society. Many girls experience pressure to do extraordinarily well and be good at everything. However, telling girls that they can do anything actually undermines their confidence. When girls set high standards for themselves, there is a risk of not meeting those standards (Simmons, 2018).

Media products for girls exploit the discourse of Girl Power, which emphasizes individualism and personal responsibility but disregards the social systems and institutions in which girls are embedded (Taft, 2004). The claim that girls can be anything as long as they work for it:

> can give girls a sense of power and esteem, it hides both the material and the discursive forces shaping identity and the ways that these gendered, raced, classed, and sexualized identities may give girls privileges or pose challenges.
>
> (Taft, 2004, p. 73)

When failing to address the social factors underlying injustices, Girl Power does not help girls to understand or even acknowledge social problems. Instead, it makes girls fully responsible for their achievements which may cause feelings of inadequacy and low self-esteem. Furthermore, the focus on individual power can weaken girls' connections with each other and reduce opportunities for social and political engagement (Taft, 2004). Putting a strong emphasis on girls' agency is problematic, as it sends them the message that they are responsible for "rescuing" themselves instead of addressing the broader sociopolitical and cultural contexts in which girls exist (Thomas, 2011). The idea that girls' agency is linked to choice, empowerment, and voice may also contradict another narrative that portrays girls as injured by patriarchal structures (Harris & Dobson, 2015). Without resolving or reconciling the dichotomy between victimhood and the capacity for agency, adolescent girls are in a difficult situation regarding developing a healthy identity.

Experiences of Ethnic and Racial Minority Girls

Girls from diverse ethnic and racial backgrounds often experience additional pressure regarding their intersectionality, that is, they represent a minority belonging to two categories that have historically been subject to discrimination: race and gender. In her ethnographic study, Thomas (2011) explored how ethnically diverse girls navigate racial and class-based reality in the American high school. She conducted a series of interviews with African American, Armenian, Latina, Filipina, and Anglo girls in a Los Angeles high school. The focus of the analysis was how girls construct the meaning of race, ethnicity, masculinity, and femininity in the context of school life. Many girls talked about racism and sexism existing in their school. Girls perceived school campuses as segregated and "demarcated territories of belonging and exclusion" (Thomas, 2011, p. 11). Even the schoolyards reflect this segregation as different groups dominate certain places in the schoolyard. Furthermore, girls experience segregated social practices not only in school, but at home and the community as well. For example, girls often do not have friends outside their own race or ethnicity. Girls from immigrant families face the almost impossible task of trying to acculturate to the idealized white, middle-class girlhood (Thomas, 2011). When talking about campus violence and interracial conflicts, girls repeatedly expressed a desire to get along with others. Thomas (2011) argues that this "getting along" motto originates from a simplistic version of multicultural education, advocating for the idea of a "postracial space where everyone is equal and happily coexists" (p. 4). The message "we are the same" contradicts life experiences of minority girls and their narrative about differences they see in others' appearance and behavior. Additionally, this idea contradicts reality, where girls feel "deep resentment to others while also feeling deeply wounded by others" (p. 4).

Thomas provides a critical analysis of multicultural education in schools. Simplistic multiculturalism can lead to problematic identities: While embracing humanistic beliefs of similarity and equality, girls are nevertheless engaged in racially and gender-segregated practices. Girls in the study sought racial recognition and resisted racial reduction by others. The study also revealed the anger and stress girls experience. When talking about injustice and violence on school campus, girls lamented that the school is unsupportive and does not want to hear their voices.

Identity development in girls of color may be challenging as these girls often have to encounter societal stereotypes about themselves. For example, African American girls often encounter false and incomplete images representing Black girlhood (Muhammad & McArthur, 2015). They have to combat myths or distorted images of femininity, which are historically derived but still present in the contemporary media. Black women are often portrayed as hypersexual, seductive "bad-black-girls" ("Jezebel" stereotype); tough, angry, and sharp-tongued ("Sapphire" stereotype); or domestic, docile, and obese ("Mammy" stereotype). These images make Black girls believe that they might be perceived as angry, loud, and sexualized. In one study, girls who endorsed the "Jezebel" stereotype perceived risky sexual behaviors as less harmful (Townsend et al., 2010). In another study, Black women attending a predominantly White university reported experiencing gendered racial microaggressions stemming from the projection of stereotypes, including Angry Black Woman, Silenced, and Marginalized, as well as assumptions about their communication style and beauty (Lewis et al., 2016). To combat these distorted images of Black femininity, girls are encouraged to write against those portrayals and pledge for social change. Such an intervention creates a space for Black adolescent girls to defy media stereotypes and negotiate their identities (Muhammad & McArthur, 2015).

At school, Black girls are often perceived as loud, assertive, and challenging to teachers' authority, and receive greater surveillance regarding their clothing than White girls (Epstein et al., 2017). This leads to increasingly disproportionate rates of school discipline for Black girls. Epstein and colleagues (2017) reported that Black girls experience the phenomenon of adultification, meaning that they are perceived as more mature and self-reliant than they actually are. They are often thought of as more knowledgeable about adult topics, including sex, and capable of assuming adult roles and responsibilities greater than what would be expected for their age. This adultification has negative implications for many aspects of adolescents' functioning. They may also receive less support, protection, and nurturance from adults.

Identity in Adolescent Girls

Girls face very complex and often contradictory social realities. Many discourses about girls are deeply contradictory (Griffin, 2004). They are "being urged, simultaneously, to be independent, assertive, and achievement oriented, yet also demure, attractive, soft-spoken, fifteen pounds underweight, and deferential to men" (Douglas, 1997, p. 21). Instead of thinking who they are and what they want, girls focus on what they can do to please others. Girls experience a social pressure to "put aside their authentic selves and to display a small portion of their gifts" (Pipher, 1994, p. 22). Girls are longing for unattainable perfection often at the expense of their authentic self (Stern, 2007).

The Internet intensifies girls' desire for perfection. "On-line, as in life, there will always be somebody thinner more successful, in a better relationship, with more friends" (Simmons, 2018, p. 28). In addition, social media reinforces "behaviors that girls have been long primed to express: pleasing others, seeking feedback, performing and looking good" (Simmons, 2018, p. 28). Girls often experience pressure to relinquish their true self and develop false selves (Pipher, 1994). This pressure comes from school, media products, and peers. Girls face a dilemma: To be true to themselves and face potential risk of peer rejection or to reject their true self for the sake of peers' acceptance. Many girls choose the second path, and as a result, they "split into two selves, one that is authentic and one that is culturally scripted. In public, they become who they are supposed to be" (Pipher, 1994, p. 38).

Identity formation continues in the virtual world (Stern, 2007). Online representations can be considered in terms of falsehood which girls can intentionally enact. These representations can also be considered as a way to experiment with different identities. Adolescents can "distribute" themselves between multiple simultaneous conversations. Social media also creates role overload as it enables girls to create "an exhausting range of identities – jock, scholar, beauty queen, party girl, best friend, and on and on – demanded by the new rules of girls' success, crammed into a twenty-four-hour day" (Simmons, 2018, p. 32). Coupled with conflicting messages from media and difficulty asserting their true self, this creates challenges for adolescent girls regarding their identity consolidation.

Gergen (1991) introduced the concept of a "saturated self," which reflects a fragmentation of identities in the modern world. The proliferation of communication technologies (e.g., radio, television, the Internet, and smartphones) transformed our everyday life and expanded the individual's repertoire of "ways of being" (e.g., attitudes, values, worldviews, and moralities). This leads to a so-called saturated self and makes it difficult to achieve a stable and consolidated sense of identity. At the interpersonal level, this leads to diminished authenticity, emotional intensity, and commitment.

Girls need to develop a consolidated narrative about who they are and what they want. They need to understand and resist messages from media and social stereotypes about themselves. They also need to take a critical look at sociocultural stereotypes and messages about female's roles and appearances (Johnson et al., 1999). Girls need to connect the dots of cultural messages and their own desires and behaviors. Awareness of and challenging these stereotypes will lead to positive change regarding the development of girls' full potential.

In order to resist negative stereotypes, ethnic minority girls need to have a stronger sense of ethnic identity and critically analyze the societal messages that they receive. The strongest protective factor shared by all ethnic minority groups is identification with their family and community. Bonding among families of color can be a protective factor for adolescent girls struggling with sociocultural stress, including discrimination and rejection based on color and language (Vasquez & Fuentes, 1999).

Developing an authentic self is essential for girls' well-being. "A girl who remains true to herself will accept her body as hers and resist others' attempts to evaluate and define her by appearance" (Pipher, 1994, p. 57). It is important to create "hardiness zones" where girls have opportunities to experience control, commitment, and challenges (Johnson et al., 1999). Such zones can be created through supportive relationships in families and schools and provide girls with opportunities to acquire and practice important life skills. Meaningful participation in school and community life are other avenues to foster healthy identity in adolescent girls (Johnson et al., 1999).

Recommended Resources

Girls Empowerment Network – https://www.girlsempowermentnetwork.org/

Originally The Ophelia Project, the Girls Empowerment Network was inspired by *Reviving Ophelia* by Dr. Mary Pipher and founded in order to combat the trend among middle school girls of declines in self-esteem, low academic achievement, and maladaptive behaviors. The Girls Empowerment Network offers an array of programs, including school-based programming, summer camps, leadership summits, and self-paced activities and curriculum in order to teach and promote self-efficacy. Girls between 3rd and 12th grade are provided opportunities to discover and learn about self-efficacy and discover their own potential.

Girls Inc. – https://www.girlsinc.org/

Girls Inc. is a nonprofit organization that serves girls between the ages of 5 and 18. Evidence-based programming delivered by trained professionals focuses on building confidence and self-esteem, empowerment and leadership, promoting girls in STEM fields, and providing girls an affirming, pro-girl environment. Girls are taught to discover and develop their strengths, adopt healthy lifestyles, develop and value their whole self, and receive support to navigate challenges.

Girls for a Change – https://www.girlsforachange.org

Girls for a Change (GFAC) has the mission of empowering young women of color. GFAC provides outreach programs for middle and high school females, after-school and summer camp programs as well as local "Girl Action Teams," which help women design, lead, fund, and implement social change projects within their communities. These projects also emphasize problem-solving skills, leadership skills, community engagement, goal-planning, and social-emotional learning. GFAC programs provide support to Black girls from youth through early adulthood, with the mission of helping girls to feel seen, heard, and celebrated.

References

Brown, C., & Leaper, C. (2010). Latina and European American girls' experiences with academic sexism and their self-concepts in mathematics and science during adolescence. *Sex Roles, 63*(11), 860–870. https://doi.org/10.1007/s11199-010-9856-5

Brown, L. M. (2003). *Girlfighting: Betrayal and rejection among girls*. New York University Press.

Choate, L., & Curry, J. R. (2009). Addressing the sexualization of girls through comprehensive programs, advocacy, and systemic change: Implications for professional school counselors. *Professional School Counseling, 12*(3), 213–222. https://doi.org/10.1177%2F2156759X0901200302

Douglas, S. (1997, August 25). Girls 'n' spice: All things nice? *The Nation*, 21–24.

Downing, S. (2018). They're not mean girls if they are adult women: Reality television's construction of women's identity and interpersonal aggression. *Sociological Research Online, 23*(1), 3–20. https://doi.org/10.1177/1360780417735781

Ellemers, N. (2018). Gender stereotypes. *Annual Review of Psychology, 69*, 275–298. https://doi.org/10.1146/annurev-psych-122216-011719

Epstein, R., Blake, J., & González, T. (2017, June 27). *Girlhood interrupted: The erasure of Black girls' childhood*. http://dx.doi.org/10.2139/ssrn.3000695

Fredrickson, B. L., & Roberts, T.-A. (1997). Objectification theory: Toward understanding women's lived experiences and mental health risks. *Psychology of Women Quarterly, 21*(2), 173–206. https://doi.org/10.1111/j.1471-6402.1997.tb00108.x

Gergen, K. J. (1991). *The saturated self: Dilemmas of identity in contemporary life.* Basic Books.

Gilligan, C. (1982). *In a different voice: Psychological theory and women's development.* Harvard University Press.

Gilligan, C., Lyons, N., & Hanmer, T. (Eds.) (1990). *Making connections: The relational worlds of adolescent girls at Emma Willard School.* Harvard University Press.

Gilligan, C., Rogers, A. G., & Tolman, D. L. (Eds.) (1991). *Women, girls and psychotherapy: Reframing resistance.* Harvard University Press.

Graff, K. A., Murnen, S. K., & Krause, A. K. (2013). Low-cut shirts and high-heeled shoes: Increased sexualization across time in magazine depictions of girls. *Sex Roles, 69,* 571–582. https://doi.org/10.1007/s11199-013-0321-0

Griffin, C. (2004). Good girls, bad girls: Anglo-centrism and diversity in the constitution of contemporary girlhood. In A. Harris (Eds.), *All about the girl: Culture, power and identity* (pp. 29–44). Routledge.

Harris, A., & Dobson, A. S. (2015). Theorizing agency in post-girlpower times. *Continuum, 29*(2), 145–156.

Heldman, C., Frankel, L. L., & Holmes, J. (2016). "Hot, black leather, whip": The (de)evolution of female protagonists in action cinema, 1960–2014. *Sexualization, Media, & Society, 2*(2), 1–19. https://doi.org/10.1177%2F2374623815627789

Jackson, S., & Vares, T. (2015). 'Perfect skin', 'pretty skinny': Girls' embodied identities and post-feminist popular culture. *Journal of Gender Studies, 24*(3), 347–360. https://doi.org/10.1080/09589236.2013.841573

Johnson, N. G., Roberts, M. C., & Worell, J. (Eds.) (1999). *Beyond appearance: A new look at adolescent girls.* American Psychological Association. https://doi.org/10.1037/10325-000

Lamb, S., & Koven, J. (2019). Sexualization of girls: Addressing criticism of the APA report, presenting new evidence. *Sage Open, 9*(4). https://doi.org/10.1177/2158244019881024

Lamb, S., & Plocha, A. (2015). Pride and sexiness: Girls of color discuss race, body image, and sexualization. *Girlhood Studies, 8*(2), 86–102. https://doi.org/10.3167/ghs.2015.080207

Leaper, C. (2002). Parenting girls and boys. In M. H. Bornstein (Ed.), *Handbook of parenting: Children and parenting* (pp. 189–225). Lawrence Erlbaum Associates Publishers.

Lewis, J. A., Mendenhall, R., Harwood, S. A., & Huntt, M. B. (2016). "Ain't I a woman?": Perceived gendered racial microaggressions experienced by Black women. *The Counseling Psychologist, 44*(5), 758–780. https://dx.doi.org/10.1177/0011000016641193

McKinley, N. M., & Hyde, J. S. (1996). The objectified body consciousness scale: Development and validation. *Psychology of Women Quarterly, 20*(2), 181–215. https://doi.org/10.1111/j.1471-6402.1996.tb00467.x

Muhammad, G. E., & McArthur, S. A. (2015). "Styled by their perceptions": Black adolescent girls interpret representations of Black females in popular culture. *Multicultural Perspectives, 17*(3), 133–140. https://doi.org/10.1080/15210960.2015.1048340

Pipher, M. (1994). *Reviving Ophelia: Saving the selves of adolescent girls.* Ballantine Books.

Ringrose, J. (2006). A new universal mean girl: Examining the discursive construction and social regulation of a new feminine pathology. *Feminism & Psychology, 16*(4), 405–424. https://doi.org/10.1177%2F0959353506068747

Ringrose, J. L., Tolman, D. L., & Ragonese, M. (2018). Hot right now: Diverse girls navigating technologies of racialized sexy femininity. *Feminism & Psychology, 29*(1), 76–95. https://doi.org/10.1177/0959353518806324

Simmons, R. (2018). *Enough as she is: How to help girls move beyond impossible standards or success to live healthy, happy, and fulfilling lives.* HarperCollins Publishers.

Steinke, J. (2017). Adolescent girls' STEM identity formation and media images of STEM professionals: Considering the influence of contextual cues. *Frontiers in Psychology, 8*, Article 716. https://doi.org/10.3389/fpsyg.2017.00716

Stern, S. T. (2007). *Instant identity: Adolescent girls and the world of instant messaging.* Peter Lang.

Taft, J. K. (2004) Girl power politics: Pop-culture barriers and organizational resistance. In A. Harris (Ed.), *All about the girl: Culture, power and identity* (pp. 69–78). Routledge.

Thomas, M. E. (2011). *Multicultural girlhood: Racism, sexuality, and the conflicted spaces of American education.* Temple University Press.

Tiggemann, M., & Slater, A. (2015). The role of self-objectification in the mental health of early adolescent girls: Predictors and consequences. *Journal of Pediatric Psychology, 40*(7), 704–711. https://doi.org/10.1093/jpepsy/jsv021

Townsend, T. G., Thomas, A. J., Neilands, T. B., & Jackson, T. R. (2010). I'm no Jezebel; I am young, gifted, and Black: Identity, sexuality, and Black girls. *Psychology of Women Quarterly, 34*(3), 273–285. https://doi.org/10.1111/j.1471-6402.2010.01574.x

Whitney, S. (2017). Kisses, bitches: Pretty Little Liars frames postfeminism's adolescent girl. *Tulsa Studies in Women's Literature, 36*(2), 353–377. https://doi.org/10.1353/tsw.2017.0026

Zhao, F., Zhang, Y., Alterman, V., Zhang, B., & Yu, G. (2018). Can math-gender stereotypes be reduced? A theory-based intervention program with adolescent girls. *Current Psychology: A Journal for Diverse Perspectives on Diverse Psychological Issues, 37*(3), 612–624. https://doi.org/10.1007/s12144-016-9543-y

4 Physical Health and Healthy Habits in Adolescent Girls

Physical health and healthy habits play an important role in adolescents' well-being, socio-emotional functioning, and school success (Ahn & Fedewa, 2011; Gangwisch et al., 2010; Gruber, 2017; Hillman, 2014; Neumark-Sztainer et al., 2008; Reid et al., 2015; Sifers & Shea, 2013). Healthy habits include, but are not limited to, regular physical activity, healthy eating, and sleep hygiene. Promoting these habits in adolescence not only contributes to young people's physical and mental health, but also creates healthy habits that will last to adulthood. Schools are a major venue for health promotion programs, including physical activity, healthy eating, and sleep hygiene.

Physical Activity in Adolescent Girls

Regular participation in physical activity is associated with many health benefits, including obesity prevention, cardiovascular fitness, and bone health (Bailey et al., 2005). It is also positively associated with youth emotional well-being and mental health (Ahn & Fedewa, 2011; Reid et al., 2015). More physically active adolescent girls experience less stress, depression, and anxiety and have higher self-esteem. They further report greater life satisfaction and feel healthier when compared to girls who are not physically active (Zullig & White, 2011). Furthermore, engagement in physical activity is associated with better cognitive and academic performance through the positive effects of physical activity on brain functioning (Hillman, 2014).

The Center for Disease Control and Prevention (2020) recommends that children and adolescents participate in at least 60 minutes of moderate to vigorous physical activity for at least three days a week. However, it is estimated that only about 28% of girls meet these guidelines (CDC, 2009). Adolescents spend less time in leisurely physical activity compared to younger children and the decline in physical activity is greater for girls than for boys (Lam & McHale, 2015). Inactive adolescents are likely to develop into inactive adults (Gordon-Larsen et al., 2004). A reduction in physical activity reflects a general cultural shift toward a more sedentary lifestyle, "despite the fact that we have inherited a genome that evolved

DOI: 10.4324/9781003105534-4

to support a chronically active lifestyle" (Hillman, 2014, p. 2). Adolescents with mental health problems have lower levels of physical activity compared to adolescents from the general population (Mangerud et al., 2014). Furthermore, a lack of physical exercise coupled with an unhealthy diet leads to obesity, which puts young people at risk for developing heart disease, stroke, bone and joint problems, and diabetes (Benjamin, 2010). Overweight and obesity are especially concerning among adolescent minority girls (Groth & Morrison-Beedy, 2011; Melnyk et al., 2009). Increased body fat is also linked to greater body dissatisfaction among adolescent girls (Olive et al., 2012).

Several factors contribute to a decline in physical activity in adolescents, including a lack of athletic competence, fear of crossing traditional gender roles, concerns about not fitting in with others, being teased about physical appearance while exercising, and time constraints due to other commitments (Kimm et al., 2006; Slater & Tiggemann, 2011; Whitehead & Biddle, 2008). In girls, sedentary behavior is also reciprocally associated with sedentary behavior of their best friends and mothers (Raudsepp & Riso, 2017).

Eating Habits in Adolescent Girls

A healthy diet is an important part of a healthy lifestyle and is essential for overall health and well-being (Johns Hopkins Medicine, 2020). Rapid physical growth in adolescents requires an adequate amount of nutrients (Iglesia et al., 2019). It is especially important for adolescent girls as they undergo significant body and hormonal changes. Diet and physical activity are the most important determinants of health. A diet rich in vegetables, fruits, legumes, and whole grains is associated with better health outcomes. At the same time, an unhealthy diet is linked to cardiovascular diseases, osteoporosis, and even cognitive problems. Furthermore, a recent line of research pointed to the importance of gut microbiota for mental health and well-being (Iglesia et al., 2019).

General guidelines for healthy eating include having three balanced meals a day and healthy snacks in between, increasing fiber in the diet, drinking plenty of water, avoiding drinks that are high in sugar and calories, and eating fruits, vegetables, and lean proteins like chicken and fish (Johns Hopkins Medicine, 2020). However, one survey study found that only 35.3% of students had eaten breakfast each day, 13.9% the recommended servings of vegetables, and 18.7% consumed at least one serving of soda or pop per day in the seven days preceding the survey (Kann et al., 2018).

Dietary behavior in adolescence is influenced by many factors, including family, peers, cultural ideals for body weight, and access to food outside the home due to the increased independence of teens. Unfortunately, adolescent girls may engage in emotional eating as a response to stress

(Jääskeläinen et al., 2014). Stress-driven female eaters are more likely to be overweight and obese. Additionally, they have fewer regular family meals, but instead consume sweets, sodas, and alcohol more frequently. Parents with higher levels of stress often use food as a reward and, consequently, have children engaged in emotional eating (Powell et al., 2017). Such a practice likely diminishes youth's ability to self-regulate food intake which contributes to emotional overeating. On the other hand, parents who respond thoughtfully, not reactively, to their children's problems (i.e., mindful parents) contribute to healthy eating habits in girls (Gouveia et al., 2019). Such parents use food as a reward less frequently and put less pressure on their children to eat.

Body Image

Body image includes thoughts, perceptions, and feelings about our body's shape and size as well as the actions we take regarding our bodies (Alleva et al., 2015). Positive body image involves having respect and acceptance of one's physical appearance and functioning (Alleva et al., 2015; Andrew et al., 2016). In adolescent girls, this is related to high self-esteem, optimism, and self-compassion. Negative body image, however, is characterized by feelings of unhappiness or dissatisfaction with one's appearance (Alleva et al., 2015). Behaviorally, this may be expressed through engagement in frequent self-weighing, appearance monitoring, or avoidance of public situations. It is estimated that 40%–70% of adolescent girls report dissatisfaction with two or more aspects of their bodies (Choate, 2007). Negative body image can lead to body dysmorphic disorder, low self-esteem, mood or eating disorders, physical inactivity, and onset of smoking (Alleva et al., 2015; Holland & Tiggemann, 2016).

Starting in elementary school, girls report restrictive eating and being teased regarding their physical appearance (Vander Wal & Thelen, 2000). Weight gain and changes in body shape during puberty may cause adolescent girls anxiety about achieving the societal ideal for physical appearance (Ata et al., 2007; Choate, 2013). A national survey ($N = 66,068$) found that a higher body mass index, overweight perception, appearance stress, and depressive mood are among the risk factors for weight control behaviors (Han et al., 2020). For adolescent girls, stress over their appearance and depressive mood contributed to the severity of weight control behaviors. Weight control and binge eating behaviors are further associated with a greater desire for thinness, body dissatisfaction, and the belief that body weight and shape are important for personal and social acceptance (Cruz-Sáez et al., 2015). Positive self-esteem protects against the development of body dissatisfaction, whereas negative self-esteem can cause body dissatisfaction which might further perpetuate low self-esteem (Hesse-Biber et al., 2004). Furthermore, girls who adopt a "superwoman ideal," characterized by a desire for excellence in schoolwork, appearance, and dating, are at a higher risk for body dissatisfaction (Mensinger et al., 2007). Being bullied regarding physical appearance is linked to body shame and self-criticism, which are further linked to depressive symptoms and eating psychopathology (Duarte et al., 2015). Therefore, targeting body shame and self-directed anger can reduce the risk of depression and eating disorders.

Body image dissatisfaction is associated with poorer health outcomes and lower well-being across all ethnic groups (i.e., Whites, African Americans, Asians, Hispanics, Native Americans, and mixed/other race; Bucchianeri et al., 2016). However, the magnitude of this association is different across racial groups. The greatest differences in depressive symptoms between girls with low and high body dissatisfaction were in mixed/other race and White girls, while the least difference was observed in African American girls. African American adolescent girls have been found to have a more positive perception of their appearance and are less dissatisfied with their weight compared to other ethnicities, especially White adolescents (Hesse-Biber et al., 2004; Mikolajczyk et al., 2012). In African American females, positive body image is linked to positive racial/Black identity and emotional support regarding their bodies received from mothers, peers, and extended family (Hesse-Biber et al., 2004).

Factors Contributing to Body Dissatisfaction

Among the factors contributing to body dissatisfaction in adolescent girls are a desire for social acceptance, perceived family and peer support, and exposure to media (Ata et al., 2007; McLean et al., 2015; Neumark-Sztainer, Bauer et al., 2010; Smith et al., 2016). Girls often affiliate with friends who have similar habits and characteristics. One study found that similarity in terms of body dissatisfaction and bulimic behaviors is likely a result of selection rather than the socialization process (Taylor & Hutchinson, 2013). Adolescent girls want to be accepted by their peers by conforming to a sociocultural ideal of image and body shape. Those who feel unsupported or rejected by their peers are more likely to report body dissatisfaction and disordered eating (Gerner & Wilson, 2005). Additionally, ethnically and racially diverse adolescent girls may be at a high risk for eating disorders if they have negative identification with their own ethnic or racial group (Bisaga et al., 2005). This risk is likely associated with the internalization of beauty stereotypes inconsistent with their own physical features.

Unhealthy eating habits and body dissatisfaction can be driven by family weight talk/teasing and dieting. In one study, about 50% of girls reported being teased regarding their weight by family members and being encouraged to diet by their mothers (Neumark-Sztainer, Bauer et al., 2010). Weight teasing was especially damaging for body image and a strong contributor to disordered eating behaviors. On the one hand, relationships with parents perceived by adolescent girls as conflictual and nonsupportive are associated with increased body concerns in girls (Ata et al., 2007; Smith et al., 2016). On the other hand, positive mother-daughter relationships can serve as a protective factor for adolescent girls from the negative effects of social media on body image (de Vries et al., 2019).

Exposure to the thin body ideal on social media is a significant risk factor for body dissatisfaction in adolescent girls. The elevated appearance exposure on social media is associated with the internalization of the thin body ideal and poorer body image (Meier & Gray, 2014; Mingoia et al., 2017). Recurrent viewing of appearance-related images likely results in perception of those images as attractive. Heavy use of Facebook and YouTube, a lower sense of empowerment, and a lack of parental involvement are also associated with poorer body image (Latzer et al., 2015). Another potential risk is visiting pro-eating disorder websites which encourages disordered eating, purging, and excessive exercising (Strasburger et al., 2010).

Adolescents with greater appearance-related media exposure take and post selfie images more frequently (Rousseau, 2021). These girls are more dissatisfied with their bodies and more likely to be engaged in dietary restrictions (McLean et al., 2015). Taking selfies and posting them online is considered a form of self-objectification associated with negative outcomes regarding body image (Salomon & Brown, 2020). Internalization and social comparison play a significant role in the association between media exposure and selfie-related behaviors, such as selfie image manipulation. Selfie posting and counting the number of likes each post receives play important roles in social acceptance for adolescent girls (Tiggemann & Slater, 2013). However, posting self-images to social media also leads users to receiving greater scrutiny and commentary from others in the public setting (McLean et al., 2019). Excessive photoshopping (e.g., altering photos to improve one's image) presents another risk factor for body-related and eating concerns. Photoshopping creates more opportunities for comparisons, self-scrutiny, and evaluation of appearance which contribute to a greater preoccupation with image and body dissatisfaction (Holland & Tiggemann, 2016; Tiggemann & Slater, 2013).

Interventions to Support Physical Activity, Healthy Eating, and Body Image

Schools play an essential role in promoting physical activity, healthy eating, and positive body image. To promote healthy eating, schools should provide healthier foods and beverages and limit access to less healthy foods and beverages (Guide to Community Preventive Services, 2016). School meal policies have to ensure that school meals meet specific nutrition requirements (e.g., School Breakfast Program, National School

Lunch Program). Schools also need to use effective food marketing strategies, such as placing healthier foods and beverages where they can be easily seen and accessed by students, making their display appealing, reducing the price for healthier foods, and providing signs and verbal prompts for healthier food choices (Guide to Community Preventive Services, 2016). The US Department of Agriculture (USDA) and the US Department of Health and Human Services created the MyPlate icon to replace the Food Pyramid as a guide to help adolescents and adults choose healthy food. The MyPlate icon is divided into five food groups, emphasizing the nutritional value of grains, vegetables, fruits, dairy, and proteins for the developing body (US Department of Agriculture, 2020). Schools can further emphasize healthy portion sizes and provide information about the nutritional value of each food group. This information as well as educational materials, visual signage, and teaching tools are all available through the USDA.

Multicomponent physical activity interventions are effective in increasing physical activity in adolescents during school hours (US Department of Health and Human Services, 2012). These interventions often combine enhanced physical education with health education, increased classroom physical activity, and promoting active transportation to school. Furthermore, school-based interventions are more effective when combined with community- and family-based interventions to promote adolescents' physical activity outside of school.

Strategies to Motivate Girls to Stay Physically Active

Motivating girls to be physically active may be a challenging task. Several studies provide an insight into how to make physical activity more appealing. In their research grounded in the self-determination theory, Mitchell and colleagues (2015) found that adolescent girls are more engaged in physical activity when the participation in that activity satisfies their needs for relatedness, competence, and autonomy. Therefore, giving girls an opportunity to choose activities, enhancing their physical activity competence, engaging peers, and reducing competition can support girls' motivation to be physically active (Mitchell et al., 2015; Owen et al., 2019).

Another important motivational factor is having positive role models who can initiate physical activity with girls (Robertson-Wilson et al., 2003; Whitehead & Biddle, 2008). Motivation to stay physically active can be further boosted by focusing on feeling good, having fun, and increasing energy levels and self-confidence (Camacho-Miñano et al., 2011; Voorhees et al., 2005). Putting girls in a position where they are advocates for active lifestyles is another way to increase motivation. In one study, underserved adolescents (83% of participants were African American) created videos where they gave their peers recommendations on how to change their physical activity habits (Wilson et al., 2005). This intervention resulted in increased levels of physical activity and motivation to stay physically active.

Additionally, the perceived motivational climate of physical education classes significantly affects adolescent girl's desire to stay physically active. One study with high school students found that a highly competitive climate was stressful and made girls feel inadequate and deficient (Hogue et al., 2019). It was further associated with shame, feeling overwhelmed, and out of control. However, a caring and task-oriented climate where youth feel respected, valued, and competent supports motivation to participate in physical activity.

Programs and Curricular to Support Healthy Habits

Health-related habits likely present a cluster of behaviors rather than separate habits (Groth & Morrison-Beedy, 2011). That is why targeting several habits may be more effective than targeting only one. Several programs incorporate physical exercise, nutrition, programs, and healthy body image components.

The COPE (Creating Opportunities for Personal Empowerment) Healthy Lifestyles TEEN (Thinking, Emotions, Exercise, and Nutrition) is a manualized educational program that targets emotional health, physical activity, and nutrition (Melnyk et al., 2009). This program was found to be effective in increasing healthy lifestyle choices and decreasing depression and anxiety in Hispanic adolescents (Melnyk et al., 2009). Additionally, overweight youth reported healthier lifestyle beliefs and nutrition knowledge. The implementation of the COPE Program with rural early adolescents yielded improvement in emotional health, self-concept, disruptive behaviors, and healthy lifestyle behaviors (Hoying et al., 2016).

A school-based obesity prevention program for adolescent girls, New Moves, integrates nutrition, social support, and physical activity in physical education class (Neumark-Sztainer et al., 2008). Additionally, girls attend individual counseling sessions and lunch meetings while their parents receive psychoeducation about obesity prevention and healthy eating habits for adolescents. The nutrition education teaches girls to avoid unhealthy weight control behaviors and to practice healthy eating, including eating breakfast, fruits, and vegetables, and reducing the intake of sweetened beverages. Girls are also trained to be attuned to their internal feelings of hunger and satiety. A program evaluation study documented an increase in girls' physical activity and healthy eating as well as improved body image (Neumark-Sztainer, Friend et al., 2010). They were also less engaged in unhealthy weight control behaviors and reported more support in their effort to implement healthy habits received from teachers, friends, and parents.

The curriculum "Full of Ourselves: A Wellness Program to Advance Girl Power, Health, and Leadership" focuses on healthy body image, healthy eating, preventing eating disorders, and promoting self-esteem (Steiner-Adair & Sjostrom, 2006). Program evaluations found significant changes in girls' knowledge and weight-related body esteem, which were maintained at a six-month follow-up (Steiner-Adair et al., 2002).

"Healthy Girls Save the World" (HGSW, 2018) is an after-school program for Black girls that provides education regarding healthy nutritional choices, benefits of physical activity, and overall healthy lifestyles. The after-school program consists of five components that are implemented over the course of 8–10 weeks in a two-hour weekly session. Sessions are organized around three pillars: healthy bodies, healthy minds, and healthy relationships (HGSW, 2018). After participating in the program, the majority of girls reported improved self-esteem and increased knowledge of healthy habits, including choices of healthy food and physical exercise (HGSW, 2018).

The "Girls on the Go!" program uses an empowerment model to improve self-esteem, body image, and confidence in adolescent girls (Tirlea et al., 2016). Educational themes covered in the program include body image, self-esteem, assertiveness, healthy habits, and positive relationships. The program was successful in improving self-esteem among girls from diverse cultural backgrounds. "Girls on Track" is a similar curriculum for adolescent girls aimed at fostering a healthy lifestyle through running (Sifers & Shea, 2013). The curriculum includes education, team building, and physical activities. Outcome studies have found improvement in girls' self-esteem in relation to physical appearance and body image (Sifers & Shea, 2013).

Specific Body Image Interventions

Positive body image intervention goals include recruiting positive influence and support from family, peers, and school; increasing global and physical self-esteem; teaching girls coping and stress reduction skills; and fostering critical thinking regarding media influences on one's body (Alleva et al., 2015; Burnette et al., 2017; Choate, 2007). Body image interventions include cognitive behavior therapy (CBT), fitness training, media literacy, self-esteem enhancement, and psychoeducation (Alleva et al., 2015). CBT is aimed at modifying dysfunctional thoughts contributing to negative body image (e.g., only beautiful people are successful) and fat talk (e.g. "I am too fat"). It further teaches girls to avoid evaluative terms when talking about their bodies (e.g., "I have a fat belly" can be modified to "I have a round belly"). Positive body talk also serves as a protective factor against thin ideal internalization (Rousseau, 2021). It is important to teach girls to deemphasize physical appearance and focus on body functions instead. They also need to recognize triggers to negative thinking about their bodies (e.g., social media). Girls also can be taught self-monitoring, for example, recording how many times they look at the mirror or weigh themselves (Alleva et al., 2015). Fitness training interventions are aimed at improving physical capacities (e.g., muscular strength) and focused on teaching healthy exercises to stay fit (Alleva et al., 2015).

Media literacy interventions are aimed at teaching girls to critically evaluate and challenge images and messages promoted by social media as the body ideal (Alleva et al., 2015). Specific strategies include educating girls about media bias toward a singular ideal, identifying harmful body-related cultural images, resisting and changing media messages, and reducing exposure to appearance-focused media (Alleva et al., 2015; Choate, 2007). Girls need understanding of the biased notion of physical beauty perpetuated by media and the unrealistic nature of those images. The intention of those images is to promote sales of various products; therefore, they are carefully photoshopped to make them appealing. In one study, exposure to the images of thin idealized models was associated with lower body satisfaction and body esteem in adolescent girls (Halliwell et al., 2011). However, when girls watched a brief video explaining the artificial nature of media images right before exposure to the models, it mitigated the negative exposure effect. Furthermore, girls can be engaged in media critique by pairing pictures of extremely attractive models with the words "fake" or "unnatural" (Alleva et al., 2015).

Another body image intervention, "Happy Being Me," focuses on increasing media literacy, reducing appearance-based conversations, and understanding the harm of body comparison (Dunstan et al., 2017). The three educator-led sessions include student interactive lessons on media literacy, cultural appearance ideal, the harm of appearance-related conversations and teasing related to appearance, and teaching skills for avoiding body comparisons (Dunstan et al., 2017). The program was found to be effective in increasing positive self-image in adolescent girls whether it was delivered as a universal intervention to a whole class or as a selective intervention to girls only.

An additional program is the "Dove Self-Esteem Project" which is a series of free, downloadable "toolkits" developed for adolescent girls, which parents or teachers can implement to address difficult topics during adolescence (Dove, 2021). The school workshops are offered as either a single lesson or a five-lesson kit and provide resources regarding self-esteem, body confidence, unrealistic "ideal" body images, and strategies to build confidence. Resources for parents are focused on building confidence and self-esteem, focusing on relationships, self-care, recognizing teasing and bullying, media, and how to talk about appearance and body image (Dove, 2021). Together, these materials help parents and teachers foster self-esteem and positive body image for adolescent girls.

Enhancing self-esteem and focusing on individual differences and strengths are other avenues to change girls' attitudes toward physical appearance. To help build self-esteem, girls should be involved in activities that are not focused on physical appearance but celebrate differences, strengths, and talents (Burnette et al., 2017; Choate, 2007). Experiential learning and drama therapy approaches can be preventative interventions for body image and self-esteem (Mora et al., 2015). In one such intervention, Theater in Health Education, adolescents were provided with media literacy training and then asked to create their own "parody making-of-video" from fashion advertisements. Results indicated that post intervention, students reported higher self-esteem which was maintained at a 13-month follow-up (Mora et al., 2015).

Sleep Habits

"Sleep in children is not merely a 'break' or leisure period, but rather an essential component of healthy growth and development from infancy through an individual's lifespan" (Gruber, 2017). Adolescents need between 8 and 10 hours of sleep per night in order to maintain their physical health, emotional well-being, and optimal school performance (Paruthi et al., 2016). Despite these recommendations, adolescents are not getting the recommended amount of sleep. A national Youth Risk Behavior Survey of US high school students (N = 12,154) evidenced that about 70% of students might have insufficient sleep (McKnight-Ely et al., 2011). Research has demonstrated that adolescence is the most vulnerable period for sleep problems, especially between the ages of 12 and 17 (Lund et al., 2010).

Quality sleep is essential for adolescents' optimal physical, cognitive, and social functioning (Tarokh et al., 2016). Adolescents' physical health can be negatively affected by a lack of sleep (Cespedes Feliciano et al., 2018). Sleep deprivation can activate a reward system, and given that adolescents are very responsive to reward stimuli, a lack of sleep might also increase reward sensitivity and potentially lead to sensation seeking and risk-taking behaviors (Zaccaro et al., 2019). Indeed, adolescents who do not get adequate sleep are more likely to engage in high-risk behaviors, such as drunk driving, drug and alcohol use, smoking, risky sexual behavior, and fights (Tarokh et al., 2016). Furthermore, a lack of sleep results in daytime drowsiness and attentional problems that have a negative impact on adolescents' academic performance (Perez-Lloret et al., 2013). Adolescents report that not having enough sleep is associated with tiredness, high levels of stress, and difficulty getting along with others (Noland et al., 2009). Unfortunately, some adolescents use problematic strategies to help with sleep, including taking sleeping pills, smoking cigarettes, and drinking alcohol before going to bed (Noland et al., 2009).

Sleep plays an important role in emotion regulation (Kaplow & Alfano, 2018; Zaccaro et al., 2019). More specifically, rapid eye movement sleep helps to separate emotional aspects of a memory of fearful experiences ("visceral charge") from the nonemotional, thus diminishing the emotional intensity. Neurophysiological mechanisms involved in this process include reducing amygdala activation through prefrontal cortex pathways and increasing hippocampal activity (Zaccaro et al., 2019). Poor sleep is associated with increased amygdala activation and reduces connectivity between the prefrontal cortex and amygdala. As a result, this increases one's reactivity to negative stimuli. A study with a nationally representative sample from the US ($N = 10,148$) indicated that adolescents with greater sleep problems also reported more depression and anxiety (Kaplow & Alfano, 2018). They were more likely to use ineffective emotion regulation strategies, including avoidance, suppression, and rumination and relied less on problem-solving. Adolescents with insufficient sleep also experience fewer positive emotions (Zaccaro et al., 2019).

Furthermore, a lack of sleep affects academic performance. Adolescents who go to bed between 10:00 PM and 11:00 PM likely have better Grade Point Averages, while those with insufficient sleep or a delayed sleep schedule have poorer academic performance (Hysing et al., 2016).

Factors Contributing to Inadequate Sleep in Adolescence

Poor sleep in adolescents is caused by a combination of biological and environmental factors. Biological factors include developmental changes, such as the shifts in circadian rhythm during puberty (Tarokh et al., 2016). Morningness/eveningness (M/E) preference is another contributing factor to sleep problems during adolescence (Susman & Dorn, 2013). M/E reflects preferences for being active in the morning or evening. Evening-oriented adolescents have less sleep than morning-oriented youth and have consecutive problems with concentration and impulse control. Furthermore, evening-type adolescent girls have more internalizing problems, especially those who are obese. Adolescents report that homework is a major barrier to having sufficient sleep, especially if they have a tendency to procrastinate or multitask (Gaarde et al., 2018). Additionally, house noise, overscheduling, and parental pressure regarding academic performance negatively affect sleep in adolescents.

Using screen media is another factor that contributes to poor sleep. One study found that 82% of adolescents watched television after 9:00 PM and this number was even higher for those who had a television in their bedroom (Calamaro et al., 2009). On average, adolescents watched TV for 1.5 hours after 9:00 PM (range: 1–8 hours) and were engaged in four technology activities (range: 0–8). After 9:00 PM, 34% of adolescents reported text messaging, 44% talking on the telephone, 55% being online,

24% playing computer games, 36% watching movies, and 42% listening to music. Some adolescents spent up to 12 hours text messaging (Calamaro et al., 2009). A longitudinal study with adolescents (N = 1,101) showed that both nighttime mobile phone use and poor sleep behavior demonstrated positive linear growth over time (Vernon et al., 2018). Nighttime mobile phone use was positively associated with externalizing behavior and negatively associated with self-esteem and coping. Sleep disruption mediated the relationship between the overuse of social networking on one hand and depression and externalizing problems on the other. Engaging in screen media during bedtime is associated with poor sleep that, in turn, leads to depressive symptoms (Li et al., 2019). Adolescents who do not get enough sleep are more likely to fall asleep during school and consume a significant amount of caffeine (Calamaro et al., 2009).

Interventions to Support Sleep Hygiene

Sleep hygiene improves good sleep and therefore enhances daytime functioning and reduces emotional, cognitive, and behavioral problems resulting from poor sleep. Mental health professionals play a critical role in developing and implementing individual and group-based programs to promote sleep hygiene in adolescents as well as providing outreach to parents about the importance of sleep hygiene. The knowledge-to-action (KTA) framework can be used to ensure the success of interventions aimed at promoting healthy sleep habits (Gruber, 2017). First, a needs assessment should determine the amount of sleep girls participating in the intervention obtain. It is also important to know how much knowledge they have about healthy sleep habits, their attitudes toward sleep, and if sleep education is present in any courses girls take (i.e., health classes). The content or sleep-related education should be age appropriate and relevant to girls' current life situations.

Psychoeducational interventions can be effective in increasing sleep duration in adolescents. In one study, high school students were educated about sleep physiology and its impact on health (Colt & Reilly, 2013). They further learned strategies to promote good sleep, such as keeping a sleep schedule, doing something relaxing and turning off electronics one hour before bedtime, avoiding caffeine, making the room darker and temperature cooler, and using the bed just for sleep. Youth completed behavior change journals in which they were asked to record the number of hours they slept each night. After the intervention, adolescents' sleep duration increased by about one hour. Adolescents should be educated about the impact of screen media use around bedtime on sleep and encouraged to reduce using screen media before going to bed. In one intervention study, adolescents were required to stop using their mobile phones during pre-bedtime (Bartel et al., 2019). After one week, adolescents stopped using their phones and turned the lights off earlier and increased sleep time. Importantly, participant recruitment for this intervention was low, which might indicate a lack of motivation to change screen use habits in many adolescents.

Parents play an important role in promoting healthy sleep in adolescents. A systematic literature review showed that longer sleep duration in adolescents was associated with parental rules for bedtime and parental sleep behavior, while sleep quality was linked with healthy parent sleep and positive family functioning (Khor et al., 2020). Although these findings were mostly obtained through self-reported measures, they provide important information for interventions. Furthermore, setting bedtime at 10:00 PM or earlier is beneficial for adolescents' emotional health; however, when parents set bedtime at midnight or later, it increases the risk for adolescent depression and suicidal ideation (Gangwisch et al., 2010).

There is emerging evidence that cognitive behavioral therapy for insomnia (CBT-I), originally designed for adults, is also effective for children and adolescents (Dewald-Kaufmann et al., 2019). CBT-I strategies include sleep restriction, stimulus control (i.e., using the bedroom for sleep only, not eating or watching TV), restructuring negative thoughts associated with sleep, psychoeducation about sleep, and relaxation. Additionally, educating parents and involving them in the intervention is important for the successful implementation of CBT-I.

How to Make Healthy Habits Interventions Work

School-based prevention programs are most beneficial when they ensure that adolescents' suggestions are noted and valued (Hermans et al., 2017). "In order to be effective, health promotion frameworks need to engage and resonate with young people's lived experiences, which may well diverge from, and indeed challenge, dominant perspectives on health" (Spencer 2014, p. 20). Adolescents often act in accordance with their own understandings of health and healthy habits and their understanding may not coincide with the health discourses offered by adults. Some young people may act in a way that is opposite to adults' suggestions, thus confirming the common public narrative about their immaturity and propensity to engage in risky behavior. Others may resist health-related recommendations through inaction or comply with adult-led perspectives in order to divert unwanted adult attention and appear to conform to adult authority (Spencer, 2014). Ignoring adolescents' sense of agency and a system of meanings might result in resistance to interventions aimed at behavioral change. Adolescents also express a desire for adults to have a more positive view of youth and their health. Exploring adolescents' health-related perspectives and values and developing trust and respect related to heath yield better outcomes in health promotion.

Yeager and colleagues (2018) argue that interventions that do not take into account adolescents' developmental needs for respect and status are not as successful as those that do. Many adolescents already have some knowledge about behaviors that are bad for their health; therefore, imparting information that does not add anything new to adolescents may be perceived as infantilizing. Furthermore, adults delivering information repeated through several sessions may be perceived as nagging and activate anger reactions. Interventions in which adolescents can lose their social status are also not well received. Yeager and colleagues (2018) give an example of how interventions targeting healthy eating can harness adolescents need for status and respect. Traditional interventions often focus on topics of how our body processes unhealthy foods and how eating healthy food makes us healthier. They also use lectures, whole school assemblies, and homework. A more effective intervention approach that empowers adolescents might focus on harmful food industry practices: "Food companies make junk food addictive to children's brains" and "Executives of food companies won't let their own children eat the junk food." After learning about those practices, adolescents can write a persuasive letter to their peers about healthy eating.

Healthy habits interventions should address adolescent girls' beliefs about change and their ability to make behavioral change ("I can make it happen," "I have the ability to learn new habits"). Girls further need to identify reasons to make new habits (e.g., being healthy, having more energy, preventing obesity). Furthermore, girls need to learn that making behavioral change requires willpower and time. Habits are automatic behaviors; therefore, it may not be easy to get rid of them even if adolescents are aware of the unhealthy nature of the habit (Nemec et al., 2015). Stopping an old habit is more difficult than learning a new habit, since habits often occur outside of one's awareness. It requires effort and perseverance (Nemec et al., 2015). Girls also have to be aware that forming a habit can be a long process. In one study, it took from 18 to 254 days for participants to reach automaticity in their new habits (Lally et al., 2010).

Mental health professionals can help girls select specific behaviors they want to learn. Reward experience is important to sustain motivation when practicing new habits. Using motivational interviewing techniques and an interactive format of intervention can keep adolescents engaged and adhere to recommendations. The success of the intervention can be increased when they involve assessment of barriers and facilitators to a desired change as well as addressing them during intervention implementation (Gruber, 2017). It is important to make an intervention a positive emotional experience. An upward spiral model of lifestyle change states that positive emotions help people to learn new positive health behaviors (Fredrickson, 2013). Positive emotions tie together "liking" and "wanting" reward systems: When one enjoys a given activity, he or she is likely to repeat the same activity.

Habit formation starts with an *initiation* phase (Gardner et al., 2012). During this stage, adolescent girls have to generate their goals regarding learning new behaviors or reducing old unhealthy behaviors. They also need to identify a context in which they will practice new behaviors. It is important to generate small and manageable behavioral changes. Additionally, girls need to identify a very concrete context where they will practice the new behavior. This can be a time of day (e.g., before breakfast) or a setting (e.g., home or school) as long as it is encountered regularly in daily life. Examples include walking three times on stairs before dinnertime or eating fruits at breakfast. During the subsequent *learning* phase, the behavior should be repeated in the selected context to strengthen the context-behavior association (Gardner et al., 2012). The ultimate goal of such a practice is to make the behavior automatic. This happens in the final *stability* phase, where the habit is performed with minimal effort or deliberation.

Recommended Resources

Markey, C. (2020). *The body image book for girls: Love yourself and grow up fearless.* **Cambridge University Press.**

This workbook helps girls to improve their body image through understanding, accepting and appreciating their bodies. It provides information on a variety of topics, including puberty, mental health, self-care, diets, and dealing with social media. It aims to nurture girls' physical and mental health and show them the positive impact they can have on others.

Resch, E. (2019). *The intuitive eating workbook for teens: A non-diet, body positive approach to building a healthy relationship with food.* **Instant Help Books.**

This workbook assists teens in cultivating body positivity and preventing unhealthy eating behaviors through noticing and respecting hunger and fullness signals, finding eating satisfaction, and building a deeper connection with their mind and body. It provides worksheets and resources related to the principles of intuitive eating.

Taylor, J. V. (2014). *The body image workbook for teens.* **Instant Help Books.**

This workbook contains practical exercises and tips that address the most common factors that lead to negative body image – social comparison, negative self-talk, unrealistic media images, societal and family pressures, perfectionism, toxic friendships, and the fear of disappointing others.

References

Ahn, S., & Fedewa, A. L. (2011). A meta-analysis of the relationship between children's physical activity and mental health. *Journal of Pediatric Psychology, 36*(4), 385–397. https://doi.org/10.1093/ jpepsy/jsql07

Alleva, J. M., Sheeran, P., Webb, T. L., Martijn, C., & Miles, E. (2015). A meta-analytic review of stand-alone interventions to improve body image. *PLoS One, 10*(9), e0139177. https://doi.org/10.1371/journal.pone.0139177

Andrew, R., Tiggemann, M., & Clark, L. (2016). Predictors and health-related outcomes of positive body image in adolescent girls: A prospective study. *Developmental Psychology, 52*(3), 463–474. https://doi.org/10.1037/dev0000095

Ata, R. N., Ludden, A. B., & Lally, M. M. (2007). The effects of gender and family, friend, and media influences on eating behaviors and body image during adolescence. *Journal of Youth and Adolescence, 36*(8), 1024–1037. https://doi.org/10.1007/s10964-006-9159-x

Bailey, R., Wellard, I., & Dismore, H. (2005). Girls' participation in physical activities and sport: Benefits, patterns, influences and ways forward. *World Health Organization.* https://www.icsspe.org/sites/default/files/Girls.pdf.

Bartel, K., Scheeren, R., & Gradisar, M. (2019). Altering adolescents' prebedtime phone use to achieve better sleep health. *Health Communication, 34*(4), 456–462. https://doi.org/10.1080/10410236.2017.1422099

Benjamin, R. M. (2010). The Surgeon General's vision for a healthy and fit nation. *Public Health Reports (Washington, D.C.:1974), 125*(4), 514–515. https://doi.org/10.1177/003335491012500402

Bisaga, K., Whitaker, A., Davies, M., Chuang, S., Feldman, J., & Walsh, B. (2005). Eating disorder and depressive symptoms in urban high school girls from different ethnic backgrounds. *Journal of Developmental and Behavioral Pediatrics, 26*(4), 257–266. https://doi.org/10.1097/00004703-200508000-00001

Bucchianeri, M. M., Fernandes, N., Loth, K., Hannan, P. J., Eisenberg, M. E., & Neumark-Sztainer, D. (2016). Body dissatisfaction: Do associations with disordered eating and psychological well-being differ across race/ethnicity in adolescent girls and boys? *Cultural Diversity & Ethnic Minority Psychology, 22*(1), 137–146. https://doi.org/10.1037/cdp0000036

Burnette, C. B., Kwitowski, M. A., & Mazzeo, S. E. (2017). "I don't need people to tell me I'm pretty on social media:" A qualitative study of social media and body image in early adolescent girls. *Body Image, 23*, 114–125. https://doi.org/10.1016/j.bodyim.2017.09.001

Calamaro, C. J., Mason, T. B., & Ratcliffe, S. J. (2009). Adolescents living the 24/7 lifestyle: Effects of caffeine and technology on sleep duration and daytime functioning. *Pediatrics, 123*(6), e1005–e1010. https://doi.org/10.1542/peds.2008-3641

Camacho-Miñano, M. J., LaVoi, N. M., & Barr-Anderson, D. J. (2011). Interventions to promote physical activity among young and adolescent girls: A systematic review. *Health Education Research, 26*(6), 1025–1049. https://doi.org/10.1093/her/cyr040

Centers for Disease Control and Prevention. (2009). Youth risk behavior surveillance. *Surveillance Summaries, Morbidity and Mortality Weekly Report, 59*(SS05), 1–142.

Centers for Disease Control and Prevention. (2020, October 7). How much physical activity do children need? *Physical activity basics.* http://www.cdc.gov/physicalactivity/basics/children/index.htm

Cespedes Feliciano, E. M., Quante, M., Rifas-Shiman, S. L., Redline, S., Oken, E., & Taveras, E. M. (2018). Objective sleep characteristics and cardiometabolic health in young adolescents. *Pediatrics, 142*(1), e20174085. https://doi.org/10.1542/peds.2017-4085

Choate, L. H. (2007). Counseling adolescent girls for body image resilience: Strategies for school counselors. *Professional School Counseling, 10*(3), 317–326. https://doi.org/10.1177/2156759X0701000314

Choate, L. H. (2013). Adolescent girls in distress: A guide for mental health treatment and prevention. Trade Paperback.

Colt, A., & Reilly, J. M. (2013). An educational intervention to improve the sleep behavior and well-being of high school students. *PRiMER, 3*(21). https://doi.org/10.22454/PRiMER.2019.871017

Cruz-Sáez, S., Pascual, A., Salaberria, K., Etxebarria, I., & Echeburúa, E. (2015). Risky eating behaviors and beliefs among adolescent girls. *Journal of Health Psychology, 20*(2), 154–163. https://doi.org/10.1177/1359105313500683

de Vries, D. A., Vossen, H., & van der Kolk-van der Boom, P. (2019). Social media and body dissatisfaction: Investigating the attenuating role of positive parent-adolescent relationships. *Journal of Youth and Adolescence, 48*(3), 527–536. https://doi.org/10.1007/s10964-018-0956-9

Dewald-Kaufmann, J., de Bruin, E., & Michael, G. (2019). Cognitive behavioral therapy for insomnia (CBT-i) in school-aged children and adolescents. *Sleep Medicine Clinics, 14*(2), 155–165. https://doi.org/10.1016/j.jsmc.2019.02.002

Dove (2021). Dove Self-Esteem Project. https://www.dove.com/us/en/dove-self-esteem-project.html

Duarte, C., Pinto-Gouveia, J., & Rodrigues, T. (2015). Being bullied and feeling ashamed: Implications for eating psychopathology and depression in adolescent girls. *Journal of Adolescence, 44*, 259–268. https://doi.org/10.1016/j.adolescence.2015.08.005

Dunstan, C. J., Paxton, S. J., & McLean, S. A. (2017). An evaluation of a body image intervention in adolescent girls delivered in single-sex versus co-educational classroom settings. *Eating Behaviors, 25*, 23–31. https://doi.org/10.1016/j.eatbeh.2016.03.016

Fredrickson, B. L. (2013). Positive emotions broaden and build. *Advances in Experimental Social Psychology, 47*, 1–53. https://doi.org/10.1016/B978-0-12-407236-7.00001-2

Gaarde, J., Hoyt, L. T., Ozer, E. J., Maslowsky, J., Deardorff, J., & Kyauk, C. (2018). So much to do before I sleep: Investigating adolescent-perceived barriers and facilitators to sleep. *Youth & Society, 52*(4), 592–617. https://doi.org/10.1177/0044118X18756468

Gangwisch, J. E., Babiss, L. A., Malaspina, D., Turner, J. B., Zammit, G. K., & Posner, K. (2010). Earlier parental set bedtimes as a protective factor against depression and suicidal ideation. *Sleep, 33*(1), 97–106. https://doi.org/10.1093/sleep/33.1.97

Gardner, B., Lally, P., & Wardle, J. (2012). Making health habitual: The psychology of 'habit-formation' and general practice. *The British Journal of General Practice, 62*(605), 664–666. https://doi.org/10.3399/bjgp12X659466

Gerner, B., & Wilson, P. H. (2005). The relationship between friendship factors and adolescent girls' body image concern, body dissatisfaction, and restrained eating. *International Journal of Eating Disorders, 37*(4), 313–320. https://doi.org/10.1002/eat.20094

Gordon-Larsen, P., Adair, L. S., Nelson, M. C., & Popkin, B. M. (2004). Five-year obesity incidence in the transition period between adolescence and adulthood: The National Longitudinal Study of Adolescent Health. *American Journal of Clinical Nutrition, 80*(3), 569–575. https://doi.org/10.1093/ajcn/80.3.569

Gouveia, M. J., Canavarro, M. C., & Moreira, H. (2019). How can mindful parenting be related to emotional eating and overeating in childhood and adolescence? The mediating role of parenting stress and parental child-feeding practices. *Appetite, 138*, 102–114. https://doi.org/10.1016/j.appet.2019.03.021

Groth, S. W., & Morrison-Beedy, D. (2011). Obesity risk in urban adolescent girls: Nutritional intentions and health behavior correlates. *The Journal of the New York State Nurses' Association, 42*(1–2), 15–28.

Gruber, R. (2017). School-based sleep education programs: A knowledge-to-action perspective regarding barriers, proposed solutions, and future directions. *Sleep Medicine Reviews, 36*, 13–28. https://doi.org/10.1016/j.smrv.2016.10.001

Guide to Community Preventive Services. (2016). Obesity: Meal or fruit and vegetable snack interventions to increase healthier foods and beverages provided by schools. https://www.thecommunityguide.org/findings/obesity-meal-fruit-vegetable-snack-interventions-increase-healthier-foods-beverages-schools

Halliwell, E., Easun, A., & Harcourt, D. (2011). Body dissatisfaction: Can a short media literacy message reduce negative media exposure effects amongst adolescent girls? *British Journal of Health Psychology, 16*(2), 396–403. https://doi.org/10.1348/135910710X515714

Han, J., Kim, S., & Park, C. G. (2020). Gender differences in risk factors influencing unhealthy weight control behaviors among adolescents. *Western Journal of Nursing Research, 42*(9), 690–697. https://doi.org/10.1177/0193945919883394

Healthy Girls Save the World (2018). After school programs & summer experience evaluation report. https://img1.wsimg.com/blobby/go/f72107a2-30d7-4ba3-98bb-6c0e985f4f80/downloads/2017-2018%20School%20year_Eval%20report.pdf?ver=1589489569402

Hermans, R., de Bruin, H., Larsen, J. K., Mensink, F., & Hoek, A. C. (2017). Adolescents' responses to a school-based prevention program promoting healthy eating at school. *Frontiers in Public Health, 5*, e309. https://doi.org/10.3389/fpubh.2017.00309

Hesse-Biber, S. N., Howling, S. A., Leavy, P., & Lovejoy, M. (2004). Racial identity and the development of body image issues among African American adolescent girls. *The Qualitative Report, 9*(1), 49–79. https://nsuworks.nova.edu/tqr/vol9/iss1/4

Hillman, C. (2014). An introduction to the relation of physical activity to cognitive and brain health and scholastic achievement. *Monographs of the Society for Research in Child Development, 79*(4), 1–6. https://doi.org/10.1111/mono.12127

Hogue, C. M., Fry, M. D., & Iwasaki, S. (2019). The impact of the perceived motivational climate in physical education classes on adolescent greater life stress, coping appraisals, and experience of shame. *Sport, Exercise, and Performance Psychology, 8*(3), 273–289. https://doi.org/10.1037/spy0000153

Holland, G., & Tiggemann, M. (2016). A systematic review of the impact of the use of social networking sites on body image and disordered eating outcomes. *Body Image, 17*, 100–110. https://doi.org/10.1016/j.bodyim.2016.02.008

Hoying, J., Melnyk, B. M., & Arcoleo, K. (2016). Effects of the COPE cognitive behavioral skills building TEEN program on the healthy lifestyle behaviors and mental health of Appalachian early adolescents. *Journal of Pediatric Health Care, 30*(1), 65–72. https://doi.org/10.1016/j.pedhc.2015.02.005

Hysing, M., Harvey, A. G., Linton, S. J., Askeland, K. G., & Sivertsen, B. (2016). Sleep and academic performance in later adolescence: results from a large population-based study. *Journal of Sleep Research, 25*(3), 318–324. https://doi.org/10.1111/jsr.12373

Iglesia I., Santaliestra-Pasías A. M., & Moreno Aznar, L. A. (2019). Habits and quality of diet. In A. Pingitore, F. Mastorci, & C. Vassalle (Eds.), *Adolescent health and well-being* (pp. 75–89). Springer. https://doi.org/10.1007/978-3-030-25816-0_4

Jääskeläinen, A., Nevanperä, N., Remes, J., Rahkonen, F., Järvelin, M. R., & Laitinen, J. (2014). Stress-related eating, obesity and associated behavioural traits in adolescents: A prospective population-based cohort study. *BMC Public Health.* https://doi.org/10.1186/1471-2458-14-321

Johns Hopkins Medicine. (2020). Healthy eating during adolescence. https://www.hopkinsmedicine.org/health/wellness-and-prevention/healthy-eating-during-adolescence

Kann, L., McManus, T., Harris, W. A., Shanklin, S. L., Flint, K. H., Queen, B., Lowry, R., Chyen, D., Whittle, L., Thornton, J., Lim, C., Bradford, D., Yamakawa, Y., Leon, M., Brener, N., & Ethier, K. A. (2018). Youth risk behavior surveillance-United States, 2017. *Morbidity and Mortality Weekly Report. Surveillance Summaries, 67*(8), 1–114. https://doi.org/10.15585/mmwr.ss6708a1

Kaplow, J. B., & Alfano, C. A. (2018). Associations among adolescent sleep problems, emotion regulation, and affective disorders: Findings from a nationally representative sample. *Journal of Psychiatric Research, 96*, 1–8. https://doi.org/10.1016/j.jpsychires.2017.09.015

Khor, S., McClure, A., Aldridge, G., Bei, B., & Yap, M. (2020). Modifiable parental factors in adolescent sleep: A systematic review and meta-analysis. *Sleep Medicine Reviews, 56*, 101408. Advance online publication. https://doi.org/10.1016/j.smrv.2020.101408

Kimm, S. Y. S., Glynn, N. W., McMahon, R. P., Voorhees, C. C., Striegel-Moore, R. H., & Daniels, S. R. (2006). Self-perceived barriers to activity participation among sedentary adolescent girls. *Medicine & Science in Sports & Exercise, 38*(3), 534–540. https://doi.org/10.1249/01.mss.0000189316.71784.dc

Lally, P., van Jaarsveld, C. H. M., Potts, H. W. W., & Wardle, J. (2010). How are habits formed: Modelling habit formation in the real world. *European Journal of Social Psychology, 40*(6), 998–1009. https://doi.org/10.1002/ejsp.674

Lam, C. B., & McHale, S. M. (2015). Developmental patterns and parental correlates of youth leisure-time physical activity. *Journal of Family Psychology, 29*(1), 100–107. https://doi.org/10.1037/fam0000049

Latzer, Y., Spivak-Lavi, Z., & Katz, R. (2015). Disordered eating and media exposure among adolescent girls: The role of parental involvement and sense of empowerment. *International Journal of Adolescence and Youth, 20*(3), 375–391. https://doi.org/10.1080/02673843.2015.1014925

Li, X., Buxton, O. M., Lee, S., Chang, A. M., Berger, L. M., & Hale, L. (2019). Sleep mediates the association between adolescent screen time and depressive symptoms. *Sleep Medicine, 57*, 51–60. https://doi.org/10.1016/j.sleep.2019.01.029

Lund, H. G., Reider, B. D., Whiting, A. B., & Prichard, J. R. (2010). Sleep patterns and predictors of disturbed sleep in a large population of college students. *Journal of Adolescent Health, 46*(2), 124–132. https://doi.org/10.1016/j.jadohealth.2009.06.016

Mangerud, W. L., Bjerkeset, O., Lydersen, S., & Indredavik, M. S. (2014). Physical activity in adolescents with psychiatric disorders and in the general population. *Child and Adolescent Psychiatry and Mental Health, 8*(2), 2–10. https://doi.org/10.1186/1753-2000-8-2

McKnight-Eily, L. R., Eaton, D. K., Lowry, R., Croft, J. B., Presley-Cantrell, L., & Perry, G. S. (2011). Relationships between hours of sleep and health-risk behaviors in US adolescent students. *Preventive Medicine, 53*(4–5), 271–273. https://doi.org/10.1016/j.ypmed.2011.06.020

McLean, S. A., Jarman, H. K., & Rodgers, R. F. (2019). How do "selfies" impact adolescents' well-being and body confidence? A narrative review. *Psychology Research and Behavior Management, 12*, 513–521. https://doi.org/10.2147/PRBM.S177834

McLean, S. A., Paxton, S. J., Wertheim, E. H., & Masters, J. (2015). Photoshopping the selfie: Selfphoto editing and photo investment are associated with body dissatisfaction in adolescent girls. *The International Journal of Eating Disorders, 48*(8), 1132–1140. https://doi.org/10.1002/eat.22449

Meier, E. P., & Gray, J. (2014). Facebook photo activity associated with body image disturbance in adolescent girls. *Cyberpsychology, Behavior and Social Networking, 17*(4), 199–206. https://doi.org/10.1089/cyber.2013.0305

Melnyk, B., Jacobson, D., Kelly, S., O'Haver, J., Small, L., & Mays, M. Z. (2009). Improving the mental health, healthy lifestyle choices, and physical health of Hispanic adolescents: A randomized controlled pilot study. *Journal of School Health, 79*(12), 575–584. https://doi.org/10.1111/j.1746-1561.2009.00451.x

Mensinger, J. L., Bonifazi, D. Z., & LaRosa, J. (2007). Perceived gender role prescriptions in schools, the superwoman ideal, and disordered eating among adolescent girls. *Sex Roles: A Journal of Research, 57*(7–8), 557–568. https://doi.org/10.1007/s11199-007-9281-6

Mikolajczyk, R. T., Iannotti, R. J., & Farhat, T. (2012). Ethnic differences in perceptions of body satisfaction and body appearance among U.S. schoolchildren: A cross-sectional study. *BMC Public Health, 12*, 425. https://doi.org/10.1186/1471-2458-12-425

Mingoia, J., Hutchinson, A. D., Wilson, C., & Gleaves, D. H. (2017). The relationship between social networking site use and the internalization of a thin ideal in females: A meta-analytic review. *Frontiers in Psychology, 8*, 1351. https://doi.org/10.3389/fpsyg.2017.01351

Mitchell, F., Gray, S., & Jo Inchley, J. (2015) 'This choice thing really works…' Changes in experiences and engagement of adolescent girls in physical education classes, during a school-based physical activity programme, *Physical Education and Sport Pedagogy, 20*(6), 593–611. doi:10.1080/17408989.2013.837433

Mora, M., Penelo, E., Gutiérrez, T., Espinoza, P., González, M. L., & Raich, R. M. (2015). Assessment of two school-based programs to prevent universal eating disorders: Media literacy and theatre-based methodology in Spanish adolescent boys and girls. *The Scientific World Journal, 2015*, 1–12. https://doi.org/10.1155/2015/328753

Nemec, P. B., Swarbrick, M. A., & Merlo, D. M. (2015). The force of habit: Creating and sustaining a wellness lifestyle. *Journal of Psychosocial Nursing and Mental Health Services, 53*(9), 24–30. https://doi.org/10.3928/02793695-20150821-01

Neumark-Sztainer, D., Bauer, K. W., Friend, S., Hannan, P. J., Story, M., & Berge, J. M. (2010). Family weight talk and dieting: How much do they matter for body dissatisfaction and disordered eating behaviors in adolescent girls? *The Journal of Adolescent Health: Official Publication of the Society for Adolescent Medicine, 47*(3), 270–276. https://doi.org/10.1016/j.jadohealth.2010.02.001

Neumark-Sztainer, D., Flattum, C. F., Story, M., Feldman, S., & Petrich, C. A. (2008). Dietary approaches to healthy weight management for adolescents: The New Moves model. *Adolescent Medicine: State of the Art Reviews, 19*(3), 421–430.

Neumark-Sztainer, D. R., Friend, S. E., Flattum, C. F., Hannan, P. J., Story, M. T., Bauer, K. W., Feldman, S. B., & Petrich, C. A. (2010). New moves-preventing weight-related problems in adolescent girls: A group-randomized study. *American Journal of Preventive Medicine, 39*(5), 421–432. https://doi.org/10.1016/j.amepre.2010.07.017

Noland, H., Price, J. H., Dake, J., & Telljohann, S. K. (2009). Adolescents' sleep behaviors and perceptions of sleep. *The Journal of School Health, 79*(5), 224–230. https://doi.org/10.1111/j.1746-1561.2009.00402.x

Olive, L. S., Byrne, D. G, Cunningham, R. B., & Telford, R. D. (2012). Effects of physical activity, fitness and fatness on children's body image: The Australian LOOK longitudinal study. *Mental Health and Physical Activity, 5*(2), 116–124. https://doi.org/10.1016/j.mhpa.2012.08.004

Owen, M., Kerner, C., Newson, L., Noonan, R., Curry, W., Kosteli, M. C., & Fairclough, S. (2019). Investigating adolescent girls' perceptions and experiences of school-based physical activity to inform the girls' peer activity intervention study. *The Journal of School Health, 89*(9), 730–738. https://doi.org/10.1111/josh.12812

Paruthi, S., Brooks, L. J., D'Ambrosio, C., Hall, W. A., Kotagal, S., Lloyd, R. M., Malow, B. A., Maski, K., Nichols, C., Quan, S. F., Rosen, C. L., Troester, M. M., & Wise, M. S. (2016). Recommended amount of sleep for pediatric populations: A consensus statement of the American Academy of Sleep Medicine. *Journal of Clinical Sleep Medicine (JCSM): Official Publication of the American Academy of Sleep Medicine, 12*(6), 785–786. https://doi.org/10.5664/jcsm.5866

Perez-Lloret, S., Videla, A. J., Richaudeau, A., Vigo, D., Rossi, M., Cardinali, D. P., & Perez-Chada, D. (2013). A multi-step pathway connecting short sleep duration to daytime somnolence, reduced attention, and poor academic performance: An exploratory cross-sectional study in teenagers. *Journal of Clinical Sleep Medicine, 9*(5), 469–473. https://doi.org10.5664/jcsm.2668

Powell, E. M., Frankel, L. A., & Hernandez, D. C. (2017). The mediating role of child self-regulation of eating in the relationship between parental use of food as a reward and child emotional overeating. *Appetite, 113*, 78–83. https://doi.org/10.1016/j.appet.2017.02.017

Raudsepp, L., & Riso, E. M. (2017). Longitudinal associations between sedentary behavior of adolescent girls, their mothers, and best friends. *Pediatric Exercise Science, 29*(3), 419–426. https://doi.org/10.1123/pes.2016-0255

Reid, M.-A., MacCormack, J., Cousins, S., & Freeman, J. G. (2015). Physical activity, school climate, and the emotional health of adolescents: Findings from 2010 Canadian health behaviour in school-aged children (HBSC) study. *School Mental Health, 7*(3), 224–234, https://doi.org/10.1007/s12310-015-9150-3

Robertson-Wilson, J., Baker, J., Derbinshyre, E., & Cote, J. (2003). Childhood sport involvement in active and inactive adult females. *AVANTE, 9*, 108.

Rousseau, A. (2021). Adolescents' selfie-activities and idealized online self-presentation: An application of the sociocultural model. *Body Image, 36*, 16–26. https://doi.org/10.1016/j.bodyim.2020.10.005

Salomon, I., & Brown, C. S. (2020). That selfie becomes you: Examining taking and posting selfies as forms of self-objectification. *Media Psychology*, 1–19. https://doi.org/10.1080/15213269.2020.1817091

Sifers, S. K., & Shea, D. N. (2013). Evaluations of Girls on the Run/Girls on Track to enhance self-esteem and well-being. *Journal of Clinical Sport Psychology, 7*(1), 77–85. https://doi.org/10.1123/jcsp.7.1.77

Slater, A., & Tiggeman, M. (2011). Gender differences in adolescent sport participation, teasing, self-objectification and body Image Concerns. *Journal of Adolescence, 34*(3), 455–463. https://doi.org/10.1016/j.adolescence.2010.06.007

Smith, J. E., Erickson, S. J., Austin, J. L., Winn, J. L., Lash, D. N., & Amrhein, P. C. (2016). Mother-daughter relationship quality and body image in preadolescent girls. *Journal of Child and Family Studies, 25*(9), 2683–2694. https://doi.org/10.1007/s10826-016-0452-3

Spencer, G. (2014). Young people and health: Towards a new conceptual framework for understanding empowerment. *Health: An Interdisciplinary Journal for the Social Study of Health, Illness and Medicine, 18*(1), 3–22. https://doi.org/10.1177/1363459312473616

Steiner-Adair, C., & Sjostrom, L. (2006). *Full of ourselves: A wellness program to advance girl power, health, and leadership.* Teachers College Press.

Steiner-Adair, C., Sjostrom, L., Franko, D. L., Pai, S., Tucker, R., Becker, A. E., & Herzog, D. B. (2002). Primary prevention of risk factors for eating disorders in adolescent girls: Learning from practice. *The International Journal of Eating Disorders, 32*(4), 401–411. https://doi.org/10.1002/eat.10089

Strasburger, V. C., Jordan, A. B., & Donnerstein, E. (2010). Health effects of media on children and adolescents. *American Academy of Pediatrics, 125*(4), 756–767. https://doi.org/10.1542/peds.2009-2563

Susman, E. J., & Dorn, L. D. (2013). Puberty: Its role in development. In R. M. Lerner, M. A. Easterbrooks, J. Mistry, & I. B. Weiner (Eds.), *Handbook of Psychology: Developmental Psychology* (pp. 289–320). John Wiley & Sons, Inc.

Tarokh, L., Saletin, J. M., & Carskadon, M. A. (2016). Sleep in adolescence: Physiology, cognition and mental health. *Neuroscience and Biobehavioral Reviews, 70*, 182–188. https://doi.org/10.1016/j.neubiorev.2016.08.008

Taylor, A., & Hutchinson, D. M. (2013). Adolescent girls' friendship networks, body dissatisfaction, and disordered eating: Examining selection and socialization processes. *Journal of Abnormal Psychology, 122*(1), 93–104. https://doi.org/10.1037/a0029304

Tiggemann, M., & Slater, A. (2013). NetGirls: The Internet, Facebook, and body image concern in adolescent girls. *International Journal of Eating Disorders, 46*(6), 630–633. https://doi.org/10.1002/eat.22141

Tirlea, L., Truby, H., & Haines, T. P. (2016). Pragmatic, randomized controlled trials of the Girls on the Go! Program to improve self-esteem in girls. *American Journal of Health Promotion, 30*(4), 231–241. https://doi.org/10.1177/0890117116639572

U.S. Department of Agriculture. (2020). Choose MyPlate. https://www.choosemyplate.gov/

U.S. Department of Health and Human Services (2012). Physical activity guidelines for Americans mid-course report: strategies to increase physical activity among youth. https://health.gov/sites/default/files/2019-09/pag-mid-course-report-final.pdf

Vander Wal, J. S., & Thelen, M. H. (2000). Predictors of body image dissatisfaction in elementary-age school girls. *Eating Behaviors, 1*(2), 105–122, https://doi.org/10.1016/S1471 0153(00)00011-8.

Vernon, L., Modecki, K. L., & Barber, B. L. (2018). Mobile phones in the bedroom: Trajectories of sleep habits and subsequent adolescent psychosocial development. *Child Development, 89*(1), 66–77. https://doi.org/10.1111/cdev.12836

Voorhees, C. C., Murray, D., Welk, G., Birnbaum, A., Ribisl, K. M., Johnson, C. C., Pfeiffer, K. A., Saksvig, B., & Jobe, J. B. (2005). The role of peer social network factors and physical activity in adolescent girls. *American Journal of Health Behavior, 29*(2), 183–190. https://doi.org/10.5993/ajhb.29.2.9

Whitehead, S., & Biddle, S. (2008). Adolescent girls' perceptions of physical activity: A focus group study. *European Physical Education Review, 14*(2), 243–262. https://doi.org/10.1177/1356336X08090708

Wilson, D. K., Evans, A. E., Williams, J., Mixon, G., & Sirard, J. R. (2005). Preliminary test of a student-centered intervention on increasing physical activity in underserved adolescents. *Annals of Behavioral Medicine: A Publication of the Society of Behavioral Medicine, 30*(2), 119–124. https://doi.org/10.1207/s15324796abm3002_4

Yeager, D. S., Dahl, R. E., & Dweck, C. S. (2018). Why interventions to influence adolescent behavior often fail but could succeed. *Perspectives on Psychological Science: A Journal of the Association for Psychological Science, 13*(1), 101–122. https://doi.org/10.1177/1745691617722620

Zaccaro, A., Conversano, C., Lai, E., & Gemignani, A. (2019). Relationship between emotions, sleep and well-being. In: A. Pingitore, F. Mastorci, & C. Vassalle (Eds.), *Adolescent Health and Well-being* (pp. 153–166). Springer.

Zullig, K. J., & White, R. J. (2011). Physical activity, life satisfaction, and self-rated health of middle school students. *Applied Research in Quality of Life, 6*(3), 277–289. https://doi.org/10.1007/s11482-010-9129-z

5 Emotional Well-Being

Emotional well-being is critical to adolescents' mental health, positive social relationships, and academic success (Chadwick et al., 2021; Hayes et al., 2012; Pekrun, 2017; Tumminia et al., 2020). It involves the ability to experience a broad range of emotions, accept one's own emotions in a nonjudgmental manner, regulate emotions effectively, and generate positive emotions.

Fostering emotional well-being becomes especially important in adolescence, as young people show heightened emotionality during this developmental period (Casey, 2015; Rapee et al., 2019; Zaccaro et al., 2019). Additionally, their emotions are often unstable and fluctuate throughout the day. High emotional reactivity, coupled with slower developing inhibitory control, represent a risk factor for emotional problems (Zaccaro et al., 2019). Furthermore, poorly regulated negative emotions can compromise adolescents' learning by their disrupting effect on cognitive processes, motivation, and relationships (Akinsola & Nwajei, 2013; Valiente et al., 2012). Therefore, targeting emotion regulation skills is one of the important avenues to prevent psychopathology.

Family represents an important context for adolescents' emotional functioning. In general, parental emotional support and validation are associated with emotional well-being in adolescents (Miller-Slough & Dunsmore, 2016). However, high family related stress may cause significant emotional problems in youth (Peris & Miklowitz, 2015). Parental behavior characterized by a high level of negative emotionality causes hypervigilance and heightened physiological stress response in youth (Miller-Slough & Dunsmore, 2016). Parents who have difficulty regulating their own emotions often invalidate their children's emotions, which, in turn, lead to emotional dysregulation (Buckholdt et al., 2014).

In adolescence, friends become an important source of emotional support (Miller-Slough & Dunsmore, 2016). They influence adolescents' emotional behavior through modeling, normalizing, and emotional contagion (Rapee et al., 2019). Observing peers' emotional behavior supplies adolescents with norms regarding emotional display and regulation of emotions. This also motivates them to resemble their peers' emotions in order to be accepted (Miller-Slough & Dunsmore, 2016). Furthermore,

DOI: 10.4324/9781003105534-5

in adolescence, peers become emotional confidants. Girls share their emotions with peers more often than boys. They also expect positive outcomes after disclosing their difficulties to friends (Miller-Slough & Dunsmore, 2016). Emotional disclosure can bring validation and comfort, but it can also expose adolescent girls to additional stress stemming from learning about peers' emotional struggles (Zaccaro et al., 2019). Resorting to peers to relieve emotional problems can also lead to adopting maladaptive emotion regulation strategies, such as consuming alcohol or cutting.

Emotion Regulation

Emotion self-regulation is a multidimensional process that targets several aspects of emotions, including their intensity, duration, and subjective experience (i.e., feeling; Gross, 2015). Gross (2002; 2015) proposed a process-oriented model of emotion regulation which consists of five families of emotions regulation strategies. The first family, called situation selection, includes strategies aimed at selecting or avoiding situations, people, and activities that might lead to a pleasant or unpleasant emotion. Situation selection can be adaptive, for example, if an adolescent girl avoids going to a party where she would likely meet her boyfriend with whom she just broke up. However, it is maladaptive if the girl regularly avoids sitting with other girls at lunch because of her social anxiety. While this can bring temporary relief, avoidant behavior can lead to missed opportunities and may make people feel guilty or more anxious (Werner & Gross, 2010). Situation selection is based on the anticipation of how one would feel in a particular situation. Therefore, it is important to teach girls to forecast positive emotions associated with certain situations or activities. It is especially important for girls with depression, as they may underestimate how much pleasure they can have in certain situations or activities.

The second family of emotion regulation strategies, situation modification, is aimed at changing the emotional impact of a situation (Gross, 2015; Werner & Gross, 2010). For instance, girls may seek support from others when feeling sad, be assertive in situations when they are unsure of themselves, or crack jokes in anxiety-producing situations. These strategies can be adaptive when used in a flexible way and in appropriate contexts. They become maladaptive when, for instance, girls over-rely on others' support and have difficulty with more independent ways of coping.

The third family of strategies, attentional deployment, is aimed at changing attentional focus in order to regulate negative emotions (Gross, 2015; Werner & Gross, 2010). Distraction is one example of attentional deployment. It involves focusing on the less emotional elements of a situation or thinking about something pleasant when distressed. This can be adaptive when not used habitually. However, when distraction becomes automatic and chronic, it may prevent adolescents from facing and processing negative emotions. Other maladaptive strategies under the attentional deployment category are rumination (i.e., excessive focusing on past events, thoughts, and feelings) and worries (i.e., anticipation of negative future events). These strategies are associated with depression and anxiety.

The fourth family of emotion regulation strategies is called cognitive change. Cognitive change allows individuals to change their emotional experience by reappraising a situation or their ability to deal with emotions (Gross, 2015; Werner & Gross, 2010). Cognitive reappraisal is effective in decreasing the experience of emotion and its behavioral manifestation (Gross, 2002). It might work well in situations characterized by low-intensity negative emotions as it allows one to process her emotions (Sheppes et al., 2011). However, in high-intensity emotional situations, distraction might be more effective as it prevents an emotion from unfolding fully. Furthermore, reappraising the situation or event is more effective than reappraising one's own emotional response (Webb et al., 2012). Importantly, appraisals that contain negative thoughts about oneself in reference to a situation (called self-elaboration) are maladaptive (Werner & Gross, 2010). For example, girls might engage in negative thoughts like "I am not competent," "I have been treated unfairly," or "I wish I could stand up for myself." Such thoughts reignite negative emotions and make them last longer.

Finally, response modulation is a family of strategies aimed at changing emotional responses directly (Gross, 2015; Werner & Gross, 2010). Adaptive strategies under this category include deep breathing, physical exercises, and relaxation. Among maladaptive strategies are expressive and experiential suppression. Expressive suppression is aimed at inhibiting the expression of emotion. This strategy not only fails to decrease the experience of emotion, but also leads to increased physiological responding and impaired memory (Gross, 2002). Moreover, expressive suppression might undermine the quality of interpersonal relationships and prevent teens from establishing close relationships (Butler et al., 2003). Experiential suppression (also called experiential avoidance) is the unwillingness to experience painful emotions, thoughts, or sensations (Hayes-Skelton & Eustis, 2020). Nonacceptance of one's own emotional experiences underlies depression and anxiety.

Beliefs about emotions may significantly affect emotion regulation (De Castella et al., 2013). Those who hold an entity theory about emotions ("I cannot change my emotions") have higher levels of distress than those who hold an incremental theory ("I can learn to change my emotions"). Furthermore, those with a perceived lack of control over their emotions use emotional avoidance more often and tend to experience higher levels of distress (De Castella et al., 2018). Importantly, simply changing beliefs in one's ability to regulate emotions can decrease avoidance of emotional experiences. Therefore, fostering a growth mindset regarding their ability to change their emotions can help adolescent girls with emotion regulation.

Emotion Regulation in Adolescents

Difficulty with emotion regulation is a transdiagnostic risk factor that can potentially lead to a wide range of mental disorders (Beauchaine & Cicchetti, 2019; McLaughlin et al., 2011). Adolescents who have difficulty with emotion regulation also show poor emotional understanding, dysregulated expression of sadness and anger, and a tendency to ruminate when feeling distressed (McLaughlin et al., 2011). Adolescents who use maladaptive emotion regulation strategies (e.g., suppression, avoidance, and rumination) have higher anxiety, depression, and aggression while those using adaptive strategies (e.g., acceptance of one's own emotions) have lower anxiety and depression (Gilbert, 2012; McLaughlin et al., 2011; Schäfer et al., 2017). Dysregulation of positive emotions also creates a risk for adolescents' psychopathology (Gilbert, 2012). This includes dampening, heightening, or not effectively modulating positive emotions. Dampening positive emotions is associated with depression (Gilbert, 2012). Girls tend to dampen positive affect more often than boys (Gentzler et al., 2014).

Temperamentally based negative and positive emotionality may significantly impact emotion regulation in adolescents (Izard et al., 2008). Negative emotionality is the tendency to experience frequently negative emotions, including anxiety, anger, and sadness, while positive emotionality involves the frequent experience of positive emotions, including interest, happiness, and excitement. Both high negative emotionality and low positive emotionality represent a temperamental risk for depression (Shankman et al., 2011). Negative emotionality is associated with a tendency to dampen positive affect (Gentzler et al., 2014) and heightened reactivity to negative emotions is associated with depression and anxiety (Gilbert, 2012). Furthermore, negative emotionality may compromise the development of emotion regulation skills (Izard et al., 2008).

Depression in Adolescent Girls

Adolescent girls are more than twice as likely as adolescent boys to develop depression (Stein & Fazel, 2015). Several risk factors contribute to higher rates of depression in girls (Nolen-Hoeksema & Girgus, 1994; Zahn-Waxler et al., 2008). Girls have a tendency to use passive, ruminative coping strategies more frequently compared to boys. They also demonstrate more relational vulnerabilities and are more sensitive to potential abandonment. Given that, unsatisfactory interpersonal relationships may be a precursor of depression. Puberty is more stressful for girls than for boys because it may be associated with undesirable body changes (e.g., increased weight). Girls also demonstrate higher empathy and care-giving behaviors (Zahn-Waxler et al., 2008). For girls from dysfunctional families, these positive qualities might increase the risk for depression associated with emotional burdens stemming from attempts to support their families emotionally. Additionally, attitudes and behaviors associated with a feminine role orientation (e.g., unassertiveness, submissiveness, and uncertainty about one's own worth) make girls more dependent on others for self-definition and vulnerable to negative self-perception (Zahn-Waxler et al., 2008).

Girls with depressive symptoms experience more intense negative emotions and tend to attribute the cause of those emotions to other people (Frost et al., 2015). They also tend to dampen their positive emotions (Gómez-Baya et al., 2017). At the same time, placing a high value on happiness also increases the probability of becoming depressed, especially when experiencing a high level of perceived stress (Gentzler et al., 2019).

A family history of depression and psychosocial stress are among the risk factors for depression (Thapar et al., 2012). Another risk factor is co-rumination, or a tendency to discuss problems with peers frequently (Stone et al., 2011). Girls who co-ruminate have more severe and prolonged depressive episodes. Insomnia is also a risk factor for depression (Casement et al., 2016). Insomnia disrupts the reward-related brain function, and adolescents may be particularly sensitive to such a disruption given their heightened sensitivity to reward. Nonrestorative sleep also alters activity in the cortical area involved in affective control that increases the risk of depression. A longitudinal study with girls found that insufficient sleep in early adolescence might be a precursor of depressive symptoms in late adolescence. Therefore, intervention aimed at improving sleep quality in early adolescence is one way to prevent depression in adolescent girls (Casement et al., 2016).

According to the interpersonal model of depression, depression is rooted in early beliefs about relationships and self-perception (Evraire & Dozois, 2011). Early negative interpersonal interactions lead to maladaptive internal working models of relationships and these models can be activated when experiencing relational stress (Mufson et al., 2004). In girls, this is associated with excessive reassurance seeking when girls rely on others' support to reduce negative emotions; however, they doubt the authenticity of the provided support and repeatedly seek reassurance (Borelli & Prinstein, 2006; Evraire & Dozois, 2011). Additionally, social comparison through social media also predicts depressive symptoms (Nesi & Prinstein, 2015). On the one hand, close friendships might represent a context for depression for adolescent girls, as girls often show similar depressive symptoms as their best friends (Giletta et al., 2011). On the other hand, emotional support from their mothers and peers is associated with lower levels of negative affect (Cui et al., 2020).

Exposure to social stressors is a potential risk factor for depression in adolescent girls (Casement et al., 2014). Like insufficient sleep, challenging social experiences disrupt neural reward circuitry. Girls with depression experience less parental warmth and acceptance (Demidenko et al., 2015). They further perceive parents as less emotionally available and report more problematic communication with them. Furthermore, they experience more negative affect toward their fathers. Low parental warmth is associated with increased brain sensitivity to potential rewards and is further associated with depressive symptoms (Cui et al., 2020). Mothers may contribute to depression and emotion dysregulation when they invalidate or dampen adolescents' positive emotions (Yap et al., 2008). Additionally, there is a link between parental depression and girls' depression: Girls who have parents with depression respond to stressful events with more depression than those who have parents without depression (Bouma et al., 2008).

Owens and colleagues (2019) found a longitudinal association between interpersonal stress and later (nine months) depressive symptoms. However, this association held only for girls with a heightened affective reactivity to stress. Furthermore, girls who had a greater increase in cortisol as a response to stress experienced the greatest depressive symptoms later on. Therefore, teaching girls stress-reduction techniques and enhancing their positive emotions at the time of stress may protect them from depression.

Hammen's stress generation model points to a bidirectional relationship between life stress events and depression (Hammen, 2006). While stressful life events contribute to depression, depressed individuals often behave in ways that generate more stressors. Additionally, abnormalities in reward processing contribute to stress sensitivity and depression (Mackin et al., 2019). One study with never-depressed adolescent girls found that girls with a blunted response to reward experienced more stress in the span of 18 months as a result of their own behavior (e.g., missing pleasurable activities and socialization with peers; Mackin et al., 2019). Later on, they reported becoming more depressed.

Interventions to Reduce Depression

Behavioral activation is one effective intervention for reducing depression (Tindall et al., 2017). Mental health professionals can help girls identify and engage in adaptive activities associated with pleasure and a sense of mastery (e.g., dancing) and decrease activities that maintain depression (e.g., social media and co-rumination with a friend). One way to increase behavioral activation is through engagement in physical activity. Indeed, studies point out that depressive symptoms can be reduced by participation in moderate- and vigorous-intensity physical activities (Conley et al., 2020; Pascoe, Bailey et al., 2020). Moreover, adding a physical activity component to traditional therapy has a positive effect on mood, sense of achievement, energy level, and provides motivation for positive change in adolescents treated for depression (Carter et al., 2016). Importantly, physical activity with a strong social component (e.g., opportunity to interact with friends) is more beneficial for reducing depressive symptoms than solitary physical activity (Conley et al., 2020).

Dancing is another way to increase behavioral activation. Dance movement interventions were found effective in reducing depression and anxiety (Anderson et al., 2014; Jeong et al., 2005; Millman et al., 2020). Dance movement engages interoception, the awareness of the body's internal sensations (Millman et al., 2020). A compromised interoception is present in many mental health problems, including anxiety and depression. Thus, tracking the body's internal experiences while engaging in dance allows girls to achieve better body awareness and control over the physiological reactions associated with emotions.

Cognitive-behavioral therapy (CBT) is a well-validated treatment option for depression in adolescents (Spirito et al., 2011). Cognitive-behavioral interventions focus on restructuring maladaptive cognitions associated with depression and deactivating dysfunctional emotion schemas. One manualized treatment program, called ACTION, trains adolescent girls to understand the relationship between emotions and cognitions, modify their maladaptive emotion schemas, learn problem-solving skills to combat stress, and modulate their irritability and depressed mood (Stark et al., 2012). Girls act like "thought judges," who evaluate the accuracy of their negative thoughts. They try to take an alternative look at a situation, find evidence for what they are feeling, and learn to evaluate the degree of their control over a negative situation. Girls are encouraged to use coping strategies when the situation cannot be changed and problem-solve when facing a changeable situation. The program also has a parental component where parents are taught to support skill acquisition in their daughters (Stark et al., 2012). Program evaluation demonstrated that the program was effective in reducing depression in adolescent girls.

Another avenue to reduce depression is to help adolescent girls deal with stresses. For example, a Positive Thoughts and Actions (PTA) program focuses on adolescents' cognitions and problem-solving skills related to school functioning, interpersonal relations, and health behavior (McCarty et al., 2013). Parents are provided with psychoeducation about adolescent development and training regarding communication skills. Adolescents who participated in the program demonstrated a reduction of depressive symptoms and improvement in personal adjustment.

Based on the interpersonal model of depression, interpersonal therapy explores adolescents' relationships with others in depth (Mufson et al., 2004). It focuses on positive and negative aspects of interpersonal relationships, expectations regarding relationships, and specific communication patterns that lead to a depressed mood (Mufson et al., 2004). Parents are also involved in treatment. Interpersonal therapy was found especially effective for depressed adolescents who experience high conflict with mothers and interpersonal problems with friends (Gunlicks-Stoessel et al., 2010).

Stress and Anxiety

Adolescents are very susceptible to stress (Sheth et al., 2017). Youth who experience chronic stress earlier in their development are especially vulnerable in this regard. Early exposure to chronic stress alters the connectivity between the prefrontal cortex and the amygdala which increases susceptibility to stress. It also alters the structure and function of the amygdala and hippocampus, both involved in emotion regulation. Such changes in brain functions result in a blunted response to rewarding stimuli, thus increasing risk for depression and substance abuse as a compensatory reward-seeking behavior (Sheth et al., 2017). High stress has an impairing impact on physical and mental health, sleep quality, and academic performance (Pascoe, Hetrick, & Parker, 2020; Sheth et al., 2017). Adolescents with high levels of stress have difficulty concentrating, staying on task, and initiating academic tasks. Furthermore, they are at an increased risk for school dropout.

Stress results from the imbalance between experienced demands and an individual's available resources to deal with these demands (Östberg et al., 2015). According to the transactional theory of stress and coping, it is the appraisal of an event rather than the event itself that leads to stress (Lazarus & Folkman, 1984). More specifically, two types of appraisal, *primary* and *secondary*, play an important role in coping with stress. Primary appraisal determines the significance of an event or situation to an individual's well-being and can be positive, irrelevant, or stressful. An appraisal of the event as stressful leads to consecutive stress and coping efforts. The aim of a secondary appraisal is to evaluate whether one can cope with stress or not. Coping involves "constantly changing cognitive and behavioral efforts to manage external and/or internal demands that are appraised as taxing or exceeding the resources of a person" (Lazarus & Folkman, 1984, p. 141). Broadly speaking, coping strategies can be divided into two groups: problem-solving, which focuses on the stressor itself, and emotion-focused, which focuses on emotions that arise as a result of stress (Lazarus & Folkman, 1984).

Stressful events alone cannot explain negative mental health outcomes (Compas et al., 1993). The way adolescents cope with stressful experiences is an important factor that links stress to psychopathology. Therefore, it is important to consider both stressful events and how adolescents appraise and cope with them. Compared to boys, girls use more maladaptive coping strategies and less distraction (Hampel & Petermann,

2006). They also engage in stress-related eating behavior more often than boys (Jääskeläinen et al., 2014). At the same time, girls use social support more often compared to boys (Hampel & Petermann, 2006). Girls who use problem-focused and emotion-focused coping experience fewer emotional and behavioral problems. However, a high degree of stress and maladaptive coping was positively associated with adjustment problems (Hampel & Petermann, 2006).

Sources of Stress

All adolescents are exposed to some level of stress, including normative daily stresses and hassles, as well as more significant stress-producing events, such as the transition from middle to high school. A survey conducted with 15–16-year-old youth in 72 countries found that 66% of students reported feeling stressed about poor grades, 55% reported test anxiety, and 37% felt very tense when studying (as cited in Pascoe, Hetrick, & Parker, 2020). Another study across 17 countries indicated that the final school years are especially stressful for youth (Wuthrich et al., 2020). Among the personal variables contributing to high stress were perfectionism, avoidant coping style, lack of self-efficacy and resilience, low self-esteem, and fear of failure of not getting into university (Schraml et al., 2011; Wuthrich et al., 2020). Environmental variables contributing to stress include increased learning requirements, pressure to perform, poor sleep routines, poor social support, and pressures coming from peer groups (e.g., through social evaluation and stress contagion).

In addition to normative stresses, some adolescents might experience traumatic events that cause significant stress (e.g., violence, death of a loved one) or be exposed to chronic stress as a part of their environment (e.g., poverty, racism; Compas et al., 1993). Ethnic minority youth, who experience discrimination and stereotype threat, experience high levels of stress (Dunbar et al., 2017). One study found that African American adolescent girls experience a significant amount of daily hassles that, in turn, are associated with greater depression and anxiety (Cooper et al., 2011). The study also found that a stronger feminine or androgynous role orientation serves as a protective factor against emotional distress (Cooper et al., 2011). Youth from immigrant families may experience stress stemming from a cultural mismatch (e.g., differences between home and school values and norms). Such a mismatch can lead to feelings of being misunderstood and inadequate (Cheah & Leung, 2014; Rogers-Sirin et al., 2014). Another source of stress is separation from relatives and close friends due to immigration. Experiencing discrepancies between parents' culture and mainstream culture can cause strained child-parent relationships and adds another layer of stress for immigrant youth (Cheah & Leung, 2014).

In general, girls experience higher stress and anxiety compared to boys (Östberg et al., 2015; Pascoe, Hetrick, & Parker, 2020; Schraml et al., 2011; Wuthrich et al., 2020). Girls experience more relational stressors, including potential or real social rejection (Compas et al, 1993; Hampel & Petermann, 2006; Östberg et al., 2015). Dissatisfaction with social contacts and experiencing a lack of social support are associated with greater distress, anxiety, and depression (Van Droogenbroeck et al., 2018). Additionally, over-involvement with social media is another potential contributor to stress. More specifically, it can cause stress associated with seeing others posting about events which adolescents have not been invited to, feeling pressure to post appealing content about themselves, and getting "likes" (Lenhart et al., 2015). Stress can also originate from having no control over content posted by others.

Test Anxiety

Testing situations are a ubiquitous source of youth's anxiety and stress. Test anxiety is triggered when students believe that the demands of the task are greater than their intellectual, attentional, or educational capacities (Zeidner, 2014). A large-scale study with high school students (N = 2435) showed that 16.4% of the sample reported having high test anxiety; more female students reported high test anxiety than male students (22.5% vs. 10.3%; Putwain & Daly, 2014). Test anxiety is also greater in students who score high on self-criticism and social anxiety and score low on self-assurance, acceptance, and mindfulness (Cunha & Paiva, 2012). Another study showed that low effortful control and a perceived threat of tests were significant predictors of test anxiety (Raymo et al., 2019). Adolescents who are uncertain about their ability to control academic outcomes tend to have higher test anxiety (Putwain & Pescod, 2018). They often anticipate failure and show a lack of confidence in their abilities. Worrying about performance, thinking about failure, and the tendency to self-deprecate have a negative impact on achievement and subjective well-being (Steinmayr et al., 2016). The worry component of test anxiety has an especially debilitating effect on academic performance, likely through its disruptive impact on working memory and attention (Putwain & Pescod, 2018).

Interventions to Reduce Stress and Anxiety

A meta-analytic study demonstrated that school-based interventions are effective in reducing stress (van Loon et al., 2020). These programs usually include mindfulness, yoga, relaxation, and stress management skills. Other strategies that work to alleviate stress include progressive muscle relaxation, guided imagery, deep breathing, and desensitization techniques (Zeidner, 2014). In one study, engaging youth in short mindfulness activities, such as free drawing/coloring and mandala coloring, before taking high-stake tests decreased their test anxiety and increased their mindfulness state (Carsley & Heath, 2018). Adolescents with dispositional mindfulness (i.e., nonreactivity and nonjudgment) experience less negative affect and rumination, while less mindful adolescents are more vulnerable to stress (Ciesla et al., 2012; Mestre et al., 2019). Therefore, dispositional mindfulness serves as a protective factor against stress. Another protective factor is emotional intelligence. In one study, youth with stronger emotional intelligence skills (e.g., labeling, expressing, understanding, and regulating emotions) experienced more positive emotions and less anxiety (Mestre et al., 2019). Therefore, emotional intelligence training can be added to other modes of stress reduction training.

Interventions based on CBT principles are effective for stress-reduction (Akinsola & Nwajei, 2013; Hains & Szyjakowski, 1990; Putwain et al., 2014). These interventions are aimed at changing maladaptive assumptions, stress-promoting self-statements, and negative attitudes that impede test performance (e.g., "If I fail this exam" or "I'm worthless"). For instance, adolescents are taught that they have the power to combat their negative thoughts. They identify their test-related negative thoughts such as "I am going to fail the test" and "I'm not as smart as the other students in class." Then, they work on replacing these thoughts with more positive ones such as "I need to try my best" and "I studied hard for this test, I know I can get through this."

Cognitive stress-reduction strategies can be integrated with mindfulness. In one study, daily mindful breathing coupled with cognitive reappraisal helped reduce test anxiety in college students (Cho et al., 2016). Additionally, mindful breathing resulted in increased positive thoughts. In another study with high school students, cognitive restructuring paired with relaxation helped to decrease anxiety and depression and improve test performance (Akinsola & Nwajei, 2013).

There is evidence about the effectiveness of computer-based CBT interventions. One intervention, named "Strategies to Tackle Exam Pressure and Stress" (STEPS), included videos of students talking about how they coped with test anxiety. It also had interactive quizzes and games to practice anxiety management techniques (Putwain et al., 2014). The adolescents were trained to identify test anxiety signs and triggers and practice relaxation. They further learned goal setting, study skills, and how to replace negative self-talk with positive. The STEPS intervention was effective in reducing test worry and tension associated with test anxiety. In a later study with the same intervention, adolescents demonstrated a reduction of uncertain control, that is, the belief that one cannot affect a successful outcome (Putwain & Pescod, 2018). They also showed a decrease in worry and tension that was partially mediated by the reduction of uncertain control. The STEPS intervention was found effective in reducing not only test anxiety, but also clinical anxiety as well (Putwain & von der Embse, 2021).

Several studies indicated that reappraising anxiety as excitement is effective in reducing test anxiety (Brady et al., 2018; Brooks, 2014; Jamieson et al., 2016). Simple strategies such as self-talk (e.g., "I am excited" or "I get excited") allows adopting an "opportunity mindset" as opposed to a "threat mindset" (Brooks, 2014). The first part of this intervention is bringing awareness to the physical symptoms of anxiety ("What does your body feel like when you are anxious?"). The second part involves asking students what happens to their body when they are excited about something. The students realize that both anxiety and excitement have similar physical symptoms. However, it is the appraisal of the situation that makes them anxious. Cognitive reappraisal helps students to focus on the test instead of worrying about being anxious. After reappraisal, students are taught to use deep breathing to calm down.

Finally, psychoeducation is an important avenue for reducing stress in adolescents. One intervention, "DeStress for Success," was found to be effective in decreasing stress level and depressive symptoms in adolescents making the transition to high school (Lupien et al., 2013). The intervention provided psychoeducation about the nature of stress and factors contributing to stress, including novelty, unpredictability, threat to personality, and lack of perceived control. Adolescents also learned about their body's response to stress and stress reduction techniques.

Fostering Emotional Awareness and Acceptance

The ability to accept one's own emotions is at the core of emotional well-being (Chambers et al., 2009; Hayes et al., 2012; Tumminia et al., 2020). Emotional acceptance involves a nonjudgmental stance toward emotions and a willingness to experience emotions, whether they are negative or positive (Chambers et al., 2009). A study with adolescents demonstrated that the ability for nonjudgmental acceptance is associated with lower rumination and consequently lower negative affect (Tumminia et al., 2020).

One empirically validated intervention aimed at accepting one's own emotions is Acceptance and Commitment Therapy (ACT; Hayes et al., 2012). ACT is based on the idea that emotional problems result from psychological rigidity and the inability to accept one's own emotional experiences. The goal of ACT is to promote flexibility and a more open, centered, and engaged way of living. There are several core concepts in the ACT framework, including contact with the present moment, acceptance, cognitive defusion, using self as a context, values, and commitment to action. Contact with the present moment involves a nonjudgmental awareness of ongoing internal experiences and environmental events, while acceptance is the ability to embrace one's own emotions and thoughts instead of attempts to control or avoid them. Cognitive defusion is aimed at creating a space between thoughts and self and understanding that one's thinking (e.g., "I am a failure") is just a thought that may not have any grounds in reality. Another ACT concept, self as a context, helps adolescents take an observer's stance and treat experiences as things that happened to them rather than defining them (e.g., "I can be anxious, but I am not an anxious person"). Attending to their values helps adolescents to recognize what is important for them and what is not. Finally, the committed action concept refers to engagement in behaviors guided by one's own values. In one study, a brief school-based group ACT intervention resulted in the reduction of depressive symptoms and stress and increased flexibility (Livheim et al., 2015).

Positive Emotions and Well-Being

The positive psychology framework has accumulated mounting evidence of the importance of positive emotions for emotional well-being (Chadwick et al., 2021; Datu & King, 2016; Hofmann et al., 2011; Lomas et al., 2014; Proctor & Linley, 2013; Weytens et al., 2014). A longitudinal study with adolescents demonstrated that focusing on and maximizing positive events (called "prioritizing positivity") is associated with higher levels of well-being (Datu & King, 2016). The broaden-and-build theory of positive emotions explains the benefits associated with positive emotions (Fredrickson, 2013). First, positive emotions increase one's scope of attention, motivation to learn, and engagement with others and the world. Second, they broaden an individual's behavioral repertoire and increase personal resources that can be used in times of emotional distress. Finally, positive emotions reduce the impact of negative emotions as they lead to a faster recovery of the cardiovascular system to a normal state after stressful experiences (Fredrickson, 2013). Different positive emotions are associated with different behavioral tendencies. For example, joy motivates one to play and get involved, while contentment to savor positive experiences and incorporate them into one's values. Gratitude leads to a desire to be generous and express kindness to others, whereas inspiration motivates us to reach our personal best. These behavioral tendencies allow us to enjoy better relationships with others and oneself and lead to higher well-being.

Strategies aimed at increasing positive emotions are relatively simple and short. One example is "loving-kindness meditation" (LKM) and compassion meditation (Hofmann et al., 2011). Some studies suggested that these activities not only increase positive and decrease negative emotions, but they may also reduce immune response to stress (Hofmann et al., 2011). Furthermore, focusing on positive experiences while engaging in LKM can amplify its positive effects and motivation to continue meditation exercises (Van Cappellen et al., 2020). This finding supports the upward spiral theory of lifestyle change, stating that positive emotions can enhance behavioral and emotional interventions (Fredrickson, 2013). One study tested a Positive Emotion Regulation program that integrated several validated techniques, including focusing on positive emotions and gratitude (Weytens et al., 2014). This program demonstrated a positive effect on subjective well-being and life satisfaction and a reduction of depression and physical symptoms in youth. Furthermore, the participants favored the integrated model over a single intervention (i.e., LKM).

As part of her broaden-and-build theory of positive emotions, Fredrickson (2016) introduced a concept of positivity resonance. Positivity resonance happens in interpersonal relationships characterized by shared positive emotions, mutual care, and behavioral and biological synchrony, which includes making eye contact, matching tone of voice, making physical contact (e.g., touching), mirroring facial expressions, and body language. These shared elements are important contributors for high-quality interpersonal relationships and have a lasting effect on one's health and well-being (Fredrickson, 2016). Strategies to increase positivity resonance can be easily integrated in interventions with adolescent girls. This can be done by encouraging girls to share positive news with each other, give and receive constructive responses regarding positive news, show respect and care, and have real-time sensory connections (e.g., laugh together; Fredrickson, 2016).

Another type of intervention aimed at increasing positive emotions comes from research on savoring. Savoring is a process of intentional engagement in thoughts or behaviors that can enhance the effect of positive events on one's emotions (Bryant & Veroff, 2007; Smith et al., 2014). In addition to increasing positive emotions, savoring also leads to increased mindfulness and a greater sense of meaning and gratitude. Adolescents' ability to savor positive emotional experiences is positively associated with well-being (Chadwick et al., 2021). Savoring involves focusing on positive past experiences (i.e., reminiscing), current positive experiences, and the anticipation of positive experiences in the future (Bryant & Veroff, 2007; Smith et al., 2014). *Positive reminiscing* includes thinking about past experiences and focusing on thoughts and emotions associated with those experiences. For example, adolescent girls can be encouraged to share positive memories with each other. In order to facilitate this process, they can use photographs and other memorabilia (e.g., souvenirs). Another strategy, called basking, is aimed at identifying positive events that happened during the day. Girls can also identify their achievements and one's personal role in them. Finally, girls can keep track of the acts of kindness toward others. *Savoring the present* involves strategies such as walking and noticing positive things (e.g., in nature); taking photographs of positive/beautiful things nearby; experiencing and expressing genuine happiness when others are talking about their accomplishments; and asking questions and encouraging others to retell their accomplishments. Finally, *anticipatory savoring* might include imagining positive events that one may anticipate in the near future and drawing future positive events. Like positivity resonance, savoring can be easily integrated in individual and group work with adolescent girls.

Last, another type of intervention aimed at capitalizing on positive emotions is gratitude intervention. Gratitude is "a sense of thankfulness and joy in response to receiving a gift, whether the gift be a tangible benefit from a specific other or a moment of peaceful bliss evoked by natural beauty" (Emmons, 2004, p. 554). Grateful people have more positive social interactions, are more empathetic, and willing to help others. Further, practicing gratitude has been shown to improve well-being and mental health (Lomas et al., 2014). A review of studies with adolescents found that gratitude interventions resulted in more positive emotions, higher life and school satisfaction, reduced physical symptoms, including headaches, and better sleep (Lomas et al., 2014). Furthermore, youth with low positive affect especially benefit from gratitude interventions. Examples of gratitude interventions include counting blessings, for example, counting five things adolescent girls are grateful for; gratitude journaling where girls record things they are grateful for on a daily basis; and a "gratitude visit" which is a letter to a benefactor whom they had not properly thanked in the past.

Recommended Resources

Alvord, M. K., & McGrath, A. (2017). *Conquer negative thinking for teens: A workbook to break the nine thought habits that are holding you back.* **Instant Help Books.**

This workbook offers cognitive restructuring activities to help teens recognize their negative thinking habits, reframe their thoughts, regulate their emotions, and become more flexible thinkers. It aims to help teens feel more in control, less anxious and sad, and see the world and themselves more clearly.

Bocci, G. S. (2019). *The social media workbook for teens.* **Instant Help Books.**

Grounded in cognitive behavioral therapy, this workbook for teens teaches the skills to promote mindful digital media use and manage the stress and anxiety that can result from excessive screen time. It covers topics such as navigating cyberbullying, differentiating between "reel" and "real" life, gaining self-confidence, and increasing engagement in the world around.

Burdick, D. (2014). *Mindfulness skills for kids & teens.* **PESI Publishing & Media.**

This guide contains 150 tools and techniques presented in a skill-building format aimed at improving self-awareness, self-regulation, mental health, and social connectedness in children and adolescents. It also contains resources for teachers and mental health practitioners on how to explain mindfulness and neurobiology. This resource improves treatment outcomes for kids and teens with ADHD, depression, anxiety, PTSD, OCD, autism, pain, poor sleep, stress, and anger.

Gray, L. (2016). *Self-compassion for teens.* PESI Publishing & Media.

This workbook contains mindfulness and compassion-building activities designed for teenagers to reduce suffering and promote kindness toward themselves and others. It includes exercises, worksheets, and activities to cope with an array of difficulties, including school challenges, bullying, anxiety, depression, autism, ADHD, trauma, addiction, body image, identity development, and illness. It is a comprehensive resource for clinicians, educators, parents, and teens.

Hallett, K., & Donelan, J. (2019). *Trauma treatment toolbox for teens.* PESI Publishing & Media.

This publication contains 144 worksheets and trauma-informed exercises to help teens understand how trauma impacts the mind and body and to promote healing and growth. Skills include emotion regulation and expression skills, self-regulation, awareness of one's stress and trauma response, increasing positive emotions and resilience, and meaning-making after an experience of trauma.

Hutt, R. (2019). *Feeling better: CBT workbook for teens.* Althea Press.

This workbook is a comprehensive resource for teens that helps them navigate common issues such as stress, anxiety, depression, self-worth, and peer relations. Based on cognitive behavioral therapy, it contains interactive exercises that help teens process negative thoughts, emotions, and behaviors, and take action toward greater mental health and well-being.

Lohmann, R. C. (2009). *The anger workbook for teens* (2nd ed.). Instant Help Books.

This workbook provides teens with a practical resource for dealing with anger and frustration. It includes 37 exercises on skills such as understanding how one's mind and body respond to anger, responding constructively to anger, calming one's anger responses, and effectively communicating one's feelings.

Schab, L. M. (2005). *The anxiety workbook for teens.* Instant Help Books.

This resource helps teens deal with the daily emotions and challenges of anxiety. It contains actionable exercises focused on helping teens develop a positive self-image, recognize their anxious thoughts, and seek help when needed.

Stark, K. D., Simpson, J., Schnoebelen, S., Hargrave, J., Molnar, J., & Glen, R. (2007). *"ACTION" workbook: Cognitive-behavioral therapy for treating depressed girls.* Workbook Publishing.

This workbook is based on an empirically supported treatment program for depressed youth. It is designed for clinicians working with girls between the ages of 9 and 13 who have a unipolar depressive disorder. The manual for this 11-week program includes 20 group sessions and two individual meetings with the girls. It also includes a parallel parent training program for those who may benefit from family intervention.

Tompkins, M. A., Barkin, J. R., & McKay, M. (2018). *The relaxation and stress reduction workbook for teens: CBT skills to help you deal with worry and anxiety.* **Instant Help Books.**

This workbook provides teens with practical tools to reduce stress and work toward their short- and long-term goals. It helps teens understand the underlying causes of their stress, teaches them mindfulness and breathing techniques to calm the mind and body, and discusses strategies to manage one's negative thoughts and emotions.

References

Akinsola, E., & Nwajei, A. (2013). Test anxiety, depression and academic performance: Assessment and management using relaxation and cognitive restructuring techniques. *Psychology, 4(6A), 18–24. https://doi.org/10.4236/psych.2013.46A1003*

Anderson, A. N., Kennedy, H., Dewitt, P., Anderson, E., & Wamboldt, M. Z. (2014). Dance/movement therapy impacts mood states of adolescents in a psychiatric hospital. *The Arts in Psychotherapy, 41*(3), 257–262. https://doi.org/10.1016/j.aip.2014.04.002

Beauchaine, T. P., & Cicchetti, D. (2019). Emotion dysregulation and emerging psychopathology: A transdiagnostic, transdisciplinary perspective. *Development and Psychopathology, 31*(3), 799–804. https://doi.org/10.1017/S0954579419000671

Borelli, J. L., & Prinstein, M. J. (2006). Reciprocal, longitudinal associations among adolescents' negative feedback-seeking, depressive symptoms, and peer relations. *Journal of Abnormal Child Psychology, 34*(2), 159–169. https://doi.org/10.1007/s10802-005-9010-y

Bouma, E. M. C., Ormel, J., Verhulst, F. C., & Oldehinkel, A. J. (2008). Stressful life events and depressive problems in early adolescent boys and girls: The influence of parental depression, temperament and family environment. *Journal of Affective Disorders, 105*(1–3), 185–193. https://doi.org/10.1016/j.jad.2007.05.007

Brady, S. T., Hard, B. M., & Gross, J. J. (2018). Reappraising test anxiety increases academic performance of first-year college students. *Journal of Educational Psychology, 110*(3), 395–406. https://doi.org/10.1037/edu0000219

Brooks, A. W. (2014). Get excited: Reappraising pre-performance anxiety as excitement. *Journal of Experimental Psychology: General, 143*(3), 1144–1158. https://doi.org/10.1037/a0035325

Bryant, F. B., & Veroff, J. (2007). *Savoring: A new model of positive experience.* Lawrence Erlbaum Associates Publishers.

Buckholdt, K. E., Parra, G. R., & Jobe-Shields, L. (2014). Intergenerational transmission of emotion dysregulation through parental invalidation of emotions: Implications for adolescent internalizing and externalizing behaviors. *Journal of Child and Family Studies, 23*, 324–332. https://doi.org/10.1007/s10826-013-9768-4

Butler, E. A., Egloff, B., Wlhelm, F. H., Smith, N. C., Erickson, E. A., & Gross, J. J. (2003). The social consequences of expressive suppression. *Emotion, 3*(1), 48–67. https://doi.org/10.1037/1528-3542.3.1.48

Carsley, D., & Heath, N. L. (2018). Effectiveness of mindfulness-based colouring for test anxiety in adolescents. *School Psychology International, 39*(3), 251–272. https://doi.org/10.1177/0143034318773523

Carter, T., Morres, I., Repper, J., & Callaghan, P. (2016). Exercise for adolescents with depression: Valued aspects of perceived change. *Journal of Psychiatric and Mental Health Nursing, 23*(1). 37–44. https://doi.org/10.1111/jpm.12261

Casement, M. D., Guyer, A. E., Hipwell, A. E., McAloon, R. L., Hoffmann, A. M., Keenan, K. E., & Forbes, E. E. (2014). Girls' challenging social experiences in early adolescence predict neural response to rewards and depressive symptoms. *Developmental Cognitive Neuroscience, 8*, 18–27. https://doi.org/10.1016/j.dcn.2013.12.003

Casement, M. D., Keenan, K. E., Hipwell, A. E., Guyer, A. E., & Forbes, E. E. (2016). Neural reward processing mediates the relationship between insomnia symptoms and depression in adolescence. *Sleep, 39*(2), 439–447. https://doi.org/10.5665/sleep.5460

Casey, B. J. (2015). Beyond simple models of self-control to circuit-based accounts of adolescent behavior. *Annual Review of Psychology, 66*(1), 295–319. https://doi.org/10.1146/annurev-psych-010814-015156

Chadwick, E. D., Jose, P. E., & Bryant, F. B. (2021). Styles of everyday savoring differentially predict well-being in adolescents over one month. *Journal of Happiness Studies, 22*, 803–824. https://doi.org/10.1007/s10902-020-00252-6

Chambers, R., Gullone, E., & Allen, N. B. (2009). Mindful emotion regulation: An integrative review. *Clinical Psychology Review, 29*(6), 560–572. https://doi.org/10.1016/j.cpr.2009.06.005

Cheah, C. S. L., & Leung, C. Y. Y. (2014). The social development of immigrant children: A focus on Asian and Hispanic children in the United States. In P. K. Smith & C. H. Hart (Eds.), *Wiley Blackwell handbooks of developmental psychology. The Wiley Blackwell handbook of childhood social development* (pp. 161–180). Wiley-Blackwell.

Cho, H., Ryu, S., Noh, J., & Lee, J. (2016). The effectiveness of daily mindful breathing practices on test anxiety of students. *PloS One, 11*(10), e0164822. https://doi.org/10.1371/journal.pone.0164822

Ciesla, J. A., Reilly, L. C., Dickson, K. S., Emanuel, A. S., & Updegraff, J. A. (2012). Dispositional mindfulness moderates the effects of stress among adolescents: Rumination as a mediator. *Journal of Clinical Child and Adolescent Psychology, 41*(6), 760–770. https://doi.org/10.1080/15374416.2012.698724

Compas, B. E., Orosan, P. G., & Grant, K. E. (1993). Adolescent stress and coping: Implications for psychopathology during adolescence. *Journal of Adolescence, 16*(3), 331–349. https://doi.org/10.1006/jado.1993.1028

Conley, M. I., Hindley, I., Baskin-Sommers, A., Gee, D. G., Casey, B. J., & Rosenberg, M. D. (2020). The importance of social factors in the association between physical activity and depression in children. *Child and Adolescent Psychiatry and Mental Health, 14*(28). https://doi.org/10.1186/s13034-020-00335-5

Cooper, S. M., Guthrie, B. J., Brown, C., & Metzger, I. (2011). Daily hassles and African American adolescent females' psychological functioning: Direct and interactive associations with gender role orientation. *Sex Roles, 65*(5–6), 397–409. https://doi.org/10.1007/s11199-011-0019-0

Cui, L., Criss, M. M., Ratliff, E., Wu, Z., Houltberg, B. J., Silk, J. S., & Morris, A. S. (2020). Longitudinal links between maternal and peer emotion socialization and adolescent girls' socioemotional adjustment. *Developmental Psychology, 56*(3), 595–607. https://doi.org/10.1037/dev0000861

Cunha, M., & Paiva M. J. (2012). Text anxiety in adolescents: The role of self-criticism and acceptance and mindfulness skills. *The Spanish Journal of Psychology, 15*(2), 533–543. https://doi.org/10.5209/rev_sjop.2012.v15.n2.38864

Datu, J. A. D., & King, R. B. (2016). Prioritizing positivity optimizes positive emotions and life satisfaction: A three-wave longitudinal study. *Personality and Individual Differences, 96*, 111–114. https://doi.org/10.1016/j.paid.2016.02.069

De Castella, K., Goldin, P., Jazaieri, H., Ziv, M., Dweck, C. S. & Gross, J. J. (2013). Beliefs about emotion: Links to emotion regulation, well-being, and psychological distress. *Basic and Applied Social Psychology, 35*(6), 497–505. https://doi.org/10.1080/01973533.2013.840632

De Castella, K., Platow, M. J., Tamir, M., & Gross, J. J. (2018). Beliefs about emotion: Implications for avoidance-based emotion regulation and psychological health. *Cognition and Emotion, 32*(4), 773–795. https://doi.org/10.1080/02699931.2017.1353485

Demidenko, N., Manion, I., & Lee, C. M. (2015). Father–daughter attachment and communication in depressed and nondepressed adolescent girls. *Journal of Child and Family Studies, 24*(6), 1727–1734. https://doi.org/10.1007/s10826-014-9976-6

Dunbar, A. S., Leerkes, E. M., Coard, S. I., Supple, A. J., & Calkins, S. (2017). An integrative conceptual model of parental racial/ethnic and emotion socialization and links to children's social-emotional development among African American families. *Child Development Perspectives, 11*(1), 16–22. https://doi.org/10.1111/cdep.12218

Emmons, R. A. (2004). Gratitude. In C. Peterson & M. E. P. Seligman (Eds.), *Character strengths and virtues: A handbook and classification* (pp. 553–568). Oxford University Press.

Evraire, L. E., & Dozois, D. J. A. (2011). An integrative model of excessive reassurance seeking and negative feedback seeking in the development and maintenance of depression. *Clinical Psychology Review, 31*(8), 1291–1303. https://doi.org/10.1016/j.cpr.2011.07.014

Fredrickson, B. L. (2013). Positive emotions broaden and build. *Advances in Experimental Social Psychology, 47*, 1–53. https://doi.org/10.1016/B978-0-12-407236-7.00001-2

Fredrickson, B. L. (2016). Love: Positivity resonance as a fresh, evidence-based perspective on an age-old topic. In L. F. Barrett, M. Lewis, & J. M. Haviland (Eds.), *Handbook of emotions* (pp. 847–858). Guilford Press.

Frost, A., Hoyt, L. T., Chung, A. L., & Adam, E. K. (2015). Daily life with depressive symptoms: Gender differences in adolescents' everyday emotional experiences. *Journal of Adolescence, 43*, 132–141. https://doi.org/10.1016/j.adolescence.2015.06.001

Gentzler, A. L., Palmer, C. A., Ford, B. Q., Moran, K. M., & Mauss, I. B. (2019). Valuing happiness in youth: Associations with depressive symptoms and well-being. *Journal of Applied Developmental Psychology, 62*, 220–230. https://doi.org/10.1016/j.appdev.2019.03.001

Gentzler, A. L., Ramsey, M. A., Yi, C. Y., Palmer, C. A., & Morey, J. N. (2014). Young adolescents' emotional and regulatory responses to positive life events: Investigating temperament, attachment, and event characteristics. *The Journal of Positive Psychology, 9*(2), 108–121. https://doi.org/10.1080/17439760.2013.848374

Gilbert, K. E. (2012). The neglected role of positive emotion in adolescent psychopathology. *Clinical Psychology Review, 32*(6), 467–481. https://doi.org/10.1016/j.cpr.2012.05.005

Giletta, M., Scholte, R. H., Burk, W. J., Engels, R. C. M. E., Larsen, J. K., Prinstein, M. J., & Ciairano, S. (2011). Similarity in depressive symptoms in adolescents' friendship dyads: Selection or socialization? *Developmental Psychology, 47*(6), 1804–1814. https://doi.org/10.1037/a0023872

Gómez-Baya, D., Mendoza, R., Paino, S., & Gillham, J. E. (2017). A two-year longitudinal study of gender differences in responses to positive affect and depressive symptoms during middle adolescence. *Journal of Adolescence, 56*, 11–23. https://doi.org/10.1016/j.adolescence.2017.01.005

Gross, J. J. (2002). Emotion regulation: Affective, cognitive, and social consequences. *Psychophysiology, 39*, 281–291. https://doi.org/10.1017/s0048577201393198

Gross, J. J. (2015). Emotion regulation: Current status and future prospects. *Psychological Inquiry, 26*(1), 1–26. *https://doi.org/10.1080/1047840X.2014.940781*

Gunlicks-Stoessel, M., Mufson, L., Jekal, A., & Turner, J. B. (2010). The impact of perceived interpersonal functioning on treatment for adolescent depression: IPT-A versus treatment as usual in school-based health clinics. *Journal of Consulting and Clinical Psychology, 78*(2), 260–267. https://doi.org/10.1037/a0018935

Hains, A. A., & Szyjakowski, M. (1990). A cognitive stress-reduction intervention program for adolescents. *Journal of Counseling Psychology, 37*(1), 79–84. https://doi.org/10.1037/0022-0167.37.1.79

Hammen, C. (2006). Stress generation in depression: Reflections on origins, research, and future directions. *Journal of Clinical Psychology, 62*(9), 1065–1082. https://doi.org/10.1002/jclp.20293

Hampel, P., & Petermann, F. (2006). Perceived stress, coping, and adjustment in adolescents. *The Journal of Adolescent Health, 38*(4), 409–415. https://doi.org/10.1016/j.jadohealth.2005.02.014

Hayes, S. C., Strosahl, K. D., & Wilson, K. G. (2012). *Acceptance and commitment therapy: The process and practice of mindful change* (2nd ed.). Guilford Press.

Hayes-Skelton, S. A., & Eustis, E. H. (2020). Experiential avoidance. In J. S. Abramowitz & S. M. Blakey (Eds.), *Clinical handbook of fear and anxiety: Maintenance processes and treatment mechanisms* (pp. 115–131). American Psychological Association. https://doi.org/10.1037/0000150-007

Hofmann, S. G., Grossman, P., & Hinton, D. E. (2011). Loving-kindness and compassion meditation: Potential for psychological interventions. *Clinical Psychology Review, 31*(7), 1126–1132. https://doi.org/10.1016/j.cpr.2011.07.003

Izard, C., Stark, K., Trentacosta, C., & Schultz, D. (2008). Beyond emotion regulation: Emotion utilization and adaptive functioning. *Child Development Perspectives, 2*(3), 156–163. https://doi.org/10.1111/j.1750-8606.2008.00058.x

Jääskeläinen, A., Nevanperä, N., Remes, J., Rahkonen, F., Järvelin, M. R., & Laitinen, J. (2014). Stress-related eating, obesity and associated behavioural traits in adolescents: A prospective population-based cohort study. *BMC Public Health, 14*(321). https://doi.org/10.1186/1471-2458-14-321

Jamieson, J. P., Peters, B. J., Greenwood, E. J., & Altose, A. J. (2016). Reappraising stress arousal improves performance and reduces evaluation anxiety in classroom exam situations. *Social Psychological and Personality Science, 7*(6), 579–587. https://doi.org/10.1177/1948550616644656

Jeong, Y. J., Hong, S. C., Lee, M. S., Park, M. C., Kim, Y. K., & Suh, C. M. (2005). Dance movement therapy improves emotional responses and modulates neurohormones in adolescents with mild depression. *The International Journal of Neuroscience, 115*(12), 1711–1720. https://doi.org/10.1080/00207450590958574

Kremer, P., Elshaug, C., Leslie, E., Toumbourou, J. W., Patton, G. C., & Williams, J. (2014). Physical activity, leisure-time screen use and depression among children and young adolescents. *Journal of Science and Medicine in Sport, 17*(2), 183–187. https://doi.org/10.1016/j.jsams.2013.03.012

Lazarus, R. S., & Folkman, S. (1984). *Stress, appraisal, and coping.* Springer.

Lenhart, A., Smith, A., Anderson, M., Duggan, M., & Perrin, A. (2015). *Teens, technology & friendships: Video games, social media and mobile phones play an integral role in how teens meet and interact with friends.* Pew Research Center. https://www.pewresearch.org/internet/2015/08/06/teens-technology-and-friendships/

Livheim, F., Hayes, L., Ghaderi, A., Magnusdottir, T., Högfeldt, A., Rowse, J., Turner, S., Hayes, S. C., & Tengström, A. (2015). The effectiveness of acceptance and commitment therapy for adolescent mental health: Swedish and Australian pilot outcomes. *Journal of Child and Family Studies, 24*(4), 1016–1030. https://doi.org/10.1007/s10826-014-9912-9

Lomas, T., Froh, J. J., Emmons, R. A., Mishra, A., & Bono, G. (2014). Gratitude interventions: A review and future agenda. In A. C. Parks & S. M. Schueller (Eds.), *The Wiley Blackwell handbook of positive psychological interventions* (pp. 3–19). Wiley-Blackwell. https://doi.org/10.1002/9781118315927.ch1

Lupien, S. J., Ouellet-Morin, I., Trépanier, L., Juster, R. P., Marin, M. F., Francois, N., Sindi, S., Wan, N., Findlay, H., Durand, N., Cooper, L., Schramek, T., Andrews, J., Corbo, V., Dedovic, K., Lai, B., & Plusquellec, P. (2013). The DeStress for Success Program: Effects of a stress education program on cortisol levels and depressive symptomatology in adolescents making the transition to high school. *Neuroscience, 249*, 74–87. https://doi.org/10.1016/j.neuroscience.2013.01.057

Mackin, D. M., Kotov, R., Perlman, G., Nelson, B. D., Goldstein, B. L., Hajcak, G., & Klein, D. N. (2019). Reward processing and future life stress: Stress generation pathway to depression. *Journal of Abnormal Psychology, 128*(4), 305–314. https://doi.org/10.1037/abn0000427

McCarty, C. A., Violette, H. D., Duong, M. T., Cruz, R. A., & McCauley, E. (2013). A randomized trial of the positive thoughts and action program for depression among early adolescents. *Journal of Clinical Child and Adolescent Psychology, 42*(4), 554–563. https://doi.org/10.1080/15374416.2013.782817

McLaughlin, K. A., Hatzenbuehler, M. L., Mennin, D. S., & Nolen-Hoeksema, S. (2011). Emotion dysregulation and adolescent psychopathology: A prospective study. *Behaviour Research and Therapy, 49*(9), 544–554. https://doi.org/10.1016/j.brat.2011.06.003

Mestre, J. M., Turanzas, J., García-Gómez, M., Guerra, J., Cordon, J. R., De La Torre, G. G., & Lopez-Ramos, V. M. (2019). Do trait emotional intelligence and dispositional mindfulness have a complementary effect on the children's and adolescents' emotional states? *Frontiers in Psychology, 10*, 2817. https://doi.org/10.3389/fpsyg.2019.02817

Miller-Slough, R. L., & Dunsmore, J. C. (2016). Parent and friend emotion socialization in adolescence: Associations with psychological adjustment. *Adolescent Research Review, 1*, 287–305. https://doi.org/10.1007/s40894-016-0026-z

Millman, L. S. M., Terhune, D. B., Hunter, E. C. M., & Orgs, G. (2020). Towards a neurocognitive approach to dance movement therapy for mental health: A systematic review. *Clinical Psychology & Psychotherapy, 28*(1), 24–38. https://doi.org/10.1002/cpp.2490

Mufson, L., Dorta, K. P., Moreau, D., & Weissman, M. M. (2004). *Interpersonal psychotherapy for depressed adolescents*. Guilford Press.

Nesi, J., & Prinstein, M. J. (2015). Using social media for social comparison and feedback-seeking: Gender and popularity moderate associations with depressive symptoms. *Journal of Abnormal Child Psychology, 43*(8), 1427–1438. https://doi.org/10.1007/s10802-015-0020-0

Nolen-Hoeksema, S., & Girgus, J. S. (1994). The emergence of gender differences in depression during adolescence. *Psychological Bulletin, 115*(3), 424–443. https://doi.org/10.1037/0033-2909.115.3.424

Östberg, V., Almquist, Y. B., Folkesson, L., Låftman, S. B., Modin, B., & Lindfors, P. (2015). The complexity of stress in mid-adolescent girls and boys: Findings from the Multiple Methods School Stress and Support study. *Child Indicators Research, 8*, 403–423. https://doi.org/10.1007/s12187-014-9245-7

Owens, S. A., Helms, S. W., Rudolph, K. D., Hastings, P. D., Nock, M. K., & Prinstein, M. J. (2019). Interpersonal stress severity longitudinally predicts adolescent girls' depressive symptoms: The moderating role of subjective and HPA axis stress responses. *Journal of Abnormal Child Psychology, 47*(5), 895–905. https://doi.org/10.1007/s10802-018-0483-x

Pascoe, M. C., Bailey, A. P., Craike, M., Carter, T., Patten, R., Stepto, N. K., & Parker, A. G. (2020). Exercise interventions for mental disorders in young people: A scoping review. *BMJ Open Sport & Exercise Medicine, 6*(1), e000678. https://doi.org/10.1136/bmjsem-2019-000678

Pascoe, M. C., Hetrick, S. E., & Parker, A. G. (2020). The impact of stress on students in secondary school and higher education. *International Journal of Adolescence and Youth, 25*(1), 104–112. https://doi.org/10.1080/02673843.2019.1596823

Peris, T. S., & Miklowitz, D. J. (2015). Parental expressed emotion and youth psychopathology: New directions for an old construct. *Child Psychiatry and Human Development, 46*(6), 863–873. https://doi.org/10.1007/s10578-014-0526-7

Pekrun, R. (2017). Emotion and achievement during adolescence. *Child Development Perspectives, 11*(3), 215–221. https://doi.org/10.1111/cdep.12237

Proctor, C., & Linley, P.A. (2013). *Research, applications, and interventions for children and adolescents: A positive psychology perspective.* Springer Science + Business Media.

Putwain, D. W., Chamberlain, S., Daly, A. L., & Sadreddini, S. (2014). Reducing test anxiety among school-aged adolescents: A field experiment. *Educational Psychology in Practice, 30*(4), 420–440. https://doi.org/10.1080/02667363.2014.964392

Putwain, D. W., & Daly, A. L. (2014). Test anxiety prevalence and gender differences in a sample of English secondary school students. *Educational Studies, 40*(5), 554–570. https://doi.org/10.1080/03055698.2014.953914

Putwain, D. W., & Pescod, M. (2018). Is reducing uncertain control the key to successful test anxiety intervention for secondary school students? Findings from a randomized control trial. *School Psychology Quarterly, 33*(2), 283–292. https://doi.org/10.1037/spq0000228

Putwain, D. W., & von der Embse, N. P. (2021). Cognitive-behavioral intervention for test anxiety in adolescent students: Do benefits extend to school-related well-being and clinical anxiety? *Anxiety, Stress, and Coping, 34*(1), 22–36. https://doi.org/10.1080/10615806.2020.1800656

Rapee, R. M., Oar, E. L., Johnco, C. J., Forbes, M. K., Fardouly, J., Magson, N. R., & Richardson, C. E. (2019). Adolescent development and risk for the onset of social-emotional disorders: A review and conceptual model. *Behaviour Research and Therapy, 123*, 103501. https://doi.org/10.1016/j.brat.2019.103501

Raymo, L. A., Somers, C. L., & Partridge, R. T. (2019). Adolescent test anxiety: An examination of intraindividual and contextual predictors. *School Mental Health, 11*, 562–577. https://doi.org/10.1007/s12310-018-09302-0

Rogers-Sirin, L., Ryce, P., & Sirin, S. R. (2014). Acculturation, acculturative stress, and cultural mismatch and their influences on immigrant children and adolescents' well-being. In R. Dimitrova, M. Bender, & F. van de Vijver (Eds.), *Global perspectives on well-being in immigrant families* (pp. 11–30). Springer Science + Business Media. https://doi.org/10.1007/978-1-4614-9129-3_2

Schäfer, J. Ö., Naumann, E., Holmes, E. A., Tuschen-Caffier, B., & Samson, A. C. (2017). Emotion regulation strategies in depressive and anxiety symptoms in youth: A meta-analytic review. *Journal of Youth and Adolescence, 46*(2), 261–276. https://doi.org/10.1007/s10964-016-0585-0

Schraml, K., Perski, A., Grossi, G., & Simonsson-Sarnecki, M. (2011). Stress symptoms among adolescents: The role of subjective psychosocial conditions, lifestyle, and self-esteem. *Journal of Adolescence, 34*(5), 987–996. https://doi.org/10.1016/j.adolescence.2010.11.010

Shankman, S. A., Klein, D. N., Torpey, D. C., Olino, T. M., Dyson, M. W., Kim, J., Durbin, C. E., Nelson, B. D., & Tenke, C. E. (2011). Do positive and negative temperament traits interact in predicting risk for depression? A resting EEG study of 329 preschoolers. *Development and Psychopathology, 23*(2), 551–562. https://doi.org/10.1017/S0954579411000022

Sheppes, G., Scheibe, S., Suri, G., & Gross, J. J. (2011). Emotion-regulation choice. *Psychological Science, 22*(11), 1391-1396. https://doi.org/10.1177/0956797611418350

Sheth, C., McGlade, E., & Yurgelun-Todd, D. (2017). Chronic stress in adolescents and its neurobiological and psychopathological consequences:

An RDoC perspective. *Chronic Stress* (Thousand Oaks). https://doi.org/10.1177/2470547017715645

Smith, J. L., Harrison, P. R., Kurtz, J. L., & Bryant, F. B. (2014). Nurturing the capacity to savor: Interventions to enhance the enjoyment of positive experiences. In A. C. Parks & S. M. Schueller (Eds.), *The Wiley Blackwell handbook of positive psychological interventions* (pp. 42–65). Wiley Blackwell. https://doi.org/10.1002/9781118315927.ch3

Spirito, A., Esposito-Smythers, C., Wolff, J., & Uhl, K. (2011). Cognitive-behavioral therapy for adolescent depression and suicidality. *Child and Adolescent Psychiatric Clinics of North America, 20*(2), 191–204. https://doi.org/10.1016/j.chc.2011.01.012

Stark, K. D., Streusand, W., Arora, P., & Patel, P. (2012). Childhood depression: The ACTION treatment program. In P. C. Kendall (Ed.), *Child and adolescent therapy: Cognitive-behavioral procedures* (pp. 190–233). Guilford Press.

Stein, K., & Fazel, M. (2015). Depression in young people often goes undetected. *The Practitioner, 259*(1782), 17–22.

Steinmayr, R., Crede, J., McElvany, N., & Wirthwein, L. (2016). Subjective well-being, test anxiety, academic achievement: Testing for reciprocal effects. *Frontiers in Psychology, 6, 1994.* https://doi.org/10.3389/fpsyg.2015.01994

Stone, L. B., Hankin, B. L., Gibb, B. E., & Abela, J. R. Z. (2011). Co-rumination predicts the onset of depressive disorders during adolescence. *Journal of Abnormal Psychology, 120*(3), 752–757. https://doi.org/10.1037/a0023384

Thapar, A., Collishaw, S., Pine, D. S., & Thapar, A. K. (2012). Depression in adolescence. *The Lancet, 379*(9820), 1056–1067. https://doi.org/10.1016/S0140-6736(11)60871-4

Tindall, L., Mikocka-Walus, A., McMillan, D., Wright, B., Hewitt, C., & Gascoyne, S. (2017). Is behavioural activation effective in the treatment of depression in young people? A systematic review and meta-analysis. *Psychology and Psychotherapy, 90*(4), 770–796. https://doi.org/10.1111/papt.12121

Tumminia, M. J., Colaianne, B. A., Roeser, R. W., & Galla, B. M. (2020). How is mindfulness linked to negative and positive affect? Rumination as an explanatory process in a prospective longitudinal study of adolescents. *Journal of Youth and Adolescence, 49*, 2136–2148. https://doi.org/10.1007/s10964-020-01238-6

Valiente, C., Swanson, J., & Eisenberg, N. (2012). Linking students' emotions and academic achievement: When and why emotions matter. *Child Development Perspectives, 6*(2), 129–135. https://doi.org/10.1111/j.1750-8606.2011.00192.x

Van Cappellen, P., Catalino, L. I., & Fredrickson, B. L. (2020). A new micro-intervention to increase the enjoyment and continued practice of meditation. *Emotion, 20*(8), 1332–1343. https://doi.org/10.1037/emo0000684

Van Droogenbroeck, F., Spruyt, B., & Keppens, G. (2018). Gender differences in mental health problems among adolescents and the role of social support: Results from the Belgian health interview surveys 2008 and 2013. *BMC Psychiatry, 18*(1), 6. https://doi.org/10.1186/s12888-018-1591-4

van Loon, A. W. G., Creemers, H. E., Beumer, W. Y., Okorn, A., Vogelaar, S., Saab, N., Miers, A. C., Westenberg, P. M., & Asscher, J. J. (2020). Can schools reduce adolescent psychological stress? A multilevel meta-analysis of the effectiveness of school-based intervention programs. *Journal of Youth and Adolescence, 49*(6), 1127–1145. https://doi.org/10.1007/s10964-020-01201-5

Webb, T. L., Miles, E., & Sheeran, P. (2012). Dealing with feeling: A meta-analysis of the effectiveness of strategies derived from the process model of emotion regulation. *Psychological Bulletin, 138*(4), 775–808. https://doi.org/10.1037/a0027600

Werner, K., & Gross, J. J. (2010). Emotion regulation and psychopathology: A conceptual framework. In A. M. Kring & D. M. Sloan (Eds.), *Emotion regulation and psychopathology: A transdiagnostic approach to etiology and treatment* (pp. 13–37). The Guilford Press.

Weytens, F., Luminet, O., Verhofstadt, L. L., & Mikolajczak, M. (2014). An integrative theory-driven positive emotion regulation intervention. *PloS One, 9*(4), e95677. https://doi.org/10.1371/journal.pone.0095677

Wuthrich, V. M., Jagiello, T., & Azzi, V. (2020). Academic stress in the final years of school: A systematic literature review. *Child Psychiatry & Human Development, 51*(6), 986–1015. https://doi.org/10.1007/s10578-020-00981-y

Yap, M. B., Allen, N. B., & Ladouceur, C. D. (2008). Maternal socialization of positive affect: The impact of invalidation on adolescent emotion regulation and depressive symptomatology. *Child Development, 79*(5), 1415–1431. https://doi.org/10.1111/j.1467-8624.2008.01196.x

Zaccaro, A., Conversano, C., Lai, E., & Gemignani, A. (2019). Relationship between emotions, sleep and well-being. In: A. Pingitore, F. Mastorci, & C. Vassalle (Eds.), *Adolescent health and well-being* (pp. 153–166). Springer.

Zahn-Waxler, C., Shirtcliff, E. A., & Marceau, K. (2008). Disorders of childhood and adolescence: Gender and psychopathology. *Annual Review of Clinical Psychology, 4*, 275–303. https://doi.org/10.1146/annurev.clinpsy.3.022806.091358

Zeidner, M. (2014). Test anxiety. In P. Emmelkamp & T. Ehring (Eds.), *The Wiley handbook of anxiety disorders, Vol. 1. Theory and research; Vol. 2. Clinical assessment and treatment* (pp. 581–595). Wiley Blackwell.

6 Interpersonal Relationships in Adolescent Girls as a Pathway to Well-Being

The need to belong and to be connected with others is one of the basic human needs (Jordan, 2010; Leary & Allen, 2011; Ryan & Deci, 2017). It results from a deeply seated desire to be accepted by others and to be a part of social groups. This need can be satisfied in caring interpersonal relationships and communities that promote a sense of belonging. Connection with others leads to a sense of self-worth and a desire for more relationships (Jordan, 2010). It is further essential for one's well-being (Ryan & Deci, 2017).

Adolescence is marked by expanding relational ecologies. Young people become engaged in many relationships outside their families and close friends' circles. Their ability to navigate successfully these relationships and the supportive nature of those relationships are central for adolescents' healthy socio-emotional development. Research findings suggest that positive interpersonal relationships during adolescence predict health outcomes in adulthood (Kim, 2020) and are positively associated with academic achievement and school well-being (Kiuru et al, 2020). This chapter discusses adolescent girls' relationships with parents, peers, romantic partners, and non-parental adults. It further provides recommendations on how to create relational ecologies to promote well-being in adolescent girls.

Relationships with Parents

Cognitive and psychosocial advances in adolescents lead to changes in their relationships with parents (Smetana & Rote, 2019; Steinberg & Silk, 2002). Adolescents become more autonomous and enjoy more opportunities outside their families. They also have more unsupervised time and greater exposure to self-selected mass media. These changes pose challenges to parents who feel that they have less control over adolescents' lives. In early adolescence, relationships with parents are marked by diminished positive interactions as children are trying to adjust to the transition to adolescence (Steinberg & Silk, 2002).

Popular culture often portrays adolescence as a time of increased relational difficulties (Smetana, 2011). More specifically, there is a perception

DOI: 10.4324/9781003105534-6

that adolescents have strained relationships with parents, reject parental values, and behave in a disrespectful manner. Parental anxiety about children entering adolescence may partially stem from these popular beliefs. However, a significant body of research evidences that these beliefs are not accurate. Only a small number of adolescents experience problematic relationships with parents and these adolescents often have relational difficulties early on (Laursen et al., 2010; Smetana, 2011). Adolescents who have a history of positive relationships with parents experience temporary and minor relational difficulties. Nevertheless, parental anxiety about raising adolescents can be justified because significant and rapid developments in adolescents require adaptation of the family system.

Establishing autonomy is one of the important developmental tasks in adolescence. Adolescents begin to reevaluate their parents and view them as less perfect – a process called de-idealization (McElhaney et al., 2009). Vertical relationships, in which parents have more knowledge, social power, and resources, become more horizontal and are characterized by more equality and reciprocity (Laursen & Bukowski, 1997). More advanced cognitive abilities allow adolescents to have a stronger voice in family discussions and question established rules and standards. This, in turn, creates challenges for parents who might feel as though their authority has been questioned. Coupled with a shift to turning to peers as emotional confidants and role models, this trend leads to emotional distancing between adolescents and parents (Steinberg & Silk, 2002). Nevertheless, parents remain important figures for adolescents who can influence their decisions and choices. Both parents and adolescents agree that parents have legitimate authority to regulate adolescents' behaviors related to others' welfare, rights, and health- and safety-related behaviors (Smetana et al., 2015).

Puberty is often associated with more frequent parent-child conflicts; however, these conflicts are not high intensity and are usually over mundane issues (Smetana, 2011). Conflicts may arise because adolescents and parents have different expectations regarding behavior related to adolescents' degree of autonomy and parental control (Branje, 2018). The frequency and intensity of conflicts depend on the parent-adolescent relational history. Those who have had positive relationships usually experience temporary and minor relational difficulties. Some conflicts between adolescents and their parents are developmentally appropriate, as they facilitate adolescents' development of autonomy and individuation (Branje, 2018). A longitudinal study of adolescents' perception of their relationships with parents concluded that conflict temporarily increases during middle adolescence, with parental power decreasing from early to late adolescents (De Goede et al., 2009). Once parents and adolescents renegotiate their relational expectations in a way satisfactory to both parties, parents reduce their control, and as a result, the level of conflicts usually decreases (Branje, 2018).

Too many conflicts may have negative consequences for adolescents' psychosocial adjustment and well-being (Branje, 2018). Adolescents who have more frequent conflicts with their parents have more emotional and behavioral problems, lower self-esteem, difficulty with school adjustment, and more frequent substance use (Tucker et al., 2003). Moreover, daily parent-teen conflicts are associated with adolescents' emotional distress (Silva, Ford & Miller, 2020). It is not surprising that on days when parents and adolescents experience more conflict than usual, they also experience lower well-being. At the same time, parental warmth can buffer adolescents' responses to interpersonal stressors; however, parental warmth might be less protective if demonstrated inconsistently.

As adolescents begin to establish autonomy, they also begin to manage information they disclose to their parents (Smetana et al., 2015). There is usually a decrease in sharing information with parents and an increase in keeping secrets from parents. Adolescents are more willing to disclose information when they have warm and responsive parents. However, when parents respond negatively to their adolescent children's disclosures and even punish them, it likely leads to increased secrecy. Adolescents' desire to disclose leads to a greater probability that parents will be informed when they attempt to solicit information from their adolescent children (Smetana et al., 2015). Adolescents who have positive relationships with their mothers share more information with them, while negative relationships were reciprocally associated with greater concealment (Rote et al., 2020).

The way adolescents navigate developmental tasks related to autonomy depends on the quality of their relationships with parents (McElhaney et al., 2009). In secure relationships, parents support adolescents' autonomy while maintaining close relationships so adolescents can still receive comfort and support from their parents. Furthermore, they begin to transfer close relationships from their families to peers who become their source of support. Parents, especially mothers, do not stop being important attachment figures from whom adolescents seek comfort in especially difficult situations (McElhaney et al., 2009). Some adolescents may struggle between an emerging need for autonomy and attachment to parents. Adolescents with more secure attachment are more likely to have parents who support their growing autonomy. They also have a better ability to deal with their emotional experiences. In contrast, adolescents with insecure attachment are more emotionally reactive and use maladaptive coping strategies for managing stress (McElhaney et al., 2009).

Beyers and colleagues (2003) identified the following four factors related to autonomy and separation: connectedness, separation, detachment, and agency. *Connectedness* describes parent-adolescent relationships, characterized by closeness, mutual reciprocity, and trust.

In this type of relationship, adolescents feel that they can easily talk to parents and receive support when necessary. *Separation* reflects the process of interpersonal distancing of adolescents from and the de-idealization of their parents. With this process in place, adolescents become less reliant on parents when encountering problems. They may also keep secrets from parents trying to establish their individuality. *Detachment* refers to feelings of mistrust and alienation toward parents. This is associated with emotional distance and a high level of conflict between parents and adolescents. Finally, *agency* refers to competence, self-governess, and self-reliance (Beyers et al., 2003).

Autonomy development may be compromised by inadequate boundaries between child and parent, which can take several forms (Mayseless & Scharf, 2009). In *role reversal* or *parentification*, children are placed in a position to satisfy parental needs for comfort and protection. In *triangulation*, the child serves as a mediator between parents and helps them to sustain their marriage. The *blurring of boundaries* (*enmeshment*) is a type of relationship where the child is perceived as an extension of the parent. Finally, *psychological control* is characterized by intrusive parenting practices that inhibit children's ability to make their own decisions and have their own desires and activities. Some parents may achieve psychological control through inducing guilt to their children. All forms of inadequate boundaries may have a detrimental effect on adolescents' emerging autonomy, their ability to deal with their emotions, and to engage with others in a healthy way. Mayseless and Scharf (2009) in their longitudinal study found a negative impact of inadequate boundary constellations on adolescent girls' transition from high school to work. More specifically, girls who experienced high guilt induction and psychological control had a difficult time during the transition. They also had the lowest level of individuation, a tendency for angry entanglement, and a desire for over-independence. Girls with blurred parentified relationships had less difficulty with transition, but nevertheless were characterized by overdependence and immaturity.

Parental beliefs about adolescents may influence the quality of communication between parents and adolescents. Positive parental beliefs are associated with more open and positive communication, while negative parental beliefs (e.g., adolescents are moody or rebellious) accounted for lower quality of communication (Silva, Robles et al., 2020). Additionally, parents and adolescents with more positive communication also had higher parent and adolescent well-being.

Recommendations for Parents to Support Positive Parent-Adolescent Relationships

Parents need to be educated about the developmental needs of their adolescent daughters. Adolescents' need for autonomy, the importance of peer relationships, sensitivity to both reward and rejection, and emotional instability should be considered by parents when interacting with their youths. Mental health professionals should validate parents' anxiety about raising adolescent girls, but at the same time, they need to dispel the popular beliefs portraying adolescence as a time of moodiness and behavioral problems. Responsive and understanding parents can facilitate a smooth transition from childhood to adolescence and help their daughters navigate this developmental period. Below are some recommendations for parents on how to create an optimal interpersonal environment for adolescent girls.

Establish clear parent-child boundaries. Parents need to be advised about establishing clear boundaries and support their adolescent daughters' need to individuate from parents. It is important for parents to accept their daughters as they are and respect their world. While adolescent girls strive to individuate from their parents, they also need parental support. However, parents have to provide this support in a manner that does not compromise girls' need for autonomy. Parents should also avoid making girls responsible for family well-being. Given girls' propensity to care about others, it may come at the cost of their own needs.

Encourage expression of emotions and emotion talk. The ability to express a range of positive and negative emotions appropriately is essential for healthy relationships. Validation and acceptance of their daughters' emotions not only assists with emotion regulation, but also helps to promote trust and closeness between parents and youths.

Set appropriate limits. Parents should be firm in setting limits but also respect their daughters' desire for autonomy. While parents often set limits in order to keep their daughters safe, they may perceive it as encroaching on their autonomy and react with anger. Parents have to be mindful that excessive parental control often leads to conflictual child-parent relationships. Rules should be discussed and agreed upon. While girls' safety takes precedence, parents have to be flexible and open to comprise in some areas.

Respect privacy. In order to maintain trust, it is important for parents to respect adolescent girls' privacy. Parents should be advised not to put pressure on them to disclose information. Girls have a right to have their own secrets as it helps them to individuate from parents. Parents need to strive to be warm and sensitive toward their daughters' needs. Such parental behavior will likely lead to girls' willingness to disclose information that may have importance for parents.

Promote open communication. Mental health professionals can teach parents positive communication skills in order to make their children feel understood and validated. Parents should be encouraged to have conversations about topics that are important for adolescent girls. These may include school, friends, hobbies and personal interests, emotions, worries about appearance, family, parents' lives and hopes, the future, and current events. Open communication will allow parents to know what is going on in their daughters' online world. This is especially important in situations when girls are at risk for being victims of cyberbullying or engaging in unsafe activities.

Reduce parental worries. Mental health professionals can help parents to explore and manage their worries about raising adolescent daughters. Parental worries can lead to excessive control and overprotection which can undermine their daughters' autonomy and cause conflicts. While some worries are justified, parents need to understand when their worries become unreasonable. Parents also need to be aware about unrealistic expectations they may have regarding their daughters.

Interventions to Support Positive Parent-Adolescent Relationships

Parent training programs were found effective in promoting parenting skills and positive relationships between parents and their adolescent children. One such program is Positive Parenting Program "Triple P," where parents are trained to build stronger relationships, negotiate boundaries, and prepare teens to handle risky situations and life problems (Sanders et al., 2014). Another program, "Parenting Adolescents Wisely," educates parents on how to deal with common difficult situations with their children such as not doing chores or fighting with siblings (Kacir & Gordon, 2000). This is a computer-based program that uses video clips depicting typical adolescent situations for parents to practice their skills. Finally, the "Adolescents ParentWays Program" uses both in-person small group as well as online formats. Parents watch videos, role-play, and do activities with adolescents at home (Taylor et al., 2015).

There is research evidence that mindful parenting can improve parent-adolescent relationships and consequently youth well-being. Mindful parenting involves the following dimensions: emotional self-awareness and acceptance, awareness and acceptance of child's emotions, effective self-regulation when interacting with a child, the ability to listen to a child, and compassion for self and child (Coatsworth et al., 2014). The "Mindfulness-enhanced Strengthening Families Program" trains parents' parenting skills and how to be mindful in their interactions with adolescents. The training program starts with the awareness of breath, a foundational mindfulness skill. The participants learn the motto "Stop, Be Calm, Be Present." Parents then learn to recognize their own emotions and explore how their emotions might influence their children's behavior. The objective is to make parents less reactive in interactions with youths. Parents also learn about triggers to their negative feelings and their impulsive reactions resulting from those feelings (e.g., blaming or yelling). They are engaged in perspective-taking activities to understand how their children feel when parents react impulsively. Additionally, parents learn to focus on the positive characteristics of their children and adopt a nonjudgmental stance toward children's thoughts and desires. It is important for parents to understand that children's thoughts and desires may not coincide with their own. Finally, parents learn to treat their youths and themselves with empathy and compassion (Coatsworth et al., 2014).

Relationships with Peers

In adolescence, peer groups play an essential role in psychosocial adjustment and well-being (Pozzi et al., 2019). Adolescents who have high-quality and satisfying relationships with peers also have better mental health and overall psychological well-being (Walsh et al., 2010). Furthermore, belonging to a popular peer group is positively associated with an ability to adapt to the social environment (Heaven et al., 2005). Additionally, positive relationships with peers serve as a protective factor against symptoms of depression and social anxiety (La Greca & Harrison, 2005). Peer pressure and competition also play a significant role in adolescent socialization (Larson et al., 2002). Establishing reputation, status, and prestige in a peer group are important motivations for adolescents' interpersonal behavior.

Friends usually share many characteristics, including background, values, and interests (Brown & Braun, 2013; Brown & Larson, 2009). Such similarity is a result of both selection and influence processes, meaning that young people tend to select friends with similar characteristics and then receive affirmation from friends regarding those characteristics. Importantly, friendship may end if adolescents begin to develop different attitudes and interests (Brown & Larson, 2009).

For adolescent girls, friendship with other girls represents an essential element of their socio-emotional development (Crothers et al, 2005):

> Female friendship is one of the most important dimensions of a girl's life, and its influence on her well-being may be surpassed only by family relationships in her growth toward adulthood. Teachers, school counselors, and parents know only too well the consuming and complex emotional struggles girls face on a daily basis on playgrounds, in hallways, during class, on the phone, and in chat rooms.
> (Hossfeld, 2008, p. 43)

Compared to boys, girls have more intimate relationships with their friends, but are also more vulnerable to interpersonal stressors (Rose & Rudolph, 2006). Girls engage in a greater level of prosocial interactions such as social conversation and self-disclosure and are more likely to have goals oriented toward connection with others. Additionally, they are more sensitive to distress in others, the status of their peer relationships, and more likely to seek and receive emotional support in their friendships (Rose & Rudolph, 2006).

Peer relationships serve several important functions (Pozzi et al., 2019). They facilitate autonomy from parents and an affirmation of personal identity. Relationships with peers allow youths to take different social roles and practice social skills, including conflict resolution. They further help explore different meanings and purposes. Girls often turn to peers for emotional support during difficult times (Miller-Slough & Dunsmore, 2016). Peer relationships can exert positive influences in several areas, including academic achievement, school engagement, extracurricular participation, health-related behaviors, prosocial behavior, and positive psychosocial adjustment (Brown & Braun, 2013). They may prevent or mitigate emotional distress during adolescence. More specifically, peers can diminish adolescents' susceptibility to bullying or aggression by reducing feelings of loneliness and anxiety. Peers also play a significant role in adolescents' identity development (Hill et al., 2007).

Despite the many benefits associated with peer relationships, they can also be linked to negative behaviors. Uncritical acceptance of group thinking, especially around risky behavior, exclusion, and rejection from peers, may present risk factors (Pozzi et al., 2019). One longitudinal study found that peer victimization and emotional problems are bidirectionally associated; they also predict poorer school connectedness, social functioning, and quality of life (Forbes et al., 2019).

Relational Aggression in Adolescent Girls

Relational aggression is a type of social or emotional manipulation aimed at compromising relationships or excluding others (Centifanti et al., 2015). Girls tend to use relational aggression more often than boys (Lansford et al., 2012). Since girls are more emotionally invested in relationships, they can use relationships as leverage against other girls. Relational aggression may take different forms, ranging from social exclusion to gossiping and stealing romantic partners. Common tactics include talking badly about others, engaging in vindictive behavior, making fun of other people, posting hurtful messages on social media, intimidating others, forming cliques or groups of friends while excluding others, and spreading rumors (Shetgiri, 2013).

There are several potential reasons for relational aggression in adolescent girls. One reason is a desire to establish and maintain social status within a group (Centifanti et al., 2015). Another reason may be related to adolescents' insecurity and their attempts to elevate their self-esteem (Atherton et al., 2017). A lack of genuine empowerment for girls can be the underlying cause of relational aggression (Brown, 2003). Traditional feminine gender schema discourages physical aggression and culturally prescribed "niceness" may lead to tempering anger reactions (Crothers et al., 2005). Therefore, girls' anger may take an indirect form of relational aggression.

Relational aggression may have a lasting negative impact for both the aggressor and the target. Research demonstrated that adolescent girls who use high levels of relational aggression also have more significant adjustment problems, including difficulty maintaining positive relationships with others (Centifanti et al., 2015). Victims of relational aggression often feel rejected, inadequate, and unlikeable (Blakely-McClure & Ostrov, 2015). They also experience symptoms of depression and suicidal ideation, low self-esteem, and may be engaged in disordered eating. It is not uncommon for them to have academic challenges and difficulty maintaining healthy friendships.

Romantic Relationships in Adolescent Girls

Romantic relationships play an increasingly important role from early to late adolescence (Furman, 2002). More than 50% of adolescents have dating experience by age 15 (Price et al., 2016). Relationship qualities vary with age: In early adolescence, relationships have more affiliative, companionate qualities, while in older adolescence they tend to be more committed, loving, and supportive (Shulman & Scharf, 2000). In mid-to-late adolescence, girls change their focus from friendship to establishing romantic partners.

Romantic relationships provide adolescents with support and companionship (Shulman et al., 2011) and are associated with a higher level of well-being (Collins & Van Dulmen, 2006). The positive qualities of relationships are associated with less isolation, positive self-image, better future outlook, and higher self-esteem (Ciairano et al., 2006). The influence of romantic relationships on well-being depends on an adolescent's level of social competence as well as on the quality of the romantic relationship (Davila et al., 2017). Peer pressure, peer rejection, and aggression experienced in romantic relationships are associated with symptoms of depression, poor psychosocial functioning, and at times substance use (Schad et al., 2007).

An analysis of referrals for counseling found that significantly more females (77.2%) than males sought help regarding relational difficulties. Younger adolescents are more concerned about how to initiate relationships, while older adolescents – how to maintain and repair relationships (Price et al., 2016). Both female and male adolescents often reported relationship breakups as a reason for counseling. Post relationship problems (including breakups) were associated with mental health concerns, including self-harm and suicide.

Volpe and colleagues (2014) conducted in-depth interviews with adolescent girls in order to explore their experiences associated with romantic relationships. One of the recurrent themes was the initiation of relationships that involved boys approaching them, calling frequently, and asking them to be their girlfriend. Girls reported that a desire for social status or peer norms is among motivations to be engaged in romantic relationships. They described romantic partners as a confidant, friend, and companion, and discussed the importance to negotiate intimacy with respect. Girls reflected on companionship as an important aspect of their romantic relationships. This included having fun together, chilling, and laughing. The majority of girls reported having positive relationships characterized by emotional support and care. However, they also experienced relational conflicts, including controlling behaviors and physical, psychological, and sexual violence. These behaviors were often bidirectional, and some girls indicated that their violence toward their boyfriends was a way to communicate anger (Volpe et al., 2014).

Parents and friends may influence the quality of romantic relationships. More specifically, attachment and friendship quality at age ten was a predictor of romantic relationship outcomes at age 12 and 15 (Kochendorfer & Kerns, 2017). Adolescent girls who had better relationships with their mothers also had better romantic relationships and entered sexual relationships at a later age (Scharf & Mayseless, 2008). Girls who had better relationships with their fathers also reported better quality romantic relationships. Killoren and colleagues (2019) found that adolescent girls were more likely to disclose information about dating and sexual matters to their mothers and sisters as opposed to their friends. Those who disclosed to their mothers and sisters also had more positive relationships with them, and those who disclosed to their mothers reported greater romantic relationship intimacy. Additionally, adolescents who discuss their sexual matters with selected friends had less conservative sexual attitudes.

While the quality of friendship is not related to involvement in romantic relationships, there is a robust association between friendship qualities and romantic relationship qualities (Kochendorfer & Kerns, 2020). Adolescents who did not have many opposite sex friends and who had more negative interactions with their best friends reported more dating anxiety. Dating anxiety is also higher in adolescents with no dating experience or negative interactions with their dating partners (La Greca & Mackey, 2007). Romantic relationships may have an impact on adolescents' friendship quality. It was found that greater levels of intimacy, encouragement, compromise, and less co-rumination in romantic relationships were linked with a more positive perception of the quality of adolescents' friendships (Thomas, 2012).

Sensitivity to rejection from peers and teachers plays an important role in the way adolescents negotiate their romantic relationships (Purdie & Downey, 2000). Girls who scored high on rejection sensitivity felt insecure in their relationships with a boyfriend and were willing to engage in behavior that could undermine those relationships. These girls also showed more physical aggression and nonphysical hostility during romantic conflicts.

Social Media and Relationships with Peers

In the past decade, social media has become an important interpersonal context for adolescents (Lenhart et al., 2015). Indeed, 57% of teens reported that they met a new friend online, mainly through social media and online gaming. Text messaging has become a common communication mode as 55% of youth admitted texting with friends daily and 88% texting with friends occasionally. Girls are more likely to use texting, social media, and phone to communicate with their close friends. Adolescents acknowledge both positive and negative impacts of social media use. While most adolescents (83%) said that social media make them feel more connected to their friends, 68% of teens reported experiencing drama with friends through social media (Lenhart et al., 2015). Additionally, about 88% of adolescents believe that people share too much information about themselves on social media.

Social media can diminish the sense of community as young people are "embedded in networks of personal relationships that are relatively loose, more flexible, and portable" (Morimoto & Friedland, 2011, p. 554). Such a cultural shift may contribute to a culture of individualism as opposed to orientation toward others. Based on adolescents' reports, screen media might replace socialization with friends and schoolwork (Livingstone et al., 2011). Some young people experienced so called "mobile entrapment" or feelings of pressure or guilt to be available and respond to friends' communications. These feelings are associated with increased relationship dissatisfaction (Hall & Baym, 2012).

"Technology is redefining the fundamental cues, content, and cadence of our communication and the improvisational, uniquely human dimension of connection" (Steiner-Adair, 2013, p. 20). Nesi and colleagues (2018a) developed a transformation framework to understand how social media is reshaping peer relationships and social experiences. They argue that social media changed the frequency and immediacy of interpersonal experiences, amplified experiences and demands, altered the qualitative nature of social interactions, and facilitated new opportunities for social behavior (Nesi et al., 2018a). Additionally, social networking allows immediate support from a large group of peers. At the same time, social media can amplify peer victimization as it is difficult to control or escape cyberbullying (Nesi et al., 2018b).

Nesi and colleagues (2018a) identified several features that distinguish social media from the traditional face-to-face interactions. The *cue absence* and *asynchronicity* (time lapse between message and response) of social media change the nature of communication as they might present challenges for the interpretation of information shared online. The inability to see facial expressions and body language or to hear the tone of voice on some forms of social media can result in misinterpretations and misunderstanding. Asynchronicity may also create uncertainty in relationships and prompt feedback-seeking and a need for reassurance. At the same time, it allows participation in multiple conversations simultaneously and the opportunity to craft carefully one's presentation online. *Permanent accessibility* of social media content, its *publicity*, and *availability* regardless of physical location may allow for social support from a large audience. Concurrently, these features of social media may facilitate social comparison, rumination over social media content, and the need to stay constantly connected with others. Another feature, called *quantifiability*, allows for countable social metrics. While in face-to-face communication, acceptance and rejection might be ambiguous and require interpretation, in social media it is unambiguous as it provides clear metrics in the form of "friends," "followers," and "likes." This can be problematic and lead to the feeling of being unpopular or rejected. Finally, *visualness*, or the ability to share photographs or videos, may exacerbate focus on appearance and an expectation to receive feedback regarding one's appearance.

Social media may change adolescents' experiences of their own and peers' status (Nesi et al., 2018b). Adolescents' social status can be compromised by deviations from socially acceptable online behaviors and from receiving negative feedback. Since negative feedback is publicly and permanently available, youths need to take steps to safeguard their online reputations. As such, social media create "a 'high stakes' environment in which online interactions may be more careful or calculated" (Nesi et al., 2018b, p. 18).

Furthermore, the online world provides many affordances for adolescents to enhance social standing. Stern (2007) conducted in-depth interviews with adolescent girls regarding their use of instant messaging. The girls admitted using various ways to manipulate their social standings. For example, they provide information to make a particular impression (e.g., exaggerate the number of dating partners) and post information about their accomplishments and possessions (real or made up). Furthermore, they fake popularity by intentionally taking a longer time to respond, creating an illusion of being busy chatting with others. The girls also reported various ways to exclude others (Stern, 2007). This can be done by blocking certain people, not answering their messages, and spreading gossip. Language is a powerful tool for social inclusion or exclusion. Abbreviation and manipulation of language in instant messaging allows creating in-group mentality, where those who do not know language norms can easily be excluded. Profanity and vulgarity were also present in online communication, even from girls who admit never using that type of language in the off-line world. Furthermore, girls reported being more confrontational and direct in online communication than off-line (Stern, 2007).

Recommendations to Support Girls' Healthy Relationships with Peers

When working with adolescent girls to support their healthy relationships with peers, mental health professionals have to take into consideration their relational and developmental needs. Girls might be especially vulnerable to interpersonal rejection and often need reassurance from their peers. They need to be educated about healthy strategies to promote and maintain their relational value and avoid being devalued and rejected by others. These include having prosocial orientation, being competent, and being a good group member. Below are some recommendations on how to help adolescent girls develop and maintain healthy peer and romantic relationships.

Teach socio-emotional skills. Having strong interpersonal skills and self-confidence serve as protective factors against peer pressure and other negative influences of peer relationships. Girls who can communicate well with others and resolve conflicts in an adaptive manner are more likely to be accepted by their peers and to develop successful friendships. Teaching emotional skills is another avenue to promote healthy relationships. These include emotional awareness, regulation, and understanding others' emotions. These skills are especially important in emotionally charged situations, as they can reduce the "heat of the moment" and approach a situation from a more rational perspective.

Provide psychoeducation about healthy relationships. Girls should be educated about healthy relationships, whether with peers or romantic partners. They need to know about problematic types of relationships, for example, overdependency, constantly seeking reassurance, or engaging in interpersonal manipulations. Girls should be aware of signs of maladaptive relational patterns. Furthermore, they need to be provided with strategies to cope with breakups, reestablish life after ending relationships, and manage relationships with an ex-partner.

Educate about causes and signs of relational aggression. Adolescent girls need to learn about the functions, signs, and consequences of relational aggression. This should include both off-line and online relational aggression. An open conversation about power and affiliation in relationships is necessary for girls to understand how to assert themselves without engaging in maladaptive interpersonal strategies. Perspective-taking activities can be effective in teaching girls to understand distress of victims of relational aggression. They further need to be equipped with skills necessary to resist or avoid relational aggression.

Educate parents about peer relationships. It is recommended to involve parents in interventions aimed at promoting healthy relationships with peers. Parents should to be educated about the developmental aspects of girls' friendships and romantic relationships. Furthermore, they can help their adolescent daughters with interpersonal skill and model positive relationships.

Prioritize face-to-face relationships. Adolescent girls should be encouraged and provided with opportunities to spend time engaging in face-to-face relationships. While respecting their desire to socialize via social media, mental health professionals should educate girls about the importance of face-to-face interactions for their well-being and mental health. Education should go hand-in-hand with creating activities and projects where girls can interact and work together.

Interventions to Support Girls' Healthy Relationships with Peers

Relational-cultural theory states that healthy relationships can be built when empathy and equal power dynamics are present (Jordan, 2010). A lack of empathetic responses from others and unequal power dynamics further leads to diminished self-worth and a lack of desire to engage in relationships with others. Mutual empathy and empowerment are essential for creating relational ecology that promotes girls' healthy socio-emotional development (Jordan, 2010). When adolescent girls feel they can openly share their experiences and that their experiences are being acknowledged, they can trust others and themselves.

Adolescent girls need a safe place where they can join a small group of peers and reflect on what is important for them, what troubles or confuses them, and feel supported (Kessler, 2000). "Girls Circle" can provide such a place. Girls Circle is a relational-cultural empowerment intervention that supports girls' healthy development through peer support (Hossfeld, 2008). The aim of this intervention was to mitigate sociocultural and interpersonal forces impeding girls' personal relationships and helping girls to use their authentic voices. It includes one-to-two-hour weekly or biweekly sessions for 8–12 weeks and can be implemented in a variety of settings such as after-school programs, schools, juvenile justice programs, and recreational programs. A small group of girls meets with a facilitator and the girls take turns talking and listening to each other about their interests and concerns. These may include friendship, trust, sexuality, drugs, and decision-making. A variety of activities can be used to help girls express their experiences such as journaling, drama, dance, drawing, and poetry. The Girls Circle intervention was found effective in increasing girls' self-efficacy and improving perceived social connection (Hossfeld, 2008).

Another similar intervention – "Talking Circles" – is aimed at instilling friendships, emotional literacy, conflict resolution, empathy, and anger management skills (Schumacher, 2014). Talking Circles provides a space for girls to help each other and improve their social understanding and skills. This intervention was implemented with adolescent girls from diverse racial and ethnic backgrounds. Each meeting consisted of four parts: checking in, sharing problems or concerns, discussing student-generated topics, and closing with a reading of inspirational quotes or making a wish for the week. After the intervention, participating girls reflected on several themes, including developing a sense of interpersonal connection; safety and trust; being accepted by others; expressing genuine emotions; and feeling empathy and compassion. Girls also reflected on helpful strategies to facilitate their conversations. For example, a talking piece (squishy ball) helped with impulse control and focused listening, while reflective questions stimulated self-reflection and an exchange of ideas (Schumacher, 2014). An adaptation of Talking Circles for African American girls called "Sisters of Nia" was found effective in decreasing relational aggression and increasing positive social identity (Belgrave et al., 2004).

Promoting Healthy Relationships through Mentoring

Many adolescents report the presence of significant non-parental adults in their lives (Beam et al., 2002). These adults can offer resources and support that adolescents may not receive in their families or relationships with peers. Adolescents who have relationships with supportive non-parental adults have higher self-esteem and lower incidents of behavioral and emotional problems (Sterrett et al., 2011).

Relationships with a significant non-parental adult can take the form of mentoring. One example of a successful mentoring program is "GirlPOWER!" (Dubois et al., 2008). The acronym POWER stands for Pride, Opportunity, Women-in-the-Making, Effort and Energy, and Relationships. This program is aimed at the development of mentoring relationships through participation in joined experiential learning activities.

High-quality mentoring relationships are characterized by regular contacts, personal compatibility, and mutual feelings of trust and positive regard (Dubois et al., 2008). They also include collaboration in working toward goals, spending time in mutually enjoyable activities, adolescents' connections to mentors' social networks, and ties between the mentors and youths' parents. Adolescents receive instrumental, informational, and emotional support in high-quality mentoring relationships (Dubois et al., 2008). Finally, mentors should be sensitive to culturally relevant relational processes. One study found that when girls of color experience cultural mistrust toward Whites, they have less satisfactory relationships with White mentors (Sánchez et al., 2019). It is important to give youths the opportunity to select their own mentor. In one study, youth-initiated mentor selection facilitated the development of close and trustworthy relationships between adolescents and mentors (Spencer et al., 2019).

Creating Caring Communities to Promote Healthy Relationships

In addition to healthy relationships with parents and peers, well-being of adolescent girls can be promoted through their engagement with a caring community. Block (2009) argued that in order to build healthy communities, we need to shift our attention "from the problems of community to the possibility of community" (p. 1). The ideas of healing, belonging, and relatedness are at the heart of a restorative community. One way to build community is through conversations. These conversations can focus on the following questions: What do we want to do together to build our community? What can we create together that would be difficult to create alone? Leaders play an important role in community building. Their job is to bring those in the margins to the center so their voices can be heard and their talents can be used. Block (2009) also emphasized the importance of physical space for building community. For example, chairs arranged in a circle are more community building than having tables with chair in rows.

A dialogue-based approach can be used to create communities characterized by responsibility, commitment, and understanding (Braghero, 2019). The core element of dialogue is creating space and time for generous and reflective listening. It is important for adults to change their view of adolescent girls: Instead of focusing on vulnerabilities and problems, girls' potential should be at the center. Another important thing is to give credit to girls' subjective experiences. Dialogue fosters a space where adolescent girls can be heard and answered, and where adults do not have preconceived notions about these girls and do not pursue their own agenda. Respect and trust are integral parts of a dialogue-based approach. The construction of respect entails the ability to listen to the experiences of others, while trust means being reliable and believing in oneself and others. "For an adolescent, being listened to, welcomed and recognized is fundamental... Suspension of judgment, practicing a healthy 'epoché' facilitates mutual recognition and respect" (Braghero, 2019, p. 192).

When relationships are compromised or broken, restorative justice practices can be used to rebuild relationships (Costello et al., 2009; Morrison & Vaandering, 2012). The restorative justice framework was initially developed to address conduct problems at schools as an alternative to sanctioning systems based on reward and punishment. However, it was found to be effective in addressing school interpersonal climate and teaching youth to resolve conflicts on their own. Restorative practice is grounded in the ideas of the primacy of human relationships and social engagement. At the school level, restorative justice practice is aimed at building relational ecologies based on responsibility and respect. When relational harm occurs, focus is placed on those who have been affected, including the whole community. Restorative practice uses a circles format where the participants discuss events that led to harm and how one's actions affected others.

Recommended Resources

Lohmann, R. C., & Taylor, J. V. (2013). *The bullying workbook for teens.* **Instant Help Books.**
This workbook consists of 42 activities to teach teens anti-bullying strategies and emotion regulation skills. It helps teens identify unhealthy friendships and build their self-confidence. It can be a practical resource for teens, parents, educators, and mental health practitioners.

Sprague, S. (2008). *Coping with cliques: A workbook to help girls deal with gossip, put-downs, bullying, and other mean behavior.* **Instant Help Books.**
This workbook helps teens develop self-confidence when facing challenging social situations. It provides practical guidance on dealing with cliques, teasing and gossip, provides strategies to stand up for oneself, and maintain one's self-esteem when bullied. It guides teens to seek out and cultivate healthy friendships.

Girls Circle Association (2011). *The girls circle model.* **http://www. girlscircle.com/how_it_works.aspx**
The Girls Circle model is a structured support group for girls. It promotes an emotionally safe setting and structure with which girls can develop caring relationships and use their authentic voices. It integrates relational theory, resilience practices, and skills training to increase positive connection, personal and collective strengths, and competence in girls.

Teen Talking Circles (2011). *About teen talking circles.* **http://www. daughters-sisters.org/content/ttc/ttc.php**
Teen Talking Circles offers workshops, books, and other resources for youths and adults with the goal of facilitating safe spaces for connection and self-expression. It seeks to educate, inspire, and empower young women and men into social action.

References

Atherton, O. E., Tackett, J. L., Ferrer, E., & Robins, R. W. (2017). Bidirectional pathways between relational aggression and temperament from late childhood to adolescence. *Journal of Research in Personality, 67,* 75–84. https://doi.org/10.1016/j.jrp.2016.04.005

Beam, M. R., Chen, C., & Greenberger, E. (2002). The nature of adolescents' relationships with their "very important" nonparental adults. *American Journal of Community Psychology, 30*(2), 305–325. https://doi.org/10.1023/A:1014641213440

Belgrave, F. Z., Reed, M. C., Plybon, L. E., Butler, D. S., Allison, K. W., & Davis, T. (2004). An evaluation of Sisters of Nia: A cultural program for African American girls. *Journal of Black Psychology, 30*(3), 329–343. https://doi.org/10.1177/0095798404266063

Beyers, W., Goossens, L., Vansant, I., & Moors, E. (2003). A structural model of autonomy in middle and late adolescence: Connectedness, separation, detachment, and agency. *Journal of Youth and Adolescence, 32*(5), 351–365.

Blakely-McClure, S. J., & Ostrov, J. M. (2015). Relational aggression, victimization and self-concept: Testing pathways from middle childhood to adolescence. *Journal of Youth and Adolescence, 45*(2), 376–390. https://doi.org/10.1007/s10964-015-0357-2

Block, P. (2009). *Community: The structure of belonging.* San Francisco, CA: Berrett-Koehler Publishers, Inc.

Braghero, M. (2019). Adolescents in the 21st century: Back to dialogue from marked lives vs dreamed lives. In A. Pingitore, F. Mastorci, & C. Vassalle (Eds.), *Adolescent Health and Well-being* (pp. 167–202). Springer. doi:10.1007/978-3-030-25816-0_9

Branje, S. (2018). Development of parent-adolescent relationships: Conflict interactions as a mechanism of change. *Child Development Perspectives, 12*(3), 171–176. https://doi.org/10.1111/cdep.12278

Brown, B. B. & Braun, M. T. (2013). Peer relations. In C. Proctor & P. A. Linley (Eds.), *Research, Applications, and Interventions for Children and Adolescents: A Positive Psychology Perspective* (pp. 131–147). Springer Science + Business Media. https://doi.org/10.1007/978-94-007-6398-2

Brown, B. B., & Larson, J. (2009). Peer relationships in adolescence. In R. M. Lerner & L. Steinberg (Eds.), *Handbook of adolescent psychology: Contextual influences on adolescent development* (pp. 74–103). John Wiley & Sons, Inc.

Brown, L. M. (2003). *Girlfighting: Betrayal and rejection among girls.* New York University Press.

Centifanti, L., Fanti, K., Thomson, N., Demetriou, V., & Anastassiou-Hadjicharalambous, X. (2015). Types of relational aggression in girls are differentiated by callous-unemotional traits, peers and parental overcontrol. *Behavioral Sciences, 5*(4), 518–536. https://doi.org/10.3390/bs5040518

Ciairano, S., Bonino, S., Kliewer, W., Miceli, R., & Jackson, S. (2006). Dating, sexual activity, and well-being in Italian adolescents. *Journal of Clinical Child & Adolescent Psychology, 35*(2), 275–282. https://doi.org/10.1207/s15374424jccp3502_11

Coatsworth, J. D., Duncan, L. G., Berrena, E., Bamberger, K. T., Loeschinger, D., Greenberg, M. T., & Nix, R. L. (2014). The Mindfulness-enhanced Strengthening Families Program: integrating brief mindfulness activities and parent training within an evidence-based prevention program. *New Directions for Youth Development, 2014*(142), 45–58. https://doi.org/10.1002/yd.20096

Collins, W. A., & Van Dulmen, M. (2006). The course of true love(s). Origins and pathways in the development of romantic relationships. In A. C. Crouter & A. Booth (Eds.), *Romance and sex in adolescence and emerging adulthood: Risks and opportunities* (pp. 63–86). Mahwah, NJ: Lawrence Erlbaum Associates Publishers.

Costello, B., Wachtel, J., & Wachtel, T. (2009). *The restorative practices handbook for teachers, disciplinarians, and administrators: Building a culture of community in schools*. Bethlehem, PA: International Institute of Restorative Practices

Crothers, L. M., Field, J., & Kolbert, J. B. (2005). Navigating power, control, and being nice: Aggression in adolescent girls' friendships. *Journal of Counseling and Development, 83*, 349–354.

Davila, J., Mattanah, J., Bhatia, V., Latack, J. A., Feinstein, B., Eaton, N. R., Daks, J. S., Kumar, S. A., Lomash, E. F., McCormick, M., & Zhou, J. (2017). Romantic competence, healthy relationship functioning, and well-being in emerging adults. *Personal Relationships, 24*(1), 162–184. https://doi.org/10.1111/pere.12175

De Goede, I. H. A., Branje, S. J. T., & Meeus, W. H. J. (2009). Developmental changes in adolescents' perceptions of relationships with their parents. *Journal of Youth and Adolescence, 38*, 75–88. https://doi.org/10.1007/s10964-008-9286-7

Dubois, D. L., Silverthorn, N., Pryce, J., Reeves, E., Sanchez, B., Silva, A., Ansu, A. A., Haqq, S., & Takehara, J. (2008). Mentorship: The GirlPOWER! Program. In C. W. LeCroy & J. E. Mann (Eds.), *Handbook of prevention and intervention programs for adolescent girls* (pp. 326–336). John Wiley & Sons Inc.

Forbes, M. K., Fitzpatrick, S., Magson, N. R., & Rapee, R. M. (2019). Depression, anxiety, and peer victimization: Bidirectional relationships and associated outcomes transitioning from childhood to adolescence. *Journal of Youth and Adolescence, 48*(4), 692–702. https://doi.org/10.1007/s10964-018-0922-6

Furman, W. (2002). The emerging field of adolescent romantic relationships. *Current Directions in Psychological Science, 11*(5), 177–180. https://doi.org/10.1111/1467-8721.00195

Hall, J. A., & Baym, N. K. (2012). Calling and texting (too much): Mobile maintenance expectations, (over)dependence, entrapment, and friendship satisfaction. *New Media & Society, 14*(2), 316–331. https://doi.org/10.1177/1461444811415047

Heaven, P. C. L., Ciarrochi, J., Vialle, W., & Cechavicuite, I. (2005). Adolescent peer crowd self-identification, attributional style and perceptions of parenting. *Journal of Community & Applied Social Psychology, 15*(4), 313–318. https://doi.org/10.1002/casp.823

Hill, N. E., Bromell, L., Tyson, D. F., & Flint, R. (2007). Developmental commentary: Ecological perspectives on parental influences during adolescence. *Journal of Clinical Child & Adolescent Psychology, 36*(3), 367–377. https://doi.org/10.1080/15374410701444322

Hossfeld, B. (2008). Developing friendships and peer relationships: Building social support with the Girls Circle program. In C. LeCroy & J. Mann (Eds.), *Handbook of prevention and intervention programs for adolescent girls* (pp. 43–80). John Wiley.

Jordan, J. V. (2010). *Relational-cultural therapy*. Washington, DC: American Psychological Association.

Kacir, C. D., & Gordon, D. A. (2000). Parenting adolescents wisely: The effectiveness of an interactive videodisk parent training program in Appalachia. *Child & Family Behavior Therapy, 21*(4), 1–22. https://doi.org/10.1300/j019v21n04_01

Kessler, R. (2000). *The soul of education: Helping students find connection, compassion and character at school*. Alexandria, VA: Association for Supervision and Curriculum Development.

Killoren, S. E., Campione-Barr, N. M., Jones, S. K., & Giron, S. E. (2019). Adolescent girls' disclosure about dating and sexuality. *Journal of Family Issues, 40*(7), 887–910. https://doi.org/10.1177/0192513X19829501

Kim, J. (2020). The quality of social relationships in schools and adult health: Differential effects of student–student versus student–teacher relationships. *School Psychology.* Advance online publication. https://doi.org/10.1037/spq0000373

Kiuru, N., Wang, M. T., Salmela-Aro, K., Kannas, L., Ahonen, T., & Hirvonen, R. (2020). Associations between adolescents' interpersonal relationships, school well-being, and academic achievement during educational transitions. *Journal of Youth and Adolescence, 49*(5), 1057–1072. https://doi.org/10.1007/s10964-019-01184

Kochendorfer, L. B., & Kerns, K. A. (2017). Perceptions of parent-child attachment relationships and friendship qualities: Predictors of romantic relationship involvement and quality in adolescence. *Journal of Youth and Adolescence, 46*(5), 1009–1021. https://doi.org/10.1007/s10964-017-0645-0

Kochendorfer, L. B., & Kerns, K. A. (2020). A meta-analysis of friendship qualities and romantic relationship outcomes in adolescence. *Journal of Research on Adolescence, 30*(1), 4–25. https://doi.org/10.1111/jora.12505

La Greca, A. M., & Harrison, H. M. (2005). Adolescent peer relations, friendships, and romantic relationships: Do they predict social anxiety and depression? *Journal of Clinical Child & Adolescent Psychology, 34*(1), 49–61. https://doi.org/10.1207/s15374424jccp3401_5

La Greca, A. M., & Mackey, E. R. (2007). Adolescents' anxiety in dating situations: The potential role of friends and romantic partners. *Journal of Clinical Child and Adolescent Psychology, 36*(4), 522–533. https://doi.org/10.1080/15374410701662097

Lansford, J. E., Skinner, A. T., Sorbring, E., Giunta, L. D., Deater-Deckard, K., Dodge, K. A., Malone, P. S., Oburu, P., Pastorelli, C., Tapanya, S., Uribe Tirado, L. M., Zelli, A., Al-Hassan, S. M., Peña Alampay, L., Bacchini, D., Bombi, A. S., Bornstein, M. H., & Chang, L. (2012). Boys' and girls' relational and physical aggression in nine countries. *Aggressive Behavior, 38*(4), 298–308. https://doi.org/10.1002/ab.21433

Larson, R. W., Wilson, S., Brown, B. B., Furstenberg, F. F., & Verma, S. (2002). Changes in adolescents' interpersonal experiences: Are they being prepared for adult relationships in the 21st century? *Journal of Research on Adolescence, 12*(1), 31–68.

Laursen, B., & Bukowski, W. M. (1997). A developmental guide to the organisation of close relationships. *International Journal of Behavioral Development, 21*, 747–770. https://doi.org/10.1080/016502597384659

Laursen, B., DeLay, D., & Adams, R. E. (2010). Trajectories of perceived support in mother–adolescent relationships: The poor (quality) get poorer. *Developmental Psychology, 46*, 1792–1798. https://doi.org/10.1037/a0020679

Leary, M. R., & Allen, A. B. (2011). Belonging motivation: Establishing, maintaining, and repairing relational value. In D. Dunning (Ed.), *Frontiers of social psychology. Social motivation* (pp. 37–55). Psychology Press.

Lenhart, A., Smith, A., Anderson, M., Duggan, M., & Perrin, A. (2015). *Teens, technology & friendships: Video games, social media and mobile phones play an integral role in how teens meet and interact with friends.* Pew Research Center. https://www.pewresearch.org/internet/2015/08/06/teens-technology-and-friendships/

Livingstone, S., Haddon, L., Görzig, A., & Ólafsson, K. (2011). *Risks and safety on the internet: The perspective of European children. Full findings. LSE, London: EU Kids Online.* http://eprints.lse.ac.uk/33731/

Mayseless, O., & Scharf, M. (2009). Too close for comfort: Inadequate boundaries with parents and individuation in late adolescent girls. *The American Journal of Orthopsychiatry, 79*(2), 191–202. https://doi.org/10.1037/a0015623

McElhaney, K. B., Allen, J. P., & Stephenson, J. C. (2009). Attachment and autonomy during adolescence. In L. Steinberg & R. M. Lerner (Eds.), *Handbook of Adolescent Psychology, Volume 1: Individual Bases of Adolescent Development* (3rd ed., pp. 358–403). Wiley. https://doi.org/10.1002/9780470479193. adlpsy001012

Miller-Slough, R. L., and Dunsmore, J. C. (2016). Parent and friend emotion socialization in adolescence: associations with psychological adjustment. *Adolescent Research Review, 1*, 287–305. doi: 10.1007/s40894-016-0026-z

Morimoto, S. A., & Friedland, L. A. (2011). The lifeworld of youth in the information society. *Youth & Society, 43*(2), 549–567. https://doi.org/10.1177%2F0044118X10383655

Morrison, B. M. & Vaandering, D. (2012). Restorative justice: Pedagogy, praxis, and discipline, *Journal of School Violence, 11*(2), 138–155, https://doi.org/10.1080/15388220.2011.653322

Nesi, J., Choukas-Bradley, S., & Prinstein, M. J. (2018a). Transformation of adolescent peer relations in the social media context: Part 1-A theoretical framework and application to dyadic peer relationships. *Clinical Child and Family Psychology Review, 21*(3), 267–294. https://doi.org/10.1007/s10567-018-0261-x

Nesi, J., Choukas-Bradley, S., & Prinstein, M. J. (2018b). Transformation of adolescent peer relations in the social media context: Part 2-application to peer group processes and future directions for research. *Clinical Child and Family Psychology Review, 21*(3), 295–319. https://doi.org/10.1007/s10567-018-0262-9

Pozzi, M., Becciu, M., & Colasanti, A. R. (2019). Two-faced Janus: The role of peers in adolescence. In A. Pingitore, F. Mastorci, & C. Vassalle (Eds.), *Adolescent Health and Well-being.* Springer. https://doi.org/10.1007/978-3-030-25816-0_12

Price, M., Hides, L., Cockshaw, W., Staneva, A. A., & Stoyanov, S. R. (2016). Young love: Romantic concerns and associated mental health issues among adolescent help-seekers. *Behavioral Sciences, 6*(2), 9. https://doi.org/10.3390/bs6020009

Purdie, V., & Downey, G. (2000). Rejection sensitivity and adolescent girls' vulnerability to relationship-centered difficulties. *Child Maltreatment, 5*(4), 338–349. https://doi.org/10.1177/1077559500005004005

Rose, A. J., & Rudolph, K. D. (2006). A review of sex differences in peer relationship processes: potential trade-offs for the emotional and behavioral development of girls and boys. *Psychological Bulletin, 132*, 98–131.

Rote, W. M., Smetana, J. G., & Feliscar, L. (2020). Longitudinal associations between adolescent information management and mother-teen relationship quality: Between- versus within-family differences. *Developmental Psychology, 56*(10), 1935–1947. https://doi.org/10.1037/dev0000947

Ryan, R. M., and Deci, E. L. (2017). *Self-determination theory: Basic psychological needs in motivation, development, and wellness.* Guilford Press.

Sánchez, B., Pryce, J., Silverthorn, N., Deane, K. L., & DuBois, D. L. (2019). "Do mentor support for ethnic–racial identity and mentee cultural mistrust matter for girls of color? A preliminary investigation": Correction to Sánchez et al (2019). *Cultural Diversity and Ethnic Minority Psychology, 25*(4), 514. https://doi.org/10.1037/cdp0000300

Sanders, M., Kirby, J., Tellegen, C. L., & Day, J. (2014). The Triple P-Positive Parenting Program: A systematic review and meta-analysis of a multi-level system of parenting support. *Clinical Psychology Review, 34*(4), 337–357.

Schad, M. M., Szwedo, D. E., Antonishak, J., Hare, A., & Allen, J. P. (2007). The broader context of relational aggression in adolescent romantic relationships: Predictions from peer pressure and links to psychosocial functioning. *Journal of Youth and Adolescence, 37*(3), 346–358. https://doi.org/10.1007/s10964-007-9226-y

Scharf, M., & Mayseless, O. (2008). Late adolescent girls' relationships with parents and romantic partner: The distinct role of mothers and fathers. *Journal of Adolescence, 31*(6), 837–855. https://doi.org/10.1016/j.adolescence.2008.06.012

Schumacher, A. (2014). Talking circles for adolescent girls in an urban high school. *SAGE Open, 4*(4), 1–13.

Shetgiri, R. (2013). Bullying and victimization among children. *Advances in Pediatrics, 60*(1), 33–51. https://doi.org/10.1016/j.yapd.2013.04.004

Shulman, S., & Scharf, M. (2000). Adolescent romantic behaviors and perceptions: Age- and gender-related differences, and links with family and peer relationships. *Journal of Research on Adolescence, 10*(1), 99–118. https://doi.org/10.1207/sjra1001_5

Shulman, S., Davila, J., & Shachar-Shapira, L. (2011). Assessing romantic competence among older adolescents. *Journal of Adolescence, 34*(3), 397–406. https://doi.org/10.1016/j.adolescence.2010.08.002

Silva, K., Robles, R., Friedrich, E., Thiel, M., Ford, C., & Miller, V.A. (2020). Stereotyped beliefs about adolescents and parent and teen well-being: The role of parent-teen communication. *Journal of Early Adolescence*, 027243162096144.

Silva, K., Ford, C. A., & Miller, V. A. (2020). Daily parent–teen conflict and parent and adolescent well-being: The moderating role of daily and person-level warmth. *Journal of Youth Adolescence, 49*, 1601–1616. https://doi.org/10.1007/s10964-020-01251-9

Smetana, J. G. (2011). *Adolescents, families, and social development: How teens construct their worlds.* Wiley-Blackwell.

Smetana, J. G., Robinson, J., & Rote, W. M. (2015). Socialization in adolescence. In J. E. Grusec & P. D. Hastings (Eds.), *Handbook of socialization: Theory and research* (pp. 60–84). The Guilford Press.

Smetana, J. G., & Rote, W. M. (2019). Adolescent–parent relationships: Progress, processes, and prospects. *Annual Review of Developmental Psychology, 1*, 41–68. https://doi.org/10.1146/annurev-devpsych-121318-084903

Spencer, R., Gowdy, G., Drew, A. L., & Rhodes, J. E. (2019). "Who knows me the best and can encourage me the most?": Matching and early relationship development in youth-initiated mentoring relationships with system-involved youth. *Journal of Adolescent Research, 34*(1), 3–29. https://doi.org/10.1177/0743558418755686

Steinberg, L., & Silk, J. S. (2002). Parenting adolescents. In M. H. Bornstein (Eds.), *Handbook of parenting: Children and parenting* (pp. 103–133). Lawrence Erlbaum Associates Publishers.

Steiner-Adair, C. (2013). *The big disconnect: Protecting childhood and family relationships in the digital age.* HarperCollins Publishers.

Stern, S. T. (2007). *Instant identity: Adolescent girls and the world of instant messaging.* Peter Lang.

Sterrett, E., Jones, D. J., McKee, L., & Kincaid, C. (2011). Supportive non-parental adults and adolescent psychosocial functioning: An integration and review of recent findings. *American Journal of Community Psychology, 48*, 484–495. https://dx.doi.org/10.1007%2Fs10464-011-9429-y

Taylor, L. C., Leary, K. A., Boyle, A. E., Bigelow, K. E., Henry, T., & DeRosier, M. (2015). Parent training and adolescent social functioning: A brief report. *Journal of Child and Family Studies, 24*(10), 3030–3037. https://doi.org/10.1007/s10826-014-0106-2

Thomas, J. J. (2012). Processes through which adolescents believe romantic relationships influence friendship quality. *The Journal of Psychology, 146*(6), 595–616. https://doi.org/10.1080/00223980.2012.665099

Tucker, C. J., McHale, S. M., & Crouter, A. C. (2003). Dimensions of mothers' and fathers' differential treatment of siblings: Links with adolescents' sex-typed personal qualities. *Family Relations, 52*, 82–89. https://doi.org/10.1111/j.1741-3729.2003.00082.x

Volpe, E. M., Morales-Alemán, M. M., & Teitelman, A. M. (2014). Urban adolescent girls' perspectives on romantic relationships: initiation, involvement, negotiation, and conflict. *Issues in Mental Health Nursing, 35*(10), 776–790. https://doi.org/10.3109/01612840.2014.910582

Walsh, S. D., Harel-Fisch, Y., & Fogel-Grinvald, H. (2010). Parents, teachers and peer relations as predictors of risk behaviors and mental well-being among immigrant and Israeli born adolescents. *Social Science & Medicine, 70*(7), 976–984. https://doi.org/10.1016/j.socscimed.2009.12.010

7 Purpose, Agency, and Identity

Exploring identity and purpose are important developmental tasks in adolescence (Crocetti, 2017; Damon, 2008; Ferrer-Wreder & Kroger, 2020). Young people are further tasked with mastering intentional self-regulation – the ability to select and pursue adaptive goals (Larson & Tran, 2014). Having a sense purpose, meaning, and a healthy identity are among the important contributors to well-being (Burrow & Hill, 2011; Mariano & Going, 2011; Ryff, 2014; Seligman, 2011). Therefore, helping adolescents successfully navigate the developmental tasks associated with exploring identity and fostering their agentic orientation regarding their developmental goals is an important pathway to resiliency and thriving.

Purpose

Purpose is defined as "a stable and generalized intention to accomplish something that is at once meaningful to the self and of consequence to the world beyond the self" (Damon et al., 2003, p. 121). Purpose is an important developmental asset and a form of identity capital necessary to have a meaningful life trajectory (Burrow & Hill, 2011). Having a sense of purpose mediates the relationships between identity commitment and positive youth adjustment and thriving. More specifically, it is associated with life satisfaction, adaptive coping, generosity, optimism, and identity consolidation (Mariano & Going, 2011). Furthermore, youths with a sense of purpose have hope and more positive affect (Burrow & Hill, 2011).

Purpose integrates the following four dimensions: personal meaningfulness, future intention, active engagement, and beyond-the-self impact (Damon, 2008; Moran, 2018). It provides direction for adolescents and drives their actions (Malin et al., 2017). Purpose is closely linked with the pursuit of long-term goals. It connects adolescents with something greater than their self, which might involve assisting people in need or participating in a community initiative, such as building a playground for young children.

Adolescents with a sense of purpose act on values central to their sense of self. They are engaged in more socially responsible behavior

DOI: 10.4324/9781003105534-7

and have an impact on the world (Malin et al., 2017). A sense of purpose coupled with values, including transcendence, humility, vitality, integrity, and spirituality, gives cohesion to emerging identity (Lerner et al., 2013). In one study, young adolescents expressed values and concerns about their family well-being, injustice, and people who experience adversity at their schools and communities. They also expressed concerns about problems in the environment and society (Malin et al., 2017). However, the majority of adolescents reported that they did not act upon their concerns. Another study found that non-White youth often have well-articulated purposes drawn from their experiences as minorities or immigrants (Moran et al., 2013). It is likely that experiences associated with discrimination or suffering stimulate their desire to promote change in both the dominant culture and within their home culture.

A lack of purpose contributes to disengagement, one of the most pressing problems in education (Damon, 2008). Youth without purpose feel disappointed and discouraged. In some adolescents, this results in feelings of emptiness and boredom, in others anxiety, and yet in some hedonism and cynicism. Disengaged students experience higher stress in school even when they are not working hard. Pressure from parents to do what youths do not want to do and making choices for them likely leads to a sense of purposelessness. Additional factors include a lack of support from adults and an absence of worthy goals. While some adolescents become disengaged, others dream big but make little progress in bringing their ideas to life. Conversely, some adolescents engage in so many activities that tasks are never accomplished. The ability to face difficulties and learn from failures are important mindsets for pursuing purpose (Damon, 2008).

Stress can be a barrier to purpose development. One study found that adolescents experiencing high stress believed that it was impossible to pursue their goals, or they felt overwhelmed so their engagement with purpose was not a priority (Gutowski et al., 2018). At the same time, stress can motivate purpose development through a desire to meet the expectations of significant others or to escape from stressors, such as violence or financial difficulties.

Family support is important for adolescents to identify and act upon a sense of purpose. In one study, adolescent girls who had close positive relationships with their parents reported more other-oriented than self-oriented goals (Liang et al., 2018). In addition to fostering prosocial values and behaviors, family can also provide emotional and financial support (Moran et al., 2013). For example, parents can give youth money for donations or participation in a community project. Another source of support is community organizations (e.g., church or local charity groups), which create opportunities for youth to act upon their purpose.

How to Foster Purpose in Adolescents

There are several ways to help youth find purpose. Among them are observing people who have purpose, having conversations with people who can inspire youth, defining purpose and identifying steps in pursing it, and mastering the needed skills and making a commitment (Damon, 2008). Adolescents can be encouraged to ask questions such as: What things do you care about? Why do you care about these things? What is most important to you in your life? Why is that important to you? They further need an opportunity to make choices and discover their interests and sparks. Other ways to introduce adolescents to purposeful activities include sports, music, theater, creating a magazine or newspaper, and engagement in activities that promote civic purpose.

Adults should be sensitive to young people's interests and concerns and provide support to help youth develop a sense of purpose (Mariano & Going, 2011). An adolescent's purpose can be further supported by mentors (White et al., 2021). Mentors play an important role in steering adolescents toward lives of meaning and purpose not only by providing support and guidance, but also by challenging youth and helping them master skills.

Education is an important avenue for promoting purpose in adolescents (Koshy & Mariano, 2011; Malin, 2018). In the classroom, a sense of purpose can be fostered through exploring and reflecting on core values, discussing roles in society, and contributing to the common good. Furthermore, it is important to create a learning environment where adolescents can openly share their dreams and personal stories. Purpose education is especially important for marginalized youth and youth who have experienced adversity (Malin, 2018). Purpose-centered systems of education help adolescents identify socially significant purposes through learning about various school subject matters (Koshy & Mariano, 2011). Experiential and service learning education also helps to foster purpose. In this type of education, youths are involved in collaborative projects in which they address socially significant issues or discuss how they can improve services outside of school. Such projects allow them to develop plans, problem-solve, cooperate, and connect with a larger purpose – to serve society.

"Make Your Work Matter" is a school-based intervention designed to help adolescents explore and enact a sense of purpose in their early career development (Dik et al., 2011). The program involves three modules. In the first, students interview a parent or another trusted adult about the role of work in their life and how work is related to their values. The second module is a classroom activity focused on exploring adolescents' interests, preferences, and work values. During the third module, adolescents are engaged in a board game, One Village, which helps them explore the social function of various occupations. Adolescents in the intervention group reported a better understanding of their interests, strengths, and weaknesses. They also reported gaining a clearer sense of career direction and being more prepared for the future (Dik et al., 2011).

Character Strengths

Character strengths are developmental assets intrinsically associated with youth well-being. They guide goal-directed behavior as they help adolescents articulate what is important for them and stay on track while pursuing their goals (Linley et al., 2010). When adolescents focus on strengths during goal pursuit, it activates intrinsic motivation and helps them make a connection between their values and goals.

Peterson and Seligman (2004) developed a character strengths framework based on core virtues highly valued by philosophers and religious thinkers across many cultures. These virtues include wisdom, courage, justice, humanity, temperance, and transcendence. The authors translated these core virtues into 24 character strengths, representing the psychological processes involved in those virtues and manifesting themselves in a trait-like manner. Here are examples of character strengths associated with each virtue. The virtue of *wisdom* consists of creativity, curiosity, and open-mindedness, while the virtue of *courage* consists of bravery, persistence, and integrity. The virtue of *humanity* includes love and kindness, while the virtue of *justice* means being a good team member and promoting fairness. The virtue of *temperance* involves strengths related to forgiveness and mercy, modesty, and self-regulation. Finally, the virtue of *transcendence* includes strengths that make connections to the larger universe and meaning, including the appreciation of beauty, gratitude, hope, spirituality, or a sense of purpose. Character strengths are important for both subjective and psychological well-being (Harzer, 2016). Zest, hope, and curiosity are found to have the most robust relationship with well-being. Character strengths are also associated with positive mental health. In one study, adolescents with other-oriented strengths (e.g., kindness and teamwork) demonstrated fewer symptoms of depression and those with transcendence strengths (e.g., meaning, love) had greater life satisfaction (Gillham et al., 2011).

Another concept related to character strength is "sparks," which reflects adolescents' talents, interests, or hobbies (Benson, 2009; Scales et al., 2011). A large-scale study ($N = 1,817$) with ethnically and racially diverse adolescents investigated their "sparks," the perceived support when pursuing those sparks, and a sense of empowerment when making civic contributions (Scales et al., 2011). The study found that linking "sparks" with a sense of voice and relational support leads to positive outcomes. However, less than 10% of adolescents reported having a high level of sparks, supportive opportunities, and a sense of voice.

Strength Building Interventions

School-based character strength interventions have a positive effect on adolescents' hope, school engagement, well-being, and life satisfaction (Lavy, 2020). The key elements of those interventions include teaching youth strength-based language, identifying strengths in oneself and others (including peers, books, and film characters); using strengths in different ways throughout school day; and reflecting on outcomes associated with using strengths. For example, in the teacher-facilitated "Strengths Gym" intervention, adolescents completed strengths-based exercises on each of the 24 strengths through in-class activities, discussions, stories, and homework where students applied their strengths in their lives (Proctor et al., 2011). The intervention had a positive effect on adolescents' life satisfaction. Strength-based education is a core feature of the Geelong Grammar School Project described in Chapter 1.

Niemiec (2018) proposed the Aware-Explore-Apply Model which can be used to work on strengths in individual and group interventions. During the Aware phase, adolescents are asked to identify their strengths. Then they explore their strengths (Explore phase) using tools, including journaling, identifying strengths in others, and reflecting on inner experiences associated with strengths. During the Apply phase, youths are encouraged to use their strengths on an everyday basis, for example, in the process of goal setting and goal pursuit.

Adolescents need a supportive social environment and relational opportunities to pursue their "sparks." It is important to encourage them to reflect on what they want to do as opposed to what they have to do. In order to promote sparks in young people, Benson (2009) recommends asking the following questions: What are your sparks? When and how do you express them? Who knows your sparks and who supports your sparks? What gets in your way? How can I help you to express your sparks?

Goal Pursuit

Goal pursuit is a self-directing and self-defining process that involves selecting goals and determining strategies to achieve them (Massey et al., 2008). It further determines the narratives adolescents create about themselves. Goals serve two main purposes, namely self-direction and self-definition (who am I and who will I become). Adolescents who can make a connection between "who they are" with "who they will become" are more successful in goal-oriented behavior (Linley et al., 2010). Setting and successfully pursuing goals is closely associated with identity development (Massey et al., 2008).

Having goals makes life meaningful; it is further associated with life satisfaction. A large-scale longitudinal study with adolescents as they transitioned to adulthood revealed that meeting goals and continued goal striving were associated with well-being (Messersmith & Schulenberg, 2010). When goals seem unattainable or beyond one's control, it might lead to dissatisfaction and depression (Brandtstädter & Rothermund, 2002). The ability to adjust personal goals to life circumstances and available resources is important for resilience (Brandtstädter & Rothermund, 2002). Goals with intrinsic motivation usually have an internal locus of causality and are integrated with the self (Sheldon & Elliot, 1999). In contrast, goals pursued because of external forces often have an external locus of causality and are not integrated with the self. Their volitional strength is likely to weaken when a person encounters obstacles while reaching his or her goals. Furthermore, the attainment of goals, consistent or concordant with one's interests and core values, is associated with well-being (Sheldon & Elliot, 1999).

Developmental Goals

Youths regulate their development by setting personal goals and striving for their attainment (Heckhausen et al., 2010; Nurmi & Salmela-Aro, 2002). Selection of personal goals depends on culturally determined age windows for the accomplishment of major developmental tasks. Massey and colleagues' (2008) systematic review found that adolescents often report having goals related to education, occupation, and social relationships. Girls have a stronger preference toward relational goals, while boys create goals related to status and being successful. Girls also reported goals related to education more often and envision themselves in arts and humanities to a greater degree than in math and business. A study with American multiethnic high school seniors revealed that the majority of them generated goals related to a future occupation (78.4%) and education (73.9%; Chang et al., 2006). The study demonstrated no significant differences in ethnic groups regarding the aforementioned goals.

Developmental regulation includes an individual's efforts to influence their development and adapt to changing life situations and circumstances (Heckhausen et al., 2010). It requires the ability to disengage from blocked developmental goals and to modify developmental options. An adaptive developmental course involves engagement with goals that are feasible in the current life situation and not inhibiting the attainment of other current or future goals (Heckhausen et al., 2010). The ability to disengage from unattainable goals and choose a different developmental pathway are important for one's well-being (Brandtstädter & Renner, 1990).

Developmental regulation involves selection, that is, developing and choosing personal goals; optimization, that is, investing resources for pursuing those goals; and compensation aimed at maintaining one's performance when facing loss or decline in goal-relevant activities (Freund & Baltes, 2000). The interaction between these processes determines the balance between developmental gains and losses. Based on this idea,

Heckhausen and colleagues (Heckhausen & Schulz, 1993; Heckhausen et al., 2010) proposed a two-dimensional model of optimizing primary and secondary controls. These controls serve two main functions: Selecting among available developmental paths and behavioral options and coping with failure when goals are not achievable. These two types of control can be selective or compensatory.

Selective primary control is aimed at attaining goals. It utilizes a person's internal resources, including time, effort, or abilities and skills (Heckhausen et al., 2010). When lacking internal resources to attain a chosen goal, adolescents may use compensatory primary control aimed at engaging external resources, such as seeking help from others or using technical aids. Primary control is adaptive if goals are diverse, congruent with opportunities, and not detrimental to other goals (Heckhausen et al., 2010). For example, adolescents' overinvestment in academic pursuits can deprive other domains (e.g., peer relationships or sports) from necessary action resources. A limited set of goals can bring adolescents to a dead end and compromise their sense of agency and efficacy if those goals do not come to fruition.

Secondary control strategies are aimed at addressing motivational processes to maximize primary control and minimize potential lost goals (Heckhausen et al., 2010). Using selective secondary control, adolescents may increase the value of a chosen goal or strengthen a sense of personal control. For example, they can envision being admitted to college and being proud of themselves. Finally, by utilizing compensatory secondary control, one might disengage from a goal to minimize the negative effects of failure on her sense of worth and motivational resources. Compensatory secondary control works to deactivate obsolete goals or uses self-protective strategies, including avoiding self-blame, focusing on previous successes or successes in other domains, or comparing oneself with others who are less fortunate. These strategies not only help to protect one's ego, but also free resources for goal pursuit in other domains. Adaptive goal disengagement involves actively restructuring goals rather than reflecting passively on failure (Heckhausen et al., 2010).

Intentional self-regulation is one of the essential variables associated with positive youth development (Lerner et al., 2013). It involves the ability to select adaptive goals, optimize the probability of achieving them, overcome obstacles, and flexibly adjust or compensate when the goal is not achievable. Intentional self-regulation is associated with a positive developmental trajectory and reduces the risk of behavioral problems. Hopeful future expectations is another important variable for positive youth development. It is closely associated with intentional self-regulation, low-risk behaviors, and lower depressive symptoms (Lerner et al., 2013).

The path to achieve a goal is usually not given to youth; often, they have to create it themselves (Larson, 2011). Additionally, goal pursuit can be derailed by two types of obstacles: Objective (e.g., lack of support from the environment) and subjective (e.g., lack of motivation or confidence). Therefore, creating and sustaining motivation and regulating frustration and potential anxiety are essential for overcoming barriers and staying on the developmental course (Larson, 2011). Young people need to foster initiative, the internal motivation to pursue a challenging goal (Larson, 2006). Personal engagement in tasks helps young people become intrinsically motivated and persevere when facing challenging tasks.

Adults should have a good understanding of when to support youths' goals and when to challenge them (Larson, 2006). Instrumental and motivational scaffolding can be used to activate motivation to pursue a goal. Instrumental scaffolding includes suggestions, clarifications, and modeling regarding task performance, whereas motivational scaffolding involves demonstrating enthusiasm and communicating confidence that a youth's effort will lead to a desired outcome. It is important to keep in mind that youths' intrinsic motivation can be weakened by stress, boredom, and competing motivational systems, such as pleasure and avoidance of failure. In addition, distraction due to screen media can also derail motivation (Larson, 2006).

Growth Mindset

The way adolescents respond to roadblocks and failures is linked to their mindset, or beliefs whether their abilities are fixed or can be improved (Dweck, 2006; Molden & Dweck, 2006). A fixed mindset, called an entity theory, considers traits and abilities fixed, stable, and not under one's control. A growth mindset, also called an incremental theory, suggests that abilities and traits are malleable. Mindset is most important when students struggle or encounter failure (Blackwell et al., 2007; Paunesku et al., 2015). A growth mindset predicts greater goal achievement (Burnette et al., 2013). Adolescents with a fixed mindset often demonstrate helplessness as a response to failure, choose easier tasks, and are more likely to be depressed and less healthy. In contrast, adolescents with a growth mindset consider failure a result of ineffective strategies, try different strategies, persevere when facing a difficult task, have better stress tolerance, and maintain a positive affect (Yeager et al., 2014). The following questions can help to promote a growth mindset (Dweck, 2006): What are the opportunities for learning today? How can I use those opportunities? If I encounter setbacks and obstacles, how will I overcome them? What resources do I already have or will I need to continue my personal growth? Who can help me in my growth process?

Hope and Goal Pursuit

Enhancing hope increases the probability of achieving desired goals. Snyder (2002) defined hope as a perceived capability to pave pathways to one's goals and engage agency thinking to use those pathways.

Furthermore, hope is associated with many positive outcomes, including life satisfaction, academic success, and personal adjustment (Edwards & McClintock, 2013; Snyder, 2002). Importantly, a hopeful narrative at the beginning of intervention makes intervention more effective by boosting a person's motivation for getting better (Snyder, 2002).

Hope has three major components: Goals, pathways, and agency. Pathway thinking entails generating possible routes to achieve desired goals and a sense of confidence in those routes. Agency thinking is a motivational component of hope, as it allows an adolescent to sustain motivation through all stages of goal achievement. It is often manifested in self-talk, such as "I can do it" or "Nothing can stop me." Individuals with high hope consider barriers and impediments in goal pursuit as less stressful compared to individuals with low hope (Snyder, 2002). Pathway and agency thinking work together in the process of goal achievement. At the beginning of this process, pathway thinking and agency become activated to "get started."

High-hope individuals enjoy goal pursuit and this enjoyment serves as a feedback loop, further motivating the process. They may use positive self-talk "This should be interesting" or "I am ready for this challenge." When having trouble with achieving goals, people with high hope generate alternate routes. Individuals with low hope, however, quickly become discouraged by obstacles and have difficulty maintaining their motivation (Snyder, 2002).

To accentuate hope, four strategies can be used: Hope-finding, -bonding, -enhancing, and -reminding (Lopez et al., 2004). Hope-finding strategies include reading stories about struggle and success; attending to situations when one overcame difficulties; and using hopeful self-talk ("I can make it happen," "I will pull through," and "I am hopeful for finding a solution"). Hope-bonding includes building supportive relationships with others who can help with goal pursuit. The following questions can be asked: Who can help you with this goal? How can they help you? What kind of help do you need to achieve your goal? Hope-enhancing strategies involve sharing one's hopeful thinking with others, attending to small changes one made, and reframing obstacles. Finally, hope-reminding involves keeping active memories about one's success in overcoming difficulties. Hope-focused strategies can be supplemented by brief psychodrama depicting goals pursuit (Pedrotti et al., 2008). Using props to designate obstacles and arrows for pathways to overcome these obstacles can increase youths' engagement in hope-related interventions. Furthermore, girls can create stories to incorporate hope language.

Agency in Adolescence

"The term *agency* refers to a person's autonomous control over his or her actions – but also much more than this, including a sense of what individuals can accomplish themselves and responsibility or ownership over one's actions" (Sokol et al., 2015, p. 284). Adolescents are embedded within relational networks and social structures (e.g., schools and communities) which can both constrain and enable their expression of agency. Opportunities for exercising agency and supplying adolescents with tools, skills, and voice pave the road to healthy and flourishing adults (Sokol et al., 2015).

Agency or self-authorship requires self-awareness and personal meaning-making. It further relates to intention, volition, purpose, and having control over one's own life (McAdams, 2013). Agency is intrinsically linked to self-efficacy, which determines the amount of effort one puts into pursuing a goal and persistence when facing obstacles. (Bandura, 1982). Those with low self-efficacy give up easily and those with a strong sense of efficacy exude more effort to master challenges.

McAdams (2013) called adolescents' stage of development of self a "motivated agent," which reflects adolescents' increased ability to be guided by purpose, values, and hopes. Through initiation and investment in personal goals, adolescents can project themselves into the future. They begin to ponder about what goals they want to achieve, who they want to become, and which directions to take. These questions are grounded in a sociocultural context and reflect beliefs and values present in youths' culture. Future orientation requires strategic thinking as youths choose to invest themselves into strivings and life goals that promise the best returns for the future (McAdams, 2013).

Lent (2004) emphasizes the importance of considering people as agents of their own well-being. This agentic stance toward one's well-being can be fostered by encouraging adolescents to ask the following questions: What do I need to change in order to feel more satisfied with my life? What gives my life meaning? How can I enhance my personal growth? What is most important for me right now? What gives me pleasure? How can I contribute to the well-being of my family, friends, or community?

Identity Development

Identity exploration is an important developmental task for adolescents. Identity refers to "personally meaningful aims and beliefs about who one is and who one hopes to become" (Bronk, 2011, p. 32). Adolescents begin to ask themselves questions, such as: Who am I? What are my goals? Who do I want to become? Identity development involves the exploration of different roles, goals, and beliefs, and orientation toward the future (Bronk, 2011; Schwartz et al., 2013). This is related to self-regulation and a sense of agency when youths take steps to shape their own lives (National Academies of Sciences, Engineering, and Medicine, 2019). Starting in late adolescence, youths begin to develop a narrative identity or life story. This narrative weaves together and helps to make sense of one's personal experiences. It also provides purpose and meaning to one's life (McAdams, 2013).

Civic engagement provides adolescents with opportunities for positive identity formation through experimenting with new roles, building relationships with adult models, exploring career and networking opportunities, and skill development (Crocetti et al., 2012). Social responsibility is a potential mechanism through which positive identity formation and civic engagement are related to each other. Furthermore, a sense of collective efficacy gives individuals power to solve their problems and improve their lives through a concerted effort (Bandura, 1982). Parents, other significant adults, and media serve as role models for adolescents to develop their identities (Oyserman & Fryberg, 2006). For minority youth, cultural metaphors, images, stories, icons, and symbols provide ideas about self-related qualities, goals, and aspirations important in their cultures.

Possible Selves

Possible selves is a type of self-knowledge that reflects future orientation and includes one's goals, hopes, and fears that motivate one's behavior (Markus & Nurius, 1986). Possible selves reflect a link between identity and future goals. It includes hopes, fears, goals, and threats related to the future, which provide incentives for the future behavior and a context for evaluating the current view of self:

> Possible selves are the selves we imagine ourselves becoming in the future, the selves we hope to become, the selves we are afraid we may become, and the selves we fully expect we will become. Possible selves can be distally imagined–'the self I will become as an adult', or more short term–'the self I will become next year'.
>
> (Oyserman & Fryberg, 2006, p. 4)

Possible selves are a social-cultural construct which is rooted in one's own values, ideals, and aspirations as well as in the perception of what significant others believe one should become (Oyserman & Fryberg, 2006). They can also be an expression of an adolescent's life tasks.

Adolescents have to figure out who they want to become in important domains, including education, work, family, and relationships. It is important for adolescents to have a balance between expected and feared possible selves, for example, setting a positive goal and understanding the personally relevant consequences of not meeting that goal (Oyserman & Fryberg, 2006). One study demonstrated that adolescents who endorsed feared possible self-narratives have higher levels of problem behavior (Pierce et al., 2015).

Unlike boys, girls are less sure about the probability to attain their possible selves (Oyserman & Fryberg, 2006). As a result, they might show reduced commitment to or even give up their possible positive selves and focus on avoiding negative selves. Given that, girls need to be supported in their strivings for possible positive selves. Additionally, since a relational context is central to girls' self-concept, it can make girls more susceptible to taking on the successes and failures of significant others as their own.

The focus on positive or best possible selves is important in order to orient adolescents toward positive goals. The "Best Possible Selves Intervention" can help adolescent girls imagine their future. One study found that this intervention was effective for increasing adolescents' subjective well-being (Liau et al., 2016). In another study, adolescents were asked to envision themselves as successful adults and connect those images with their current school involvement (Oyserman et al., 2002). After the intervention, youths reported a stronger bond with the school, a desire to do well in school, and better school attendance.

The following script can be used to facilitate reflection on Best Possible Selves (Niemiec, 2013):

> Think about a future time period – this can be 6 months, 1 year, 5 years from now. Imagine that at that time you are fully expressing your best possible self. Envision your best possible self in as many details as possible. Reflect on how you would you feel when reaching your full potential or accomplishing an important goal. Focus on a future that is attainable within reason. Once you have a clear vision, write down as many details as possible. Now, think about strengths, skills, or resources you can use on your path to becoming your best possible self. Then, focus on personal strengths or resources that you would have when you are at your best in the future.

Several strategies can be used with the Best Possible Selves intervention. For example, adolescents can draw or paint their future selves and contemplate strategies and the pathway to get there. They can use images and cutouts from magazines or the Internet to create a Possible Self collage. Youths can create an image or narrative that encompasses many possible selves, including academic, career, and social possible selves.

Social Identity

While personal identity reflects our values, goals, and aspirations, social identity reflects how those values, goals, and aspirations are aligned with those of other members of the group to which one belongs (Cruwys et al., 2014). Social identity makes one distinguishable from other people and at the same time satisfies a need for belongingness (Verkuyten, 2016). It also makes life meaningful and gives an individual a sense of being competent and capable of influencing one's own environment. While exploration and commitment are essential for personal identity, self-stereotyping and assimilation are key processes for establishing social identity (Verkuyten, 2016). The self becomes depersonalized and redefined toward group-based characteristics and attributes. The "mental overlap between self and ethnic-racial group emerges via self-stereotyping, top down ('I am like my group'), and self-projection, bottom-up ('the group is like me')" (Verkuyten, 2016, p. 1800).

Social identity is a psychological resource associated with shared perceptions of others, the world, and ourselves (Cruwys et al., 2014; Jetten et al., 2017). It supplies adolescents with a sense of meaning, purpose, and direction. As such, it is essential for eudaimonic well-being. Individuals with a stronger social identity can capitalize on social relationships with support. They can also be more agentic in influencing others' feelings, beliefs, and behaviors.

Physical and mental health are significantly influenced by social identity (Jetten et al., 2017). When social identity is associated with positive resources, including meaning, support, and agency, it has a positive impact on well-being by providing a so-called "social cure." However, when social identity is not linked to positive psychological resources or when it is challenged (e.g., group membership is devalued or stigmatized), it can threaten and potentially harm physical and psychological well-being. Social identities can protect against depression when they are associated with a sense of belongingness, meaning of life, and social support (Cruwys et al., 2014).

Cultural/ethnic identity is a type of social identity that refers to the extent to which individuals share goals, values, and beliefs of the members of their ethnic or cultural group (Schwartz et al., 2013). Ethnic identity serves as a protective factor against the effects of daily discrimination on the mental health of ethnic minority group members (Torres & Ong, 2010). More specifically, ethnic identity commitment serves as a stress buffer that reduces the intensity of and promotes recovery from daily discrimination. A meta-analytic study evidenced that feeling positively about one's ethnicity or race (e.g., positive ethnic-racial affect) is associated with youths' well-being, self-esteem, and positive social and academic functioning (Rivas-Drake et al., 2014).

Experiences with discrimination and exclusion stimulate an adolescent's ethnic identity development (Verkuyten, 2016). For some adolescents, it can lead to a reactive ethnicity characterized by strong ethnic minority group identification and the creation of an oppositional culture that rejects dominant cultural norms and values. Yet, some adolescents may distance themselves from their ethnic-racial group. Youths can use cues, such as dressing, acting, or speaking in a way that distinguishes their ethnic/racial group from others. Furthermore, their acceptance as members of a particular group depends on how they have mastered identity cues. An example of an identity cue is African American hip-hop culture, with rap music being a main component of that culture (Verkuyten, 2016).

The process of identity development during adolescence can be complicated among ethnic minority adolescents due to acculturative stress as they try to adapt to sociocultural contexts (Vasquez & de las Fuentes, 1999). For example, a study with recently immigrated Hispanic adolescents found a bidirectional relationship between identity and depressive symptoms (Meca et al., 2019). Identity coherence predicted fewer depressive symptoms and depressive symptoms predicted weaker identity coherence and stronger identity confusion.

Identity development can present a unique challenge for Black adolescent girls. They may struggle with constructing their selfhood and meaning of themselves, especially when confronted with racial discrimination and stereotypical images of Black women (Muhammad, 2012). For instance, one girl reflected that she sometimes cries "because not knowing who you are is the worst feeling in the world" (Muhammad, 2012, p. 207). African American girls might internalize societal biases associated with their race and gender (Duke & Fripp, 2020). Such biases are associated with perceived stress. At the same time, positive collective self-esteem, for example, positive perception of and identification with African American racial group, buffers such an association (Barrie et al., 2016).

Racial socialization and racial identity are important cultural protective factors against mental health problems in African American adolescent girls (Stokes et al., 2020). In one study, girls who felt proud of being a Black woman had fewer depressive symptoms, while those who internalized oppressive messages about Black women experienced more depressive symptoms and had negative feelings about their racial identity.

African American girls who feel positive about being Black and who feel supported at and connected to school are more engaged in learning (Buckley & Carter, 2005; Butler-Barnes et al., 2018). Furthermore, feeling positive about being African American might protect against the negative effects of a lower sense of belonging to school. Girls who endorse the importance of being a member of the African American racial group and who feel good about being Black also have higher achievement motivation. A strong racial identity serves as a cultural strength-based asset protecting African American girls against a negative racial school climate (Butler-Barnes et al., 2018).

Interventions to Support Identity Development in Girls of Color

Youth Participatory Action Research (Youth-PAR) is one avenue to support healthy identity development in adolescent girls. Youth-PAR engages adolescents in identifying and exploring problems relevant to their own lives through research inquiry and advocating for social change (Sabo-Flores, 2008). Taking part in a group research project empowers adolescent girls and increases their sense of agency. It also represents a powerful developmental context to explore adolescents' identity, power, and stereotypes (Duke & Fripp, 2020). Additionally, it helps with community building and provides an opportunity to practice collaborative description-making. Participating in Youth-PAR is especially powerful for girls of color. In one study, engaging African American girls in Youth-PAR helped to disrupt internalized biases and promote prosocial attitudes and skills (Duke & Fripp, 2020). Working in a group allowed these adolescents to challenge their negative self-narratives, create counter-narratives, and acknowledge that competence and diversity lead to more positive attitudes and deeper respect for others (Duke & Fripp, 2020).

Taft (2004) conducted a similar intervention called the Teen Women's Action Program (TWAP). The TWAP is a multicultural after-school/summer program that involves primarily African American, Latina, and Vietnamese-American adolescent girls and young women. The mission of the program is to support adolescent girls so they can improve their lives and become community change agents. Girls received training in problem-solving, self-advocacy, decision-making, conflict resolution, and self-assessment skills. The educational component included topics related to reproductive health, violence, stress, and oppression. Adolescent girls further worked collaboratively on problems existing in their school community. They designed and conducted community needs assessments and action plans.

Finally, writing can help adolescent girls explore and assert their identities. Muhammad (2012) conducted a writing institute for African American girls called Write it Out! At the beginning of each meeting, girls created and recited a powerful oral preface. Group facilitators encouraged using the opening words "We the sister authors" in their preamble. The institute curriculum was grounded in four themes: Identity, resiliency, solidarity, and advocacy. Girls were given mentor texts that served as models for their writing. These included writings from Harriet Jacobs, Ellen Watkins Harper, Mari Evans, Toni Morrison, Alice Walker, Ntozake Shange, and Sharon Flake. The writing institute allowed girls to find their voices, explore their identity, and express themselves.

Recommended Resources

Quaglia Institute for School Voice and Aspirations –- https://quagliainstitute.org/

The Quaglia for School Voice and Aspirations provides advocacy and leadership training for students and staff tailored to meet the needs and goals of school districts. This training seeks to foster school environments that listen to the voices of teachers and students and promote critical thinking, problem-solving skills, creativity, engagement and open communication. The goals of the institute include building internal capacity, inspiring meaningful improvements in teaching and learning, and helping schools foster everyone's – educators and students – voice and aspirations in schools.

Life Purpose and Career – http://parentingteenagersacademy.com/life-purpose/

This is a resource for parents to help their teens find their life purpose or career path. It provides parents with a 14-step process that they can use to guide their teens toward their purpose. These steps include not projecting one's fears onto one's child, encouraging curiosity, guiding teens to trust their excitement, and leading by example, among others.

References

Bandura, A. (1982). Self-efficacy mechanism in human agency. *American Psychologist, 37*(2), 122–147. https://doi.org/10.1037/0003-066X.37.2.122

Barrie, R., Langrehr, K. J., Jérémie-Brink, G., Alder, N., Hewitt, A. A., & Thomas, A. (2016). Stereotypical beliefs and psychological well-being of African American adolescent girls: Collective self-esteem as a moderator. *Counselling Psychology Quarterly, 29*(4), 423–442. https://doi.org/10.1080/09515070.2015.1129494

Benson, P. L. (2009, November 1). *The six essential questions.* Youth Today. https://youthtoday.org/2009/11/the-six-essential-questions/

Blackwell, L. S., Trzesniewski, K. H., & Dweck, C. S. (2007). Implicit theories of intelligence predict achievement across an adolescent transition: A longitudinal study and an intervention. *Child Development, 78*(1), 246–263. https://doi.org/10.1111/j.1467-8624.2007.00995.x

Brandtstädter, J., & Renner, G. (1990). Tenacious goal pursuit and flexible goal adjustment: Explication and age-related analysis of assimilative and accommodative strategies of coping. *Psychology and Aging, 5*, 58–67. doi:10.1037/0882-7974.5.1.5

Brandtstädter, J., & Rothermund, K. (2002). The life-course dynamics of goal pursuit and goal adjustment: A two-process framework. *Developmental Review, 22*(1), 117–150. https://doi.org/10.1006/drev.2001.0539

Bronk, K. C. (2011). The role of purpose in life in healthy identity formation: A grounded model. *New Directions for Youth Development, 2011*(32), 31–44. https://doi.org/10.1002/yd.426

Buckley, T. R., & Carter, R. T. (2005). Black adolescent girls: Do gender role and racial identity impact their self-esteem? *Sex Roles, 53*, 647–661. https://doi.org/10.1007/s11199-005-7731-6

Burnette, J. L., O'Boyle, E. H., VanEpps, E. M., Pollack, J. M., & Finkel, E. J. (2013). Mind-sets matter: A meta-analytic review of implicit theories and self-regulation. *Psychological Bulletin, 139*(3), 655–701. https://doi.org/10.1037/a0029531

Burrow, A. L., & Hill, P. L. (2011). Purpose as a form of identity capital for positive youth adjustment. *Developmental Psychology, 47*(4), 1196–1206. https://doi.org/10.1037/a0023818

Butler-Barnes, S. T., Leath, S., Williams, A., Byrd, C., Carter, R., & Chavous, T. M. (2018). Promoting resilience among African American girls: Racial identity as a protective factor. *Child Development, 89*(6), e552–e571. https://doi. org/10.1111/cdev.12995

Chang, E. S., Chen, C., Greenberger, E., Dooley, D., & Heckhausen, J. (2006). What do they want in life? The life goals of a multi-ethnic, multi-generational sample of high school seniors. *Journal of Youth and Adolescence, 35*(3), 321–332. https://doi.org/10.1007/s10964-006-9034-9

Crocetti, E. (2017). Identity formation in adolescence: The dynamic of forming and consolidating identity commitments. *Child Development Perspectives, 11*(2), 145–150. https://doi.org/10.1111/cdep.12226

Crocetti, E., Jahromi, P., & Meeus, W. (2012). Identity and civic engagement in adolescence. *Journal of Adolescence, 35*(3), 521–532. https://doi.org/10.1016/j. adolescence.2011.08.003

Cruwys, T., Haslam, S. A., Dingle, G. A., Haslam, C., & Jetten, J. (2014). Depression and social identity: An integrative review. *Personality and Social Psychology Review, 18*(3), 215–238. https://doi.org/10.1177/1088868314523839

Damon, W. (2008). *The path to purpose: How young people find their calling in life.* Free Press.

Damon, W., Menon, J. L., & Bronk, K. C. (2003). The development of purpose during adolescence. *Journal of Applied Developmental Science, 7*(3), 119–128. https://doi.org/10.1207/S1532480XADS0703_2

Dik, B. J., Steger, M. F., Gibson, A., & Peisner, W. (2011). Make your work matter: Development and pilot evaluation of a purpose-centered career education intervention. *New Directions for Youth Development, 2011*(132), 59–73. https:// doi.org/10.1002/yd.428

Duke, A. M., & Fripp, J. A. (2020). Examining youth participatory action research as a context to disrupt implicit bias in African American adolescent girls. *Educational Action Research*, 1–15. https://doi.org/10.1080/09650792.2020. 1774404

Dweck, C. S. (2006). *Mindset: The new psychology of success*. Random House Incorporated.

Edwards, L. M., & McClintock, J. B. (2013). Promoting hope among youth: Theory, research, and practice. In C. Proctor & P. A. Linley (Eds.), *Research, applications, and interventions for children and adolescents: A positive psychology perspective* (pp. 43–55). Springer. https://doi.org/10.1007/978-94-007-6398-2_4

Ferrer-Wreder, L., & Kroger, J. (2020). Identity in adolescence: The balance between self and other. Routledge.

Freund, A. M., & Baltes, P. B. (2000). The orchestration of selection, optimization, and compensation: An action-theoretical conceptualization of a theory of developmental regulation. In W. J. Perrig & A. Grob (Eds.), *Control of human behavior, mental processes, and consciousness: Essays in honor of 60th birthday of August Flammer* (pp. 35–58). Lawrence Erlbaum Associates Publishers.

Gillham, J., Adams-Deutsch, Z., Werner, J., Reivich, K., Coulter-Heindl, V., Linkins, M., Winder, B., Peterson, C., Park, N., Abenavoli, R., Contero, A., & Seligman, M. E. P. (2011). Character strengths predict subjective well-being during adolescence. *The Journal of Positive Psychology, 6*(1), 31–44. https://doi. org/10.1080/17439760.2010.536773

Gutowski, E., White, A. E., Liang, B., Diamonti, A.-J., & Berado, D. (2018). How stress influences purpose development: The importance of social support. *Journal of Adolescent Research, 33*(5), 571–597. https://doi.org/10.1177/0743558417737754

Harzer, C. (2016). The eudaimonics of human strengths: The relations between character strengths and well-being. In J. Vitterso (Ed.), *Handbook of eudaimonic well-being* (pp. 307–322). Springer International Publishing. https://doi.org/10.1007/978-3-319-42445-3_20

Heckhausen, J., & Schulz, R. (1993). Optimisation by selection and compensation: Balancing primary and secondary control in life span development. *International Journal of Behavioral Development, 16*(2), 287–303. https://doi.org/10.1177/016502549301600210

Heckhausen, J., Wrosch, C., & Schulz, R. (2010). A motivational theory of lifespan development. *Psychological Review, 117*(1), 32–60. https://doi.org/10.1037/a0017668

Jetten, J., Haslam, S. A., Cruwys, T., Greenaway, K. H., Haslam, C., & Steffens, N. K. (2017). Advancing the social identity approach to health and well-being: Progressing the social cure research agenda. *European Journal of Social Psychology, 47*(7), 789–802. https://doi.org/10.1002/ejsp.2333

Koshy, S. I., & Mariano, J. M. (2011). Promoting youth purpose: A review of the literature. *New Directions for Youth Development, 132*, 13–29. https://doi.org/10.1002/yd.425

Larson, R. (2006). Positive youth development, willful adolescents, and mentoring. *Journal of Community Psychology, 34*(6), 677–689. https://doi.org/10.1002/jcop.20123

Larson, R. W. (2011). Positive development in a disorderly world: SRA presidential address. *Journal of Research on Adolescence, 21*(3), 317–334. https://doi.org/10.1111/j.1532-7795.2010.00707.x

Larson, R. W., & Tran, S. P. (2014). Invited commentary: Positive youth development and human complexity. *Journal of Youth and Adolescence, 43*, 1012–1017. https://doi.org/10.1007/s10964-014-0124-9

Lavy, S. (2020). A review of character strengths interventions in twenty-first-century schools: Their importance and how they can be fostered. *Applied Research in Quality of Life, 15*, 573–596. https://doi.org/10.1007/s11482-018-9700-6

Lent, R. W. (2004). Toward a unifying theoretical and practical perspective on well-being and psychosocial adjustment. *Journal of Counseling Psychology, 51*(4), 482–509. https://doi.org/10.1037/0022-0167.51.4.482

Lerner, J. V., Bowers, E. P., Minor, K., Boyd, M. J., Mueller, M. K., Schmid, K. L., Napolitano, C. M., Lewin-Bizan, S., & Lerner, R. M. (2013). Positive youth development: Processes, philosophies, and programs. In R. M. Lerner, M. A., Easterbrooks, J. Mistry, & I. B. Weiner (Eds.), *Handbook of psychology, Vol. 6: Developmental Psychology* (2nd ed., pp. 365–392). John Wiley & Sons, Inc.

Liang, B., Lund, T., Mousseau, A., White, A. E., Spencer, R., & Walsh, J. (2018). Adolescent girls finding purpose: The role of parents and prosociality. *Youth & Society, 50*(6), 801–817. https://doi.org/10.1177/0044118X17697850

Liau, A. K., Neihart, M. F., Teo, C. T., & Lo, C. H. (2016). Effects of the best possible self activity on subjective well-being and depressive symptoms. *The Asia-Pacific Education Researcher, 25*, 473–481. https://doi.org/10.1007/s40299-015-0272-z

Linley, P. A., Nielsen, K. M., Gillett, R., & Biswas-Diener, R. (2010). Using signature strengths in pursuit of goals: Effects on goal progress, need satisfaction, and well-being, and implications for coaching psychologists. *International Coaching Psychology Review, 5*(1), 6–15.

Lopez, S. J., Snyder, C. R., Magyar-Moe, J. L., Edwards, L. M., Pedrotti, J. T., Janowski, K., Turner, J. L., & Pressgrove, C. (2004). Strategies for accentuating hope. In P. A. Linley & S. Joseph (Eds.), *Positive psychology in practice* (pp. 388–404). John Wiley & Sons, Inc.

Malin, H. (2018). *Teaching for purpose: Preparing students for lives of meaning.* Harvard Education Press.

Malin, H., Liauw, I., & Damon, W. (2017). Purpose and character development in early adolescence. *Journal of Youth and Adolescence, 46*(6), 1200–1215. https://doi.org/10.1007/s10964-017-0642-3

Mariano, J. M., & Going, J. (2011). Youth purpose and positive youth development. *Advances in Child Development and Behavior, 41*, 39–68. https://doi.org/10.1016/b978-0-12-386492-5.00003-8

Markus, H., & Nurius, P. (1986). Possible selves. *American Psychologist, 41*(9), 954–969. https://doi.org/10.1037/0003-066X.41.9.954

Massey, E. K., Gebhardt, W. A., & Garnefski, N. (2008). Adolescent goal content and pursuit: A review of the literature from the past 16 years. *Developmental Review, 28*(4), 421–460. https://doi.org/10.1016/j.dr.2008.03.002

McAdams, D. P. (2013). The psychological self as actor, agent, and author. *Perspectives on Psychological Science, 8*(3), 272–295. https://doi.org/10.1177/1745691612464657

Meca, A., Rodil, J. C., Paulson, J. F., Kelley, M., Schwartz, S. J., Unger, J. B., Lorenzo-Blanco, E. I., Des Rosiers, S. E., Gonzales-Backen, M., Baezconde-Garbanati & Zamboanga, B. L. (2019). Examining the directionality between identity development and depressive symptoms among recently immigrated Hispanic adolescents. *Journal of Youth and Adolescence, 48*, 2114–2124. https://doi.org/10.1007/s10964-019-01086-z

Messersmith, E. E., & Schulenberg, J. E. (2010). Goal attainment, goal striving, and well-being during the transition to adulthood: A ten-year U.S. national longitudinal study. *New Directions for Child and Adolescent Development, 2010*(130), 27–40. https://doi.org/10.1002/cd.279

Molden, D. C., & Dweck, C. S. (2006). Finding "meaning" in psychology: A lay theories approach to self-regulation, social perception, and social development. *American Psychologist, 61*(3), 192–203. https://doi.org/10.1037/0003-066X.61.3.192

Moran, S. (2018) Purpose-in-action education: Introduction and implications, *Journal of Moral Education, 47*(2), 145–158. https://doi.org/10.1080/03057240.2018.1444001

Moran, S., Bundick, M. J., Malin, H., & Reilly, T. S. (2013). How supportive of their specific purposes do youth believe their family and friends are? *Journal of Adolescent Research, 28*(3), 348–377. https://doi.org/10.1177/0743558412457816

Muhammad, G. E. (2012). Creating spaces for Black adolescent girls to "Write It Out!" *Journal of Adolescent & Adult Literacy, 56*(3), 203–211. https://doi.org/10.1002/JAAL.00129

National Academies of Sciences, Engineering, and Medicine. (2019). *The promise of adolescence: Realizing opportunity for all youth.* The National Academies Press. https://doi.org/10.17226/25388

Niemiec, R. M. (2013). VIA character strengths: Research and practice (the first 10 years). In H. H. Knoop & A. Delle Fave (Eds.), *Cross-cultural advancements in positive psychology: Vol. 3. Well-being and cultures: Perspectives from positive psychology* (pp. 11–29). Springer Science + Business Media. https://doi.org/10.1007/978-94-007-4611-4_2

Niemiec, R. M. (2018). *Character strengths interventions: A field guide for practitioners*. Hogrefe.

Nurmi, J.E., & Salmela-Aro, K. (2002). Goal construction, reconstruction and depressive symptoms in a life-span context: The transition from school to work. *Journal of Personality, 70*(3), 385–420. https://doi.org/10.1111/1467-6494.05009

Oyserman, D., & Fryberg, S. (2006). The possible selves of diverse adolescents: Content and function across gender, race and national origin. In C. Dunkel & J. Kerpelman (Eds.), *Possible selves: Theory, research and applications* (pp. 17–39). Nova Science Publishers.

Oyserman, D., Terry, K., & Bybee, D. (2002). A possible selves intervention to enhance school involvement. *Journal of Adolescence, 25*(3), 313–26. https://doi.org/10.1006/jado.2002.0474

Paunesku, D., Walton, G. M., Romero, C., Smith, E. N., Yeager, D. S., & Dweck, C. S. (2015). Mind-set interventions are a scalable treatment for academic underachievement. *Psychological Science, 26*(6), 784–793. https://doi.org/10.1177/0956797615571017

Pedrotti, J. T., Edwards, L. M., & Lopez, S. J. (2008). Promoting hope: Suggestions for school counselors. *Professional School Counseling, 12*(2), 100–107. https://doi.org/10.5330/PSC.n.2010-12.100

Peterson, C., & Seligman, M. E. P. (2004). *Character strengths and virtues: A handbook and classification*. Oxford University Press and American Psychological Association.

Pierce, J., Schmidt, C., & Stoddard, S. A. (2015). The role of feared possible selves in the relationship between peer influence and delinquency. *Journal of Adolescence, 38*, 17–26. https://doi.org/10.1016/j.adolescence.2014.10.009

Proctor, C., Tsukayama, E., Wood, A. M., Maltby, J., Fox Eades, J. F., & Linley, P. A. (2011). Strengths gym: The impact of a character strengths-based intervention on the life satisfaction and well-being of adolescents. *The Journal of Positive Psychology, 6*(5), 377–388. https://doi.org/10.1080/17439760.2011.594079

Rivas-Drake, D., Syed, M., Umaña-Taylor, A., Markstrom, C., French, S., Schwartz, S. J., Lee, R., & Ethnic and Racial Identity in the 21st Century Study Group. (2014). Feeling good, happy, and proud: A meta-analysis of positive ethnic–racial affect and adjustment. *Child Development, 85*(1), 77–102. https://doi.org/10.1111/cdev.12175

Ryff, C. D. (2014). Psychological well-being revisited: Advances in the science and practice of eudaimonia. *Psychotherapy and Psychosomatics, 83*, 10–28. https://doi.org/10.1159/000353263

Sabo-Flores, K. (2008). *Youth participatory evaluation: Strategies for engaging young people*. John Wiley & Sons.

Scales, P. C., Benson, P. L., & Roehlkepartain, E. C. (2011). Adolescent thriving: The role of sparks, relationships, and empowerment. *Journal of Youth and Adolescence, 40*(3), 263–277. https://doi.org/10.1007/s10964-010-9578-6

Schwartz, S. J., Donnellan, M. B., Ravert, R. D., Luyckx, K., & Zamboanga, B. L. (2013). Identity development, personality, and well-being in adolescence and emerging adulthood: Theory, research, and recent advances. In R. M. Lerner, M. A. Easterbrooks, J. Mistry, & I. B. Weiner (Eds.), *Handbook of psychology: Developmental psychology* (pp. 339–364). John Wiley & Sons, Inc.

Seligman, M. E. P. (2011). *Flourish: A visionary new understanding of happiness and well-being*. Free Press.

Sheldon, K. M., & Elliot, A. J. (1999). Goal striving, need satisfaction, and longitudinal well-being: The self-concordance model. *Journal of Personality and Social Psychology, 76*(3), 482–497. https://doi.org/10.1037//0022-3514.76.3.482

Snyder, C. R. (2002). Hope theory: Rainbows in the mind. *Psychological Inquiry, 13*(4), 249–275. https://doi.org/10.1207/S15327965PLI1304_01

Sokol, B. W., Hammond, S. I., Kuebli, J., & Sweetman, L. (2015). The development of agency. In W. F. Overton, P. C. M. Molenaar, & R. M. Lerner (Eds.), *Handbook of child psychology and developmental science, volume 1: Theory and method* (pp. 284–323). John Wiley & Sons, Inc. https://doi.org/10.1002/9781118963418.childpsy108

Stokes, M. N., Hope, E. C., Cryer-Coupet, Q. R., & Elliot, E. (2020). Black girl blues: The roles of racial socialization, gendered racial socialization, and racial identity on depressive symptoms among Black girls. *Journal of Youth and Adolescence, 49*(11), 2175–2189. https://doi.org/10.1007/s10964-020-01317-8

Taft, J. K. (2004). Girl power politics: Pop-culture barriers and organizational resistance. In A. Harris (Ed.), *All about the girl: Culture, power and identity* (pp. 69–78). Routledge.

Torres, L., & Ong, A. D. (2010). A daily diary investigation of Latino ethnic identity, discrimination, and depression. *Cultural Diversity and Ethnic Minority Psychology, 16*(4), 561–568. https://doi.org/10.1037/a0020652

Vasquez, M. J. T., & de las Fuentes, C. (1999). American-born Asian, African, Latina, and American Indian adolescent girls: Challenges and strengths. In N. G. Johnson, M. C. Roberts, & J. Worell (Eds.), *Beyond appearance: A new look at adolescent girls* (pp. 151–173). American Psychological Association. https://doi.org/10.1037/10325-006

Verkuyten, M. (2016). Further conceptualizing ethnic and racial identity research: The social identity approach and its dynamic model. *Child Development, 87*(6), 1796–1812. https://doi.org/10.1111/cdev.12555

White, A. E., Lincoln, B., Liang, B., Sepulveda, J., Matyjaszczyk, V., Kupersmith, C., Hill, N. E., & Perella, J. (2021). "My mentor thinks that I can be someone amazing": Drawing out youths' passions and purpose. *Journal of Adolescent Research, 36*(1), 98–123. https://doi.org/10.1177/0743558420942481

Yeager, D. S., Johnson, R., Spitzer, B. J., Trzesniewski, K. H., Powers, J., & Dweck, C. S. (2014). The far-reaching effects of believing people can change: Implicit theories of personality shape stress, health, and achievement during adolescence. *Journal of Personality & Social Psychology, 106*(6), 867–884. https://doi.org/10.1037/a0036335

Yeager, D. S., Trzesniewski, K. H., Tirri, K., Nokelainen, P., & Dweck, C. S. (2011). Adolescents' implicit theories predict desire for vengeance after peer conflicts: Correlational and experimental evidence. *Developmental Psychology, 47*(4), 1090–1107. https://doi.org/10.1037/a0023769

Index

acceptance: emotional 84; fostering emotional awareness and 84–85; self-acceptance 4
Acceptance and Commitment Therapy (ACT) 84–85
accomplishment 4
ACTION 79
adolescence 15; agency in 129–130; barriers to health and well-being 21–23; brain development in 16–18; developmental processes in 20; dietary behavior in 51–52; emotion regulation in 76; expanding relational ecologies 98; factors for inadequate sleep in 60–61; mental health 20–24; models of well-being in 7–8; purpose in 123–124; relationships with peers 104–112; *see also* youth
adolescent girls: depression in 76–78; eating habits in 51–52; identity in 45–46; physical activity in 50–51; power and agency in 42–43; puberty in 18–19; relational aggression in 105–106; romantic relationships in 106–107; school-based obesity prevention program for 56; sexualization and body image in 38–40; well-being in 36; *see also* girls
adolescent psychopathology 21
Adolescents ParentWays Program 103
African American adolescent girls 41, 53
African American girls 44, 134
after-school program, for Black girls 57
agency 37, 40, 101, 129; in adolescence 129–130; in adolescent girls 42–43
anticipatory savoring 87
anxiety 56, 80–81; interventions to reduce 82–84

appearance and ideal of femininity 40–41
appearance-related media exposure 54
asynchronicity 108, 109
attentional deployment 74–75
autonomy 5; developmental tasks in adolescence 99, 100; factors related to 100–101; need for 3
autonomy development 101
Aware-Explore-Apply Model 125

behavioral activation 78
belief-in-others 8
belief-in-self 8
beliefs: about emotions 75–76; control 40; parental 101; positive parental 101
Best Possible Selves intervention 132
binge eating behaviors 52
Black girls 41, 44, 45; after-school program for 57
Black women 44; racial discrimination and stereotypical images of 134
Block, P. 113
blurring of boundaries (enmeshment) 101
body image 52–53; in adolescent girls 38–40; factors contributing to body dissatisfaction 53–54; specific interventions 57–59
body surveillance 40
brain development, in adolescence 16–18
broaden-and-build theory of positive emotions 10, 85, 86

character strengths 124; strength building interventions 125
civic engagement 131

cognitive-behavioral therapy (CBT) 57, 79
cognitive behavioral therapy for insomnia (CBT-I) 62
cognitive change 75
cognitive reappraisal 75, 84
cognitive stress-reduction strategies 83
compensatory secondary control 127
computer-based CBT interventions 83
conflicts 99–100
connectedness 100–101
control beliefs 40
COPE Healthy Lifestyles TEEN 56
covitality 8
cultural identity 133

dancing 79
dating anxiety 107
depression 20, 23, 56; in adolescent girls 76–78; family history of 77; interventions to reduce 78–80
depression prevention program 9
"DeStress for Success" 84
detachment 101
developmental assets 26
developmental goals 126–128
developmental regulation 126
developmental tasks 15
dialogue-based approach 113
diet 51–52
dietary behavior 51–52
digital media: and adolescents' mental health 23–24; *see also* media
dispositional mindfulness 83
distraction 74–75
dopaminergic activity 17
"Dove Self-Esteem Project" 58

eating habits, in adolescent girls 51–52
education: promoting purpose in adolescents 123; strength-based 125
emotional acceptance 84
emotional competence 8
emotional difficulties 21
emotional disclosure 74
emotional intelligence 83
emotional well-being 6, 73, 84
emotion regulation 74–76; in adolescents 76; sleep role in 60
emotions: beliefs about 75–76; expression of 102
emotion self-regulation 74

emotion talk, expression of 102
empowerment 26, 28, 54, 57, 105, 111, 124
engagement 3–4; civic 131; personal 128; psychological 28
environmental mastery 5
ethnic identity 133
ethnic minority girls, experiences of 43–45
ethnic minority youth 81
eudaimonic well-being 3–6
experiential learning education 123
expressive suppression 75
external assets 26

Facebook 23, 24
face-to-face interactions 108, 111
family: adolescents' emotional functioning 73; of emotion regulation strategies 74–75
family support 122
fear extinction 20
Fear of Missing Out (FoMO) 24
femininity: consumer-oriented construct of 40; ideal of 40–41
fostering emotional awareness 84–85
fostering emotional well-being 73
4-H Study of Positive Youth Development 28
friends 104; emotional support 73
"Full of Ourselves: A Wellness Program to Advance Girl Power, Health, and Leadership" 57

Geelong Grammar School Project 10–11
gender socialization 37–38
gender stereotyping 37–38
Gilligan, Carol: *In a Different Voice: Psychological Theory and Women's Development* 36
Girl Power 42, 43
"GirlPOWER!" 112
girls 36; from diverse ethnic and racial backgrounds 43–45; identity development in 44; levels of internalized self-sexualization 40; in media 38; media products for 43; physical and physiological changes 37; *see also* adolescent girls
Girls Circle 111

"Girls on the Go!" program 57
"Girls on Track" 57
goal pursuit 125–126; developmental goals 126–128; growth mindset 128; hope and goal pursuit 128–129
gratitude intervention 85–87
growth mindset 128

habit formation: initiation phase 63–64; learning phase 64; stability phase 64
"Happy Being Me" 58
health and functioning domain 7
health, defined as 1
healthy development 27
healthy eating, interventions to support 56–57
Healthy Girls Save the World (HGSW) 57
healthy habits 50; interventions to work 62–64
healthy relationships: creating caring communities to promote 113–114; promoting through mentoring 112; psychoeducation about 110
hedonic well-being 2–3
Hispanic adolescents, depression and anxiety in 56
hope 128–129
hope-bonding strategies 129
hope-enhancing strategies 129
hope-finding strategies 129
hope-focused strategies 129
hope-reminding strategies 129
hormonal changes 17, 20
human flourishing framework 3
hypersexualization 39

identity coherence 22
identity development 130–131; interventions to support girls of color 134–135; possible selves 131–132; social identity 132–134
identity, in adolescent girls 45–46
"iDisorders" 23
incremental theory *see* growth mindset
insomnia 77
integrative models of well-being 6–7
intentional self-regulation 127
internal assets 26
International Positive Education Network (IPEN) 11

interpersonal model of depression 77, 79–80
interpersonal relationships, with peers 17
interventions 54–55; motivation strategies for girls, physically active 55–56; programs and curricular to support healthy habits 56–57; to reduce depression 78–80; to reduce stress and anxiety 82–84; specific body image 57–59; to support girls' healthy relationships with peers 111–112; to support identity development in girls of color 134–135; to support sleep hygiene 61–62; well-being 8–11
IPEN *see* International Positive Education Network (IPEN)

knowledge-to-action (KTA) framework 61

life satisfaction 2
lifestyle habits 8
loving-kindness meditation (LKM) 85

"Make Your Work Matter" 123
"mean girls" 41–42
meaning 4, 105, 123
meaningful life 2, 3, 11
media 42; girls in 38; products for girls 43; *see also* digital media
media literacy interventions 58
mental health 1; adolescence 20–24; digital media and 23–24; as flourishing 6; social identity 133
mentors 112, 123
mindful breathing 83
"Mindfulness-enhanced Strengthening Families Program" 103
mindful parenting 103
"mobile entrapment" 108
morningness/eveningness (M/E) 60
motivation 29; intrinsic 126; for mastery and competence 4; to stay physically active 55; strategies for girls, physically active 55–56
motivational scaffolding 128
multicomponent physical activity interventions 55
multicultural education 44

mutual empathy 111
MyPlate icon 55

negative body image 52
negative emotions 10, 76
Nested Model of Well-Being 6
neural plasticity 16
nonrestorative sleep 77
normative stresses 81
nutrition education 56

objectification theory 39
open communication 102–103
optimal adolescent development:
    Positive Youth Development 24–26,
    28–30; resilience 26–27
optimal mental health 4

parent-adolescent relationships
    98–101; interventions to support
    positive 103–104; recommendations
    for parents to support positive
    101–103
parental anxiety 99
parental behavior 73
parental beliefs 101
parent-child boundaries 102
parentification 101
Parenting Adolescents Wisely
    program 103
parents: educate about peer
    relationships 110; role in promoting
    healthy sleep 62
parent-teen conflicts 99–100
peer relationships 104–105; educate
    parents about 110; interventions
    to support girls 111–112;
    recommendations to support girls
    110–111; relational aggression in
    adolescent girls 105–106; romantic
    relationships in adolescent girls
    106–107; social media and 108–109
peers 73–74
Penn Resiliency Program (PRP) 9
PERMA 3–4, 10
personal growth 5–6, 10
person-and-context relationship 25
photoshopping 54
physical activity 78–79; in adolescent
    girls 50–51; interventions to support
    55–56
physical exercise 7, 51, 56, 57, 75
physical health 50; social identity 133
poor sleep 60, 61

positive attitudes 4
positive body image 52;
    intervention 57
positive education 10–11
positive emotion 2, 3, 9, 63, 78;
    dysregulation of 76; for emotional
    well-being 85; and well-being 85–87
Positive Emotion Regulation
    program 86
positive mental health domains 8
Positive Parenting Program (Triple
    P) 103
positive psychology 1; framework 85
positive psychology interventions
    (PPIs) 9
positive relations 4–5
positive reminiscing 86
Positive Thoughts and Actions (PTA)
    program 79
Positive Youth Development (PYD)
    24–26, 28–30
positivity resonance 86
possible selves 131–132
post-feminist media 40
poverty 22
POWER 112
power, in adolescent girls 42–43
PPIs *see* positive psychology
    interventions (PPIs)
primary appraisal 80
primary control 127
problematic smartphone use 23
PRP *see* Penn Resiliency Program
    (PRP)
psychoeducation 84; about healthy
    relationships 110
psychoeducational interventions 61
psychological well-being (PWB)
    framework 4
psychology, well-being in 2
psychosocial stress, family history
    of 77
pubertal changes 17
puberty 76–77, 99; in adolescent girls
    18–19; defined as 18; risk to develop
    depressive symptoms 21
purpose in adolescents 123–124
purpose in life 5

quality sleep 59

racial identity 134
racial minority girls, experiences of
    43–45

racial socialization 134
rejection sensitivity 107
relational aggression: in adolescent girls 105–106; causes and signs of 110
relational-cultural theory 111
relationships 4; with parents 98–104; with peers 104–112; secure 100; vertical 99
resilience 26–27
response modulation 75
restorative justice framework 113–114
romantic relationships, in adolescent girls 106–107

"saturated self" 46
savoring 86
scaffolding, instrumental and motivational 128
school-based character strength interventions 125
school-based intervention 123
school-based obesity prevention program 56
school-based positive education 10
school-based prevention programs 62
science, technology, engineering, and mathematics (STEM) 38
screen media 24, 60
secondary appraisal 80
secondary control 127
secure relationships 100
SEHS *see* Social Emotional Health Survey (SEHS)
SEL *see* Social-Emotional Learning (SEL)
self-acceptance 4
self-esteem 26, 59, 105
selfie-related behaviors 54
self-improvement practices 40
self-objectification 40
self-regulation 16, 17
Seligman, M. E. P. 1, 3, 4, 11, 124
separation 101; factors related to 100–101
service learning education 123
sex differences 21
sexualization, in adolescent girls 38–40
sexy femininity 38, 41
situation modification 74
situation selection 74
sleep deficit 20
sleep deprivation 59

sleep disruption 61
sleep habits 59–60; factors for inadequate sleep in adolescence 60–61; interventions to support sleep hygiene 61–62
social cure 133
Social Emotional Health Survey (SEHS) 8
Social-Emotional Learning (SEL) 9
social identity 132–134
social interactions 17, 21
socialization practices 18; gender 37–38
social media 23, 24, 45; features of 109; over-involvement with 82; and peers relationships 108–109; thin body ideal on 54
social networking 108
social stressors, exposure to 78
"sparks" 124
stereotype threat 38
"Stop, Be Calm, Be Present" 103
Strategies to Tackle Exam Pressure and Stress (STEPS) 83–84
strength-based education 125
strength building interventions 125
"Strengths Gym" intervention 125
stress 80–81; interventions to reduce 82–84; purpose development 122; sources of 81–82
stress exposure 20
stress generation model 78
subjective well-being (SWB) 2, 3, 9

Talking Circles 111–112
Teen Women's Action Program (TWAP) 135
test anxiety 82
Theater in Health Education 59
Theokas, C. 25
traditional feminine gender schema 105

unhealthy diet 51, 53

values and ideology domain 7
vertical relationships 99
virtue of courage 124
virtue of humanity 124
virtue of justice 124
virtue of temperance 124
virtue of transcendence 124
virtue of wisdom 124

weight control 52
well-being: in adolescent girls 36;
   construct of 2; eudaimonic 3–6;
   hedonic 2–3; integrative models
   of 6–7; models in adolescents 7–8;
   positive emotions and 85–87
well-being interventions 8–11
well-being therapy (WBT) 4, 10
Write it Out! 135

youth 15; adaptive development 27;
   psychological engagement 28; *see
   also* adolescence
Youth Participatory Action Research
   (Youth-PAR) 29–30,
   134, 135
youth programs 28
Youth Risk Behavior
   Survey 59

For Product Safety Concerns and Information please contact our EU
representative GPSR@taylorandfrancis.com
Taylor & Francis Verlag GmbH, Kaufingerstraße 24, 80331 München, Germany